Dazed and Confused

Dazed and Confused

America Confronts the 1970s

Blaine T. Browne

Rowman & Littlefield
Lanham • Boulder • New York • London

Published by Rowman & Littlefield
An imprint of The Rowman & Littlefield Publishing Group, Inc.
4501 Forbes Boulevard, Suite 200, Lanham, Maryland 20706
www.rowman.com

86-90 Paul Street, London EC2A 4NE

British Library Cataloguing in Publication Information Available

Library of Congress Cataloging-in-Publication Data

Names: Browne, Blaine T. (Blaine Terry), author.
Title: Dazed and confused : America confronts the 1970s / Blaine T. Browne.
Other titles: America confronts the 1970s
Description: Lanham : Rowman & Littlefield, [2023] | Includes
  bibliographical references and index.
Identifiers: LCCN 2023021554 (print) | LCCN 2023021555 (ebook) | ISBN
  9781538166093 (cloth) | ISBN 9781538166109 (ebook)
Subjects: LCSH: United States—History—1969– | United
  States—Civilization—1970– | Nineteen seventies.
Classification: LCC E741 .B75 2023 (print) | LCC E741 (ebook) | DDC
  973.92—dc23/eng/20230602
LC record available at https://lccn.loc.gov/2023021554
LC ebook record available at https://lccn.loc.gov/2023021555

This book is dedicated to those who succeeded in balancing the pursuit of personal growth goals with the struggles for social, economic, racial, and political justice and environmental activism during the 1970s.

CONTENTS

CONTENTS

PREFACE

As of the publication of this book, more than a half century will have passed since Americans began their dizzying journey through the 1970s, which was made more challenging because of the national hangover induced by the tumultuous 1960s. Many of the social and political pathologies of that chaotic decade lingered beyond 1969; the paramount issues of war and race remained unresolved, even as the age of mass mobilization and violence in American streets gradually receded. The social, political, and cultural consequences of years of turmoil were yet uncertain. What was clear by 1970, however, was that the national consensus born during the World War II years had been torn asunder.

By the late 1960s, it was clear that Americans were no longer bound by the unity that wartime had nurtured. The struggle to achieve full civil rights for African Americans and the often-violent resistance to it revealed that the nation had not fully realized its proclaimed ideals. The rediscovery of poverty, among whites as well as blacks, exposed economic inequities that belied the promise of democratic capitalism, which the wartime boom had temporarily obscured. In the midst of unprecedented postwar prosperity for many, the promise of economic advancement for others remained in doubt. Political assassinations and violent protests in the streets brought into question the viability of the ostensibly peaceful democratic political process that Americans hailed. As the war in Vietnam dragged on, the assurances of national political leaders as to progress in that conflict seemed increasingly at odds with the realities evident in the print and broadcast media. Doubts about the viability of the American political system's ability to meet challenges were amplified during the chaotic general election of 1968, which saw a sitting president challenged from within his own party over his war policies, campaigns founded on resentment and racial hatred, assassination, and the most violent presidential nominating convention in the nation's history. Ramped-up violence by political radicals in the last year of the decade further fueled national despair and uncertainty.

It was not by chance that one of the most popular television series of the 1970s was *Happy Days*, a historically myopic and vapid effort to capitalize on the public desire to shelter in the belief that there had once been a golden age when the nation was unshaken by any significant social, political, or economic turmoil. Those who experienced the 1950s realized that this was a thinly concocted fantasy largely at odds with the realities of that decade. *Back to the Future*, in 1985, touched upon similar themes, as did the later film *Pleasantville*; both transported contemporary teenagers to a supposedly more tranquil time in the 1950s. The reality was that there were no "good old days," though the longing to relive a fictional past was compelling in a decade in which the "American Dream" seemed to be slipping away.

The primary motivation for this foray into the 1970s is the realization that, other than books that deal with specific topics, the decade has been underserved by historians. The 1960s have understandably commanded considerable attention, given the dramatic events of those years. The 1980s have drawn much examination, as the nation entered an era of conservatism that drastically altered the political universe of the Cold War. By comparison, the 1970s have remained a largely ignored stepchild, with some asserting that nothing of great significance occurred. Often remembered only as a decade of streaking, mood rings, pet rocks, shag carpeting, leisure suits, and hideous home color palettes, as the airwaves filled with insipid songs, the era is often dismissed as insignificant. Indeed, one of the first histories of the decade was Peter N. Carroll's *It Seemed Like Nothing Happened* (1988), which was not a thesis that the author argued but, rather, a widespread public perception.

This volume was written with the intention of filling a noticeable gap in the literature on America's modern history. It is not intended as a comprehensive examination of the 1970s but, rather, as an overview of a decade that deserves greater attention than it has received. This book is designed to appeal to the general public as well as to serve as supplemental reading for courses in American history, hence its relative brevity. Thus, the reader will find chapters dedicated to essential subjects such as politics, foreign policy, and social, economic, and cultural change. Readers will find that each chapter includes two brief biographies of individuals who were central to that chapter's subject. Some are well known, others less so, but all deserve inclusion in the story of the American nation in the 1970s.

This book is dedicated to those who successfully navigated one of the most challenging decades in modern American history and, of course, to my wife Marian, who gamely tolerates my incessant writing projects. Many thanks also to the faculty at the University of Oklahoma who guided my study of American history and educated me in the art of historical writing, as well as my editor Jon Sisk and the excellent editing, art, and production staff at Rowman & Littlefield.

PROLOGUE

It's like the "every other decade theory," you know. The fifties were boring—the sixties rocked. The seventies, oh my God, they obviously suck.
. . . Maybe the eighties will be radical.

—"Cynthia" in the film *Dazed and Confused* (1993)

In early January 1969, the song "Dazed and Confused" (composed
by Jake Holmes) was featured on the first album of the English rock
group Led Zeppelin, whose music combined blues and rock with
thunderous electric guitar chords, screaming guitar and vocal solos, and
a percussion-heavy sound that quickly found an audience as the 1960s
raced toward an apocalyptic end. The album went gold that July, and
Led Zeppelin's success grew exponentially in subsequent years. *Dazed
and Confused* emerged again as the title of a film released in 1993, but set
in May 1976. Director Richard Linklater's film dealt with the last day of
class at an Austin, Texas, high school during which the graduates celebrate
their newfound freedom but face uncertainty as to their futures. This classic
coming-of-age comedy was only moderately successful upon initial release
but, in subsequent years, gained numerous critical proponents and became
something of a cult classic.

Thus, the genesis of the title of this work, which seeks to capture not
only the major events and trends of the 1970s but also to emphasize the
bewilderment and uncertainty that bedeviled both new high school graduates and almost all Americans during the decade. There is an appreciable

continuity in the decade's musical prelude and cinematic final years being bookended with the same phrase, "dazed and confused," leaving even historians hard-pressed to characterize the often-baffling cognitive dissonance of those years.

Perhaps the best summation of the significance of the 1970s is that of Jefferson Cowie, who writes in *Stayin' Alive: The 1970s and the Last Days of the Working Class*, "The rapidity of the change in the nation's sense of destiny is one of the most profound yet unacknowledged transformations in American culture." The 1970s were a crucial period of transition to a future that had yet to come into focus. By 1969, it was clear that many of the hopes of the 1960s were dying or dead, and the public was growing exhausted with the seemingly endless war in Vietnam, rising racial hostilities, constant civil violence, and serial political assassinations. The fracturing of the long-dominant Democratic Party over issues of war and peace betokened not only the passing of an era of stability but also the inescapable arrival of a new era in which uncertainty would prevail.

Many of the developments that characterized the late 1960s continued into the 1970s, some struggling against irrelevance and countervailing currents, while others gained new dynamism and adherents. This book necessarily begins with an examination of the intense political and cultural radicalism that had evolved by 1969. Chapter 1 seeks to present a comprehensive understanding of the year that immediately preceded that decade, as the 1970s cannot be comprehended otherwise. The racial antagonisms that spawned revolutionary groups like the Black Panthers gave birth to other lesser-known entities such as the Black Liberation Army, which grew in number and violence even as the Panthers declined. As the Vietnam War ground to its painful conclusion, the political radicalism that the war engendered did not disappear at war's end. Rather, the fractured remains of the New Left underwent a rapid transition that embraced violence and terrorism before imploding. The counterculture, which some feared threatened traditional American society, was eventually absorbed by mainstream culture and left a discernible and not entirely negative imprint. The women's rights movement, various ethnic rights movements, Native American rights, the racial justice movement, the gay rights movement, and environmentalism were destined to become permanent and significant elements in American society.

By 1969, the one issue that most divided and troubled Americans was the Vietnam War, which is examined in chapter 2. President Richard Nixon struggled to find the policies that could bring about the "peace with honor" that he had promised. Rather, as violence in Vietnam accelerated in 1969, to assuage domestic concerns, Nixon initiated a policy of the gradual withdrawal of US forces in parallel with the military strengthening of South Vietnam and more intense bombing of the North. In January 1973, the United States, South Vietnam, and North Vietnam signed the Paris Peace Accords, which ended the US role in the war, leading to the end of the American military presence and an inevitable North Vietnamese military victory in April 1975. The war had cost the lives of more than 58,000 US troops and millions of Vietnamese, and led to the devastation of that nation. Americans were compelled to come to grips with the realization that they had, for the first time, lost a war.

Chapter 3 focuses on the presidency of Richard Nixon, who after winning the Republican presidential nomination in 1968 had promised to "bring us together." Rather, Nixon opted for a policy of "positive polarization," pitting the "Silent Majority" that he claimed to speak for against liberals, the antiwar movement, black militants, and the national media. Vice President Spiro T. Agnew was delegated to unleash a barrage of attacks on all Nixon administration critics and opponents. Nixon hoped to build his presidency on foreign policy successes, which would be contingent on ending the war in Vietnam. As that conflict dragged on, and as the antiwar movement and domestic radicalism intensified, Nixon became more obsessed with "political counterintelligence," culminating in the Watergate Scandal, which unfolded between 1972 and 1974. Vice President Spiro Agnew was forced to resign in a separate scandal in 1973, less than a year before Nixon resigned rather than face impeachment, conviction, and removal from office. One of the first great disillusionments of the decade was the realization that an American president had committed criminal acts, as had many of his underlings. This was Nixon's most poisonous legacy, leading to a distrust of government that fueled the popular belief that elected officials were not to be trusted. This cynicism blossomed in future decades, undermining democratic habits of mind and action well into the first two decades of the twenty-first century with serious consequences.

The left-wing radicalism that continued to sputter on with increasingly irrational violence into the 1970s is the subject of chapter 4. Even as the Black Panther Party was decimated by factionalism, incarceration, and police murders, the Black Liberation Army launched a campaign of violence against police nationwide. As groups like Students for a Democratic Society fractured into the Maoist Progressive Labor Party and Weatherman in 1969, smaller but more radical memberships brought about a greater dedication to terrorist violence. The Brown Berets, a Chicano organization taking its cues from the Black Panthers but eschewing violence, instead directed its efforts toward community improvement and opposing police harassment. A dramatic spasm of increasingly incoherent leftist radicalism drew public attention between 1973 and 1975, as the Symbionese Liberation Army (SLA) gained infamy through a series of bank robberies and the kidnapping of newspaper heiress Patty Hearst, culminating in a wild shoot-out with Los Angeles police in 1974. The radicalism of the 1960s, it seemed, was determined not to end with a whimper, as even minor groups like the Sojourner Truth Organization and M19 coming together, the latter bombing the US Capitol, demonstrated.

America's decline from global industrial preeminence is examined in chapter 5. As inflation grew due to government borrowing to fund the Vietnam War and unprecedentedly high energy prices resulting from the Arab oil embargo against the United States in 1973, Americans also found that the economy they had known since World War II was being rapidly transformed. The most crucial victim of this surprisingly rapid reshuffling of the global economy was American manufacturing. American iron and steel production gradually gave way to products manufactured in Japan and South Korea, where cheaper wages and less workplace protection prevailed. A corollary to these developments, the American automobile industry, long a world leader, began to feel the impact of imports from two of the very nations that the United States had defeated in World War II. Germany's Volkswagen and a multitude of Japanese imports contributed to Detroit's declining share of the market.

At the same time, as US iron and steel production shrank, the nation's coal industry likewise felt the effects of these fundamental changes. In industries that had once been widely unionized, decent wages and benefits had served as rungs on the ladder to a more affluent lifestyle. By the 1970s, those crucial rungs were disappearing. Service industries took up some of the slack, but offered considerably lower wages, came with few or no benefits, and were dependent on consumer spending, which was shrinking. Not until the later 1970s did new technology industries seem to offer some promise for the future as the first primitive personal computers began to make their appearance, foreshadowing a technological boom that would reshape the American economy again in later years.

Chapter 6 addresses one of the most puzzling questions about the 1970s, that being whether it was chiefly a decade in which the disaffected, disillusioned with the failure of social or political reform in the 1960s, retreated into themselves seeking personal fulfillment and/or improvement, or whether it was a decade in which surviving social justice and reform movements gained strength. A case, it seems, could be made for either. Any number of 1960s radicals gave up the cause and either pursued the quiet life or joined the establishment. Others sought to gain self-fulfillment through various therapies, cults, and self-improvement fads. Some found renewal through physical improvement, most notably through the jogging craze that enriched athletic shoe manufacturers and undoubtedly improved the health of many Americans.

On the other hand, the 1970s saw the reorganization of the civil rights movement, as new tactics were adopted and new battles engaged. The movement for Native American rights grew throughout the decade. The women's rights and feminist movements dealt successfully with crucial internal disputes and expanded the field of engagement as their numbers increased. The modern environmental movement celebrated its birth in April 1970 with the first Earth Day and, in subsequent years, gained mass support for legislative protections through a plethora of established and new organizations. As Americans grew increasingly aware of the need to ensure clean air and water, others engaged in the crusade to preserve and protect the natural world.

Given the immense changes that film and television programming underwent in the 1970s, chapter 7 is devoted chiefly to those topics. A discernible transformation in popular film became evident as early as 1967 with the release of *Bonnie and Clyde*. *2001: A Space Odyssey*, released in 1968, hinted at new directions in film. Two 1969 films that provoked considerable controversy as well as critical acclaim, *Easy Rider* and *Midnight Cowboy*, opened the path for new directors and the New Cinema. During the first half of the 1970s, the trend toward films featuring antiheroes, provocative subjects, and moral ambiguity characterized an era that produced some of the most critically acclaimed American films of the modern era, offering a much darker vision of the nation. At mid-decade, audiences were increasingly drawn to "blockbuster" films dealing with topics as varied as killer sharks, the supernatural, science fiction, and science fiction/fantasy, which began to supplant the more controversial and innovative films of the early 1970s.

As much as any medium, television reflected the transformations reshaping American life. Before the era of cable television, American viewers had limited choices, represented by the national networks ABC, CBS, and NBC, as well as the Public Broadcasting System (PBS). PBS, which was not a network but a program distributor for member stations, went on the air in October 1970, offering a variety of documentaries, cultural events, and general entertainment, and introducing American children to *Sesame Street*, among other things. Shows featuring independent women, minorities, and once-avoided controversial subjects quickly found receptive audiences on all networks as the decade began.

American theater in the 1970s forwent some of the more shocking cultural productions of the previous decade such as *Hair*, *Oh! Calcutta!*, or even *Cabaret*, opting instead for less controversial entertainment. Religious motifs found their way onto Broadway with the blockbusters *Jesus Christ Superstar*, *Godspell*, and *Joseph and the Amazing Technicolor Dreamcoat*. Audiences seeking more traditional fare could see *A Chorus Line*, *Chicago*, and *Annie*. Those seeking an ostensibly less anxiety-producing era might attend *Grease*. The latter years of the decade witnessed the surprising success of the audience-participation cult musical *The Rocky Horror Show* (1975) and the grim *Sweeney Todd: The Demon Barber of Fleet Street* (1979).

Chapter 8 focuses on popular music in the 1970s, as by the end of the 1960s, the era of musical psychedelia was fading, while familiar genres such as rock 'n' roll and blues found continued popularity as the parameters of those realms were redefined. Though the age of the supergroup receded with the breakup of the Beatles in 1970, some survivors of the previous decade, such as the Rolling Stones, carried on with notable success. Others reappeared under new names and personnel. Disco, seemingly triumphant by 1978, soon gave way to new groups and genres, with bands like the Eagles sharing *Billboard*'s Top 100 with the founders of punk rock and New Wave.

The latter years of the 1970s were among the worst peacetime years in the nation's modern history and are detailed in chapter 9, which focuses on national politics and foreign policy. It was a politically confused era, which seemed to promise Democratic predominance in both houses of Congress following the collapse of the corrupt Nixon administration— Democrats increased their majority in both houses in the election of 1974. Gerald Ford's brief presidency was weakened by his unpopular full pardon of former President Nixon in September 1974 and his inability to deal with the mounting challenge of inflation. Ford also had the misfortune to be president when South Vietnam finally collapsed in April 1975, and a new regional crisis erupted as the radical communist Khmer Rouge gained control of Cambodia (renamed Kampuchea) and briefly seized the US merchant ship *Mayaguez*. The Southeast Asian debacles fueled growing concerns about American military competence that evolved into the "Vietnam Syndrome," a fear that the United States would be reluctant to deploy military resources in the future under any circumstances.

The presidential election of 1976 proved uninspiring, with Georgian Jimmy Carter defeating Ford chiefly through depicting himself as a Washington outsider. Faced with the intertwined issues of energy independence, renewable energy sources, related taxation issues, stagflation, and inflation, Carter was unable to resolve them, due both to their intractability and his poor relationship with the Democratic Congress. As Democratic policies seemed increasingly ineffective, the New Right, a grassroots movement born among those who believed the nation's ills were the result of decades of unfettered liberalism, gained strength. Joined to the New Right were the adherents of the Christian Right, chiefly evangelical Christians who believed that American decline resulted from 1960s immorality and a drift away from biblical foundations. This New Right gathered strength as the decade proceeded, though its growing potential went largely unrecognized by liberals until 1980.

The Carter administration's popularity and Democratic congressional strength were also undercut by a seemingly endless cascade of foreign policy crises that appeared to defy resolution. The Arab nationalism that began reshaping the Middle East in the 1960s, and threatened US oil supplies, emerged in 1969 with Libya's Muammar al-Qadhafi's (his name was spelled a confusing welter of ways in the Western press) overthrow of the corrupt regime of King Idris. The nationalization of American oil companies there prefigured a growing trend. The 1979 Islamic Revolution in Iran led to a hostage crisis as well as the end of US influence in that crucial oil-producing nation. Arab nations raised the price of oil, producing yet another energy crisis. A Soviet invasion of Afghanistan brought only a weak response from the Carter administration, while the victory of the Sandinista regime in Nicaragua seemed to signal another penetration of the Western hemisphere by Marxism. The failure of a military mission to rescue the American hostages in Tehran in April 1980 was yet another blow to the foundering Carter administration.

As the nation prepared for a general election, Democratic fortunes seemed at a low ebb. Many of the disaffected were drawn to the candidacy of former California governor Ronald Reagan. During the 1980 presidential campaign, Reagan capitalized on the public's blossoming concern about America's decline with the simple but devastating question, "Are you better off now than you were four years ago?" There were few who could have answered affirmatively, and many were willing to overlook Reagan's evident lack of factual knowledge. The Californian's quip might well have served as an epitaph for a decade.

The epilogue will speak briefly about what followed Ronald Reagan's election to the presidency. *Dazed and Confused*'s Cynthia did not get her wish—the 1980s were not radical in any sense of which she might have conceived. While neoconservatives and Republicans hailed the "Reagan Revolution" as inaugurating a new era of conservative dominance, they were only partially correct. Much of the early dynamism of the Reagan Revolution had evaporated by the late 1980s, and the George H. W. Bush and George W. Bush administrations were little more than reiterations of traditional conservative positions. The reality was that the quantitative liberalism of the New Deal and the qualitative liberalism of the Great Society, which had dominated federal governance for most of four decades, had run their course by the end of the 1970s—the public was ready to give conservatism a chance to resolve the nation's difficulties. The epilogue speaks to the rightward turn in government, which would have undreamt-of consequences by the second decade of the twenty-first century.

As with many examinations of a broad subject, this book is selective in topics covered. Discerning readers will find that there is little significant attention given to what might qualify as academic intellectual pursuits, or the scientific, artistic, and sports developments of the decade. Though this is due in part to editorial considerations, it also reflects my conclusions as to what topics were of greatest concern, what most greatly impacted the majority of Americans, and what reflected their fears and hopes.

CHAPTER ONE

"I'M WASTED, AND I CAN'T FIND MY WAY HOME"
The End of the 1960s

For most Americans, awareness of the counterculture and the "hippie" movement came in 1967, when events in California awakened the nation to the youth culture that had taken form since the mid part of the decade. Nationwide, newspapers reported on the "Human Be-In" that took place in San Francisco's Golden Gate Park on January 14, as some 20,000 participants gathered. Hailed as a "Gathering of the Tribes" by the "underground" newspaper *San Francisco Oracle*, the occasion was to mark and mock the state assembly's recent banning of the psychedelic drug LSD (lysergic acid diethylamide), large quantities of which were provided for free by famed hippie chemist Owsley Stanley. The Diggers, a local antiestablishment group, offered free turkey sandwiches to those who could still discern what they were after taking Owsley's "White Lightning" acid.

The Be-In featured speakers such as Timothy Leary, whose "Turn on, tune in, drop out" became the counterculture's creed; liberated lifestyle advocate Richard Alpert, soon to be known as Baba Ram Dass; as well as Beat poets Allen Ginsberg, Gary Snyder, and Michael McClure. Music was provided by Jefferson Airplane, the Grateful Dead, Big Brother and the Holding Company, Blue Cheer, and other bands that defined the sounds of the psychedelic era. *San Francisco Chronicle* contributor Ralph Gleason reported that the dominant fashions among Be-In attendees were "a wild polyglot mixture of Mod, Paladin, Ringling Brothers, Cochise, and Hell's Angels' Formal." Four hours of an anarchic mixture of drug-fueled hip philosophy, poetry, loud rock music, dancing, frisbee-tossing, and general

1

frolicking defined the event. Observer Helen Swick, a sociologist, believed she saw something "mystical" in this first major gathering of the peace and love generation. "The dogs did not fight," she marveled, "and the children did not cry." The Age of Aquarius, it seemed, had dawned in the United States.

Within months, the city's Haight-Ashbury district became the epicenter of a widely hailed "Summer of Love." Scott McKenzie's hit single "San Francisco (Be Sure to Wear Flowers in Your Hair)" made the number four slot among the nation's top-selling records in May, undoubtedly influencing some of the estimated 75,000 young Americans who flocked to the West Coast Nirvana. Ralph Gleason enthused, "At no time in American history has American youth possessed the strength it possesses now. Trained by music and linked by music, it has the power for good to change the world." *Time* magazine sought to enlighten readers about the counterculture in a May 7, 1967, cover story, "The Hippies: Philosophy of a Subculture." According to the writer, the "hippie code" was: "Do your own thing, wherever you have to do it and whenever you want. Drop out. Leave society as you have known it. Leave it utterly. Blow the mind of every straight person you can reach. Turn them on, if not to drugs, then to beauty, love, honesty, fun."

The 1967 Monterey Pop Festival, planned as a nonprofit event (hippies disdained profits), gave further impetus to the counterculture. It was Paul McCartney who pressed festival organizers to invite a young African American guitarist and his band, which was as yet largely unknown to Americans but had wowed English audiences. The Jimi Hendrix Experience, which featured a twenty-four-year-old lead guitarist and vocalist who could neither read nor write music, would show the world just what might be done with an electric guitar. The Jimi Hendrix Experience, consisting of singer and lead guitarist Jimi, bassist Noel Redding, and drummer Mitch Mitchell, had toured widely in the United Kingdom and Europe in 1966; the band's initial album, *Are You Experienced*, which introduced American listeners to Hendrix's astonishing electronic pyrotechnics in songs like "Purple Haze," was rapidly climbing the charts.

As to the man and his music, critics were baffled and divided. His eclectic and colorful attire combined with an anarchic Afro hairstyle joined to his band's unique sound, which was built around thunderous electrically amplified chords and soaring, often dissonant guitar solo flights matched to poetic and mystical lyrics that simply defied categorization. A *Melody Maker* writer resorted to the terms "mau-mau" and "wild man" in describing the young musician. An *Ebony* critic described Hendrix as looking like "a cross between Bob Dylan and the Wild Man of Borneo." *Rolling Stone*'s John Morthland later offered one of the least charitable assessments, mocking Hendrix as "the flower generation's electric nigger dandy—its king stud and golden calf, its maker of mighty dope music, its most outrageous visible force." Critic Robert Christgau denigrated the guitarist as "a psychedelic Uncle Tom." But the negative criticism was heavily outweighed by the response that Hendrix drew from his astounded Monterey audience. Scheduled for a nighttime performance on the festival's second day, the left-handed guitarist, whose large hands and lengthy fingers afforded him a reach that eluded many others, turned his soft smile on Eric Burdon of the Animals as he prepared to go onstage. "I'm really looking forward to tonight, man," he enthused. "I'm so high, livin' on my nerves. The spaceship's really gonna take off tonight!"

Figure 1.1. Premiering in the United States in 1967, left-handed guitarist Jimi Hendrix astounded audiences with his sonic pyrotechnics and was at the forefront of the era of psychedelic music, a major component of the counterculture. *Source:* Wikimedia Commons

The son of Al and Lucille Hendrix, Johnny Allen Hendrix was born in Seattle, Washington, on November 27, 1942. Light-complected like his mother, Johnny Allen also showed evidence of his father's part-Cherokee ancestry. The family's early history was one of transience, due both to Al's army service and Lucille's emotional immaturity, as she had been only sixteen when her son was born. Female relatives often filled in as caretakers. When Al left the army in November 1945, he retrieved his son from Berkeley, California, where the boy had been living with an aunt, after which he headed back to Seattle where he renamed his son John Marshall Hendrix. Though Al reunited with Lucille long enough to produce son Leon, the marriage was doomed to brevity, as Lucille died in 1958, having been found unconscious outside a bar. Jimi never castigated his mother for her carefree lifestyle. "She died when I was ten," he remarked. "She was a real groovy mother."

While Al struggled to keep the remnants of his family together through a series of menial jobs, James Marshall, now known as Jimmy, performed marginally in elementary school, doing poorly in music class but showing a talent for fantasy artwork. An introvert, Jimmy began to show an interest in music, often playing a "broom guitar" at home until he received his first real guitar in 1958. Drawn to the music of Elvis Presley and Little Richard, he rapidly developed his skills on the guitar and was soon playing local gigs while familiarizing himself with the rock, jazz, and blues that were favored in Seattle's black nightclubs. Jimmy was also drawn to the music of B.B. King, Muddy Waters, Jimmy Reed, John Lee Hooker, and other blues guitarists. Dropping out of high school in 1960, he seemed headed for a life of petty crime, getting a two-year sentence for multiple auto thefts in May 1961. Offered the alternative of military service, Jimmy ended up as a parachutist with the US Army's 101st Airborne Division at Fort Ord, California. His military career ended in July 1962, when he was discharged after having suffered an ankle injury stemming from a parachuting accident.

Four years of a transient existence backing artists like the Marvelettes, Curtis Mayfield, and the Isley Brothers gave Hendrix an opportunity to begin experimenting with techniques to draw new sounds from the electric guitar, and he bought his first new instrument, a Fender Duo-Sonic. By 1966, Hendrix had established a presence in Greenwich Village with his band Jimmy James and the Blue Flames. Giving up the Duo-Sonic for a

Stratocaster and leaving traditional blues behind, Hendrix tested new musical boundaries with lengthy solos and feedback. During this period, he was inevitably drawn into the Village's drug scene, trying both marijuana and methedrine. Hendrix's life took another turn during an English tour, now billing himself as "Jimi." There the Experience laid down the tracks that comprised their debut album, long-playing (LP) *Are You Experienced.* Though the LP featured such psychedelic anthems as "Manic Depression" and "Purple Haze," Hendrix claimed that their genesis was not in drugs. "I put a lot of dreams down in songs," he declared. After a whirlwind tour of Europe, the Jimi Hendrix Experience headed for America.

Hendrix's explosion onto the American music scene began with his performance at the Monterey Pop Festival. The Experience was one of the last groups to perform on the evening of Sunday, June 18, and left an unforgettable impression with thunderous versions of "Hey, Joe," "Foxy Lady, "Killing Floor," and, perhaps most notably, a cover of the Kingsmen's "Wild Thing." In an a completely unhinged performance that left listeners open-mouthed, Hendrix concluded with a memorable finale, setting his instrument on fire with lighter fluid before smashing it against the stage floor and finally hurling the shattered, still-burning remnants into the audience. That night, a music critic for the *Los Angeles Times* commented that the man from Seattle "had graduated from rumor to legend."

In 1968, the Experience won further critical success with the release of *Electric Ladyland*, which featured songs of diverse genres ranging from blues, soul, and pop to the indescribable, including a cover of Bob Dylan's "All Along the Watchtower" and the apocalyptic "Voodoo Child (Slight Return)." By 1969, Hendrix was determined to rediscover his American roots, abandoning his British sidemen and dissolving the Experience in favor of what he spoke of as an "electric church," which would feature new instrumentation as well as further experimentation. To that end, he constructed Electric Lady Studios in New York City that summer. An arrest for drug possession at the Toronto airport in May did not deter Hendrix from making what was perhaps his most famous appearance at the Woodstock Music and Art Fair of August 15 through 18, 1969. It was Hendrix, now performing with the Gypsy Sun and Rainbows, who brought the festival to a close with "Purple Haze" and an unforgettable screaming version of "The Star-Spangled Banner."

Though hailed by some as a triumph for the counterculture, Woodstock proved to be its swan song. Only four months later, the disastrous Altamont Festival in California, organized by the Rolling Stones as a free concert, turned into an anarchic nightmare of drug overdoses, violence, and death. Hendrix was not among the performers, being more focused on his drug possession trial, at which he was found not guilty. Still, any serious attention to his music was offset by quarrels over contracts and royalties, as well as disputes with girlfriends and musicians. Nevertheless, he brought together Billy Cox and Buddy Miles, who performed at the Fillmore East as the Band of Gypsies, releasing an eponymous album in 1970. It soon became apparent that Hendrix's personal life was unraveling, as at a benefit concert for the Vietnam Moratorium Committee in January of that year, Hendrix appeared disoriented and wandered offstage, possibly because of bad LSD. It was the end of the Band of Gypsies.

Fighting a growing drug habit, Hendrix sought to focus on a planned album to be called *First Rays of the New Rising Sun*, even as he was contracted to compose music for the proposed film *Rainbow Bridge*. These endeavors were made more difficult by his deteriorating health, which included ulcers, anxiety, and drug abuse that contributed to a growing moodiness and outbursts of temper. These personal issues reflected the negative changes that had overtaken the counterculture. Concert audiences were increasingly unruly and hostile, demanding free admission. The Isle of Wight Festival in August was a harbinger of what was to come. The misnamed "Love and Peace Concert" on the island of Fehmarn in West Germany was rife with apocalyptic violence. The concert began amid a howling gale as armed German bikers robbed the box office and terrorized the crowd, extorting money from concertgoers. When Hendrix finally took the stage, he was booed and taunted. Bikers shot one stagehand and assaulted others, sending Hendrix and his band fleeing from the stage, which the bikers then set ablaze. It was Jimi's last concert.

The remainder of the ill-fated tour was canceled as Billy Cox fell victim to some LSD-spiked punch, leading to his hospitalization. As his world came apart, Hendrix was increasingly erratic and distracted. On September 17, while staying at London's Samarkand Hotel, Hendrix took LSD and methedrine before retiring with his girlfriend Monika Dannemann. Later, unable to awaken Hendrix and finding her sleeping pills missing, she called for an ambulance. An hour later, at St. Mary

Abbots Hospital, Jimi Hendrix was declared dead, the coroner's report listing "inhalation of vomit" and "barbiturate intoxication" as the causes of death. Jimi Hendrix may have succeeded in his efforts to "kiss the sky," but at the cost of his life. He was not the last to succumb to the ethos of counterculture, which hailed the rejection of conventional restraints in the quest for personal liberation.

⁙

Just when did the 1960s end? The question has baffled many historians, and as Philip Jenkins writes in *Decade of Nightmares: The End of the Sixties and the Making of Eighties America* (2006), "Historical eras rarely begin or end at neat or precise points." Jenkins asserts that the 1960s "began with the assassination of John Kennedy in 1963 and ended with the resignation of Richard Nixon in 1974." Historian Bruce J. Schulman argues more broadly that the 1960s ended in 1968, bringing about the birth of "the sickly, neglected, disappointing stepsister to that brash, bruising blockbuster of a decade." Historian Andreas Killen and journalist Bryan Burrough both cite 1973 as the year that "the '60s era finally ended." For folk singer Joni Mitchell, "Woodstock was the culmination of it. . . . My generation for most of the '70s fell into apathy, sucked their thumb, heavy drugs followed light drugs, you know, the thing got darker and darker, and they didn't know where to take it."

To identify the end of the 1960s, one must identify the events and trends popularly associated with that decade. Even that approach leads one down a rock-strewn road. It has been argued that the 1960s was a bifurcated ten-year period, shaped in the first half of the decade by hopes that sprang from the promises of the invigorated leadership of the Kennedy presidency, civil rights triumphs, and the multitudinous legislative achievements of Lyndon Johnson's Great Society. Those hopes and aspirations died after 1965 in the jungles of Southeast Asia, the ghetto rebellions sweeping urban America, serial political assassinations, and civil unrest. As of 1968, reform through established political institutions looked increasingly impossible. An age of resistance, rebellion, and revolution already aborning was easily rationalized by those who once espoused peaceful, progressive reform through the establishment. By 1969, the national mood of growing hopelessness and fear produced deep political polarization. In this atmosphere, the self-destructive radicalism of three movements prospered, drawing the attention of the national media and authorities. In the course of a series of rapid mutations the counterculture, the Black Power movement, and the New Left helped speed the decade toward an unforgettable, cataclysmic end.

In early October 1967 the San Francisco Diggers, who had done much to inspire hippie culture, announced "The Death of Hippie" in a printed broadside that placed blame on the media. On October 6, some two hundred residents of the Haight-Ashbury area marched solemnly behind a fifteen-foot-long coffin in what a *Time* article the following week described as "the most frolicsome funeral in history." Ron and Jay Thelin, founders of the Haight's Psychedelic Shop, closed the shop the next day. It was the mass media, Ron charged, that "made us into hippies. We wanted to be free men and build a free community. . . . Well, the hippies are dead." Thelin's anger and the disgust voiced by the Diggers did not so much signal the "death" of hippie but, rather, anger at the rapidity with which inauthenticity had infected the phenomenon. It was *Time*'s correspondent who suggested that the "Death of Hippie" event sprang chiefly from the irritation of the "hip" founders of the pre-1967 inhabitants of Haight-Ashbury at the massive influx of "plastic" and part-time hippies, most often white, middle-class kids who had grown bored with life at home and sought out the excitement that they had heard was aborning in San Francisco. Many of the thousands flocking to "the Haight" were fascinated by the opportunity to "live free" while somehow obtaining room, board, and medical treatment at minimum or no cost, wearing outrageous clothing and hairstyles while experimenting with communal living, psychedelic drugs, and (for males at least) "free sex." The lure of such indulgences was almost irresistible.

Most of the later arrivals in the Haight had little or no idea of the roots of the hippie movement. It could be traced back to the 1940s and the founders of the "Beat Generation," like Allen Ginsberg (who made the transition to hippie), Gary Snyder, William S. Burroughs, and Jack Kerouac, whose fascination with jazz, poetry, drugs, and sex (including homosexuality) reflected their rejection of conventional boundaries. This grew out of rejection of a materialistic, consumer society that mindlessly coexisted with the horrors of imminent nuclear annihilation. Many of the same participants made the transition into writer Ken Kesey's band of

Merry Pranksters, who explored the country on an aging bus and through psychedelic drugs. Kesey's "Acid Tests" in the San Francisco Bay area in 1965 to 1967 helped lay the foundation for Haight-Ashbury's culture.

By the early 1960s, the main currents that the Beats and other non-conformists embraced had gained academic and intellectual support. As early as 1953, English author Aldous Huxley had experimented with mescaline under supervision of a psychiatrist and wrote of his experiences in *The Doors of Perception*, published in 1954 (and yes, the rock group took its name from the book). Timothy Leary, a Yale psychologist, experimented with psilocybin obtained from Mexican mushrooms a few years later and claimed that the experience fundamentally changed his understanding of reality. A later advocate of the synthesized psychedelic LSD as a treatment for mental illness and alcoholism, Leary gradually came to celebrate the drug chiefly as a means to a means of expanding one's consciousness. Together with colleague Richard Alpert, who like himself had been fired from Yale, and Ralph Metzner, an advocate of consciousness research, Leary published *The Psychedelic Experience* in 1964, deeming the psychedelic experience as "a journey to new realms of consciousness." Even as LSD was declared illegal in 1967, Leary became famous as the drug's most prominent public advocate. That did not spare him from jail, and after a series of drug arrests between 1965 and 1968, Leary began serving a twenty-year sentence in 1970.

Sexual liberation gained a popular advocate as early as 1953 when Hugh Hefner published the first issue of *Playboy* magazine and by the 1960s had created an empire of Playboy Clubs featuring "playmates" and a Playboy Mansion in Chicago, as well as publishing monthly ponderings on the "playboy philosophy," which was little more than a justification for sex as recreation. On the more serious side, philosopher Norman O. Brown, in addition to writing two best-selling books, *Life Against Death* (1959) and *Love's Body* (1966), advocated the eroticization of the body, endorsing a "polymorphous perversity." Counterculture concepts of unrestrained sexuality were also influenced by two works of the German philosopher Herbert Marcuse: *Eros and Civilization* (1955) and *One-Dimensional Man* (1964). *Eros and Civilization* countered Freud's theory of a "reality principle" that prioritized work, discipline, and social order in favor of a "pleasure principle" and "resexualization of the body." *One-Dimensional Man* argued that sexual liberation was a crucial political weapon.

Doubtless, few hippies knew of or had read Brown or Marcuse, but their works were hailed as justifications for "free sex."

Music, as the *lingua franca* of the counterculture, reflects the gradual though noticeable infusion of increasingly sexual language and drug references into the era's sounds. The Beatles' 1963 hit single "I Want to Hold Your Hand" morphed into the Rolling Stones' release of "Let's Spend the Night Together" in only four short years. Examples of the shift to lyrics about drug use (primarily psychedelics) during the same few years are legion. From the Amboy Dukes' "Journey to the Center of the Mind" (1968), the First Edition's "I Just Dropped In (to See What Condition My Condition Was In)" of the same year, and the Fraternity of Man's "Don't Bogart Me," much music explicitly or otherwise celebrating drug use became as ubiquitous as tie-dye T-shirts as the decade wore on. Though Grace Slick's haunting "White Rabbit" from Jefferson Airplane's album *Surrealistic Pillow* (1967) could be read as a warning of the potential disorientation of a psychedelic experience, Steppenwolf's "The Pusher" offered criticism only of "heavy" drugs. Lyrics alone did not define psychedelic music, which often incorporated experimental sounds, electronic feedback, swooping electric guitar solos, thunderous chords, and pounding rhythms, all of which could be found in albums by ephemeral groups like Iron Butterfly. One need only compare the Animals' 1964 hit version of "House of the Rising Sun" with that recorded by Frijid Pink in 1969 to comprehend the sonic revolution that reshaped popular music in those years.

Those who had in 1967 forecast that the insidious commercialization of the counterculture would bring about its death through absorption into mainstream culture proved correct. As much as anything, the popularity of the 1968 musical *Hair*, with its witless celebration of the "Age of Aquarius," signified the demise of the genuine counterculture. By the end of the decade, the vast majority of those youth who self-identified as hippies were simply middle-class, mostly white kids who adopted the accoutrements and hairstyles that had at one time been the sole property of the genuine counterculture. These same youth eagerly embraced both drugs and sexual liberation for recreational purposes, rather than out of a search for personal liberation or higher spirituality.

At the two epicenters of the counterculture, and in its wide-flung outposts across the nation, troublesome social pathologies had become evident as early as 1967. San Francisco's Haight district saw an explosion of drug abuse, the sexual abuse of runaways, sexually transmitted diseases, and illegitimate births as crime proliferated. Greenwich Village in New York City was the scene of a similar decline. In San Francisco, among the many new arrivals was thirty-two-year-old Charles Manson, a sociopath who had already spent half his life in jail. By 1968, the charismatic Manson had become the leader of a doomsday cult; on his orders, some of his followers murdered seven people in the Los Angeles area in August 1969. The potential violence and anarchy that hovered at the edge of the counterculture manifested itself again that December at the Altamont Festival, held only four months after Woodstock. Organized by the Rolling Stones as a free concert, Altamont was a nightmare of bad drugs, frequent violence, and death. The hastily planned event drew 300,000 people, who were "policed" by drunken Hell's Angels, one of whom stabbed a man to death. The chaos was accurately captured in the documentary film *Gimme Shelter* (1970). Historian Todd Gitlin concludes that Altamont was "the end of the Age of Aquarius."

Even as the counterculture foundered on its own limits, the Black Power movement was headed in a similar direction. That movement, which grew out of a slogan popularized by Student Nonviolent Coordinating Committee (SNCC) activist Stokely Carmichael in 1966, reflected a fracture in the civil rights movement as younger, less patient activists sought more rapid change and began to question the goal of integration, as some embraced a vaguely defined black nationalism. Only four years later, Carmichael and his wife, despairing of a black revolution in the United States, moved to Conakry, Guinea, in West Africa, where he adopted the name Kwame Ture and the cause of Pan-Africanism.

During the years of Carmichael's transition to an increasingly radical vision, the Black Panther Party for Self-Defense (BPP) was founded in Oakland, California, in October 1966 by Bobby Seale and Huey P. Newton. Formed to monitor police brutality against Oakland's black citizens and establish community service programs such as free breakfast programs and health clinics, BPP members more regularly drew media through armed clashes with white police. Between 1966 and 1969, the BPP gained national notoriety for violent confrontations with police, which became more frequent, leading racist FBI director J. Edgar Hoover to denounce the BPP as "the greatest threat to the internal security of the country." By

1969, as its membership reached five thousand, much of the BPP's leadership was incarcerated, in exile abroad (as was Eldridge Cleaver), or dead. Many considered the deaths of Panthers Bobby Hutton, Fred Hampton, and Mark Clark to be police executions. The BPP was targeted by local, state, and federal authorities, most notably through Hoover's Counterintelligence Program (COINTELPRO). A short-lived White Panther Party took shape in November 1968 under the leadership of the MC5's John Sinclair, who was soon was imprisoned for a terrorist bombing, after which the group dissolved. The BPP continued limited activities into the 1970s, often under Newton's leadership, but was riven by internecine strife.

For white radicals, Students for a Democratic Society (SDS) played a central role in charting the course of the antiwar movement and leftist radicalism. Founded in Ann Arbor, Michigan, in 1959, SDS became the flagship organization of the New Left, a phrase crafted by sociologist C. Wright Mills, who advocated a leftist course that rejected Marxist orthodoxies. SDS's founding document, the *Port Huron Statement*, seemed harmless enough with its call for "participatory democracy" as a solution to political alienation, and SDS devoted its energy to that quest, joining the struggle for civil rights, women's rights, minority rights in general, black power, and the antiwar movement—holding that the revolutionary struggle would be led by students and intellectuals. SDS organizers found college campuses congenial for recruiting. As the Vietnam War intensified, the course of the conflict drove antiwar groups like the National Mobilization Committee to End the War in Vietnam (known as the Mobe or SMC) and SDS into ever more radical stances. When resistance failed to halt the war, rebellion was embraced as protestors took to the streets and discarded the nonviolence of earlier days. The Columbia University revolt of April 1968 galvanized the New Left as students battled New York City police over the university's plans to repurpose some neighborhood property regardless of the objections of local residents. Radicals readily perceived such local injustices as reflective of deeper national and international inequities, and the scent of global youth rebellion soon wafted through the springtime air as students took to the streets of Paris, Berlin, Rome, and Tokyo. In this heady atmosphere, SDS's national membership swelled to 100,000, with more than an estimated 40,000 local chapters, with some 140,000 college students claiming an affiliation with SDS.

The SDS national conventions in 1968 and 1969 reflected the rapid radicalization of the once liberal organization. Fractures within the organization grew, as many in the National Office expressed skepticism about immediate revolution, while some of the more radical delegates such as Mark Rudd, president of the Columbia University chapter, embraced a more radical path at the 1968 meeting at Michigan State University. Of like mind was Bernardine Dohrn, a young lawyer who decided to stand for election as interorganizational secretary, proudly proclaiming to the delegates, "I consider myself a revolutionary communist!" The charismatic Dohrn won the election with no opposition and was destined to play a central role in the direction of SDS in subsequent years.

Ironically, internal strife left the national SDS organization rudderless during some of the most politically tumultuous months in American history. The National Office only belatedly supported demonstrations at the 1968 Democratic National Convention in Chicago in August, where leading figures in the peace and antiwar movements were arrested and later tried as the "Chicago Eight." Street violence there convinced national secretary Michael Klonsky that students alone would be incapable of bringing about the revolution and that they should join with working-class youth "to bring about the downfall of capitalism." The National Office's position paper "Toward a Revolutionary Youth Movement" (RYM I) was narrowly approved at a National Council meeting in Ann Arbor, Michigan, in June. Inevitably, an RYM II faction, opposed to immediate revolution, took shape.

In 1969, a year of swelling campus protest, SDS remained in a weak position to offer any direction. Unending ideological quarrels, internal factionalism, and paranoia had severely eroded SDS's campus base. At the 1969 national convention beginning on June 18 in Chicago, all of the latent fractures weakening the organization became evident, as advocates of RYM I, RYM II, and Progressive Labor (PL), a Maoist faction, prepared to do ideological battle. Dohrn and ten other RYM I proponents composed the 16,000-word document "You Don't Need a Weatherman to Know Which Way the Wind Blows," which took its title from the Bob Dylan song "Subterranean Homesick Blues." This was the genesis of Weatherman, whose wordy manifesto asserted that the objective of revolution was "the destruction of US imperialism and the achievement of a classless world: world communism." For the next five days, the floor fight among the two thousand attendees was chiefly between the Weatherman faction and PL. The tedium was broken only when Black Panther minister of information Chaka Walls, invited by the National Office faction, welcomed women into the movement by proclaiming, "We believe in pussy power!" The atmosphere grew more intense as Panther Jewel Cook confirmed that "the position for you sisters is . . . prone!" A reporter observed that the remark produced "pandemonium" in the audience, making clear that the fiasco was a setback for the Weatherman faction, but they were determined to crush PL once and for all. Dohrn seized the microphone, denounced PL, and demanded that all right-minded radicals follow her in a walkout. National Office supporters complied and, the following day, voted to expel PL from SDS. That evening, the National Office Group returned to the hall in triumph, proclaimed itself to be the sole legitimate SDS convention, and departed, retaining the keys to the Chicago office with its crucial membership files. The June 1969 convention marked the end of SDS as a coherent organization. A disillusioned radical captured the disgust of many that year when he summarized the catastrophic factionalism that had devastated SDS: "You don't need a rectal thermometer," he mused, "to know who the assholes are."

Both PL and the remnants of RYM II quickly faded into irrelevance, but the dedicated five hundred who now comprised the core of Weatherman under the leadership of Dohrn, Rudd, Bill Ayers, Jeff Jones, Terry Robbins, and Kathy Boudin were destined for a dramatic future. Determined to forge disciplined "political collectives" that would abjure "bourgeois individualism," Weatherman radicals dedicated themselves to relentless "self-criticism" sessions, martial arts, stringent diets, and abstinence from drugs and alcohol and indulgent sexual orgies for the purpose of eradicating "bourgeois sentiments." That summer, Weatherman collectives sought to energize white, working-class youth with dramatic "jailbreaks," in which the radicals invaded high school and college classrooms, subjecting captive student audiences to rants about the need for revolution. Perhaps most dramatically, in early September, a "jailbreak" at Pittsburgh's Southern Hills High School involved seventy-five Weatherwomen who rampaged through hallways with bare breasts, shouting revolutionary slogans. The radical women attacked the first police officers arriving on the scene and retreated only after eight patrol cars full of reinforcements arrived.

On October 8, the long-awaited National Action, which was planned to draw thousands of radical youths to Chicago with such slogans as "Bring the War Home!" began inauspiciously as only a few hundred radicals gathered at the southern end of Lincoln Park. Undeterred, slightly after 10:00 p.m., the radicals ran whooping from the park into the wealthy Gold Coast neighborhood, where they smashed car windshields, apartment windows, and glass storefronts. As the protestors fled in numerous directions, many were beaten by police; six were shot. Three days later, a second action was undertaken but with even less success, as police were reinforced and ready. More than 120 radicals were arrested, including all of the Weatherman leadership. The "Days of Rage," as the National Action came to be known, was an abject failure in its intended goal: white and black urban working-class youth did not join the revolution. At a final National War Council in December 1969 in Flint, Michigan, some four hundred attendees heard Dohrn's infamous remarks, which quickly caught the attention of the national news media. From the podium, Dohrn hailed cult leader Charles Manson, whose followers had recently murdered seven people, as betokening some obscure revolutionary significance. "Dig it," Dohrn exulted, "first they killed these pigs and then they ate dinner in the same room with them, then they even stuck a fork into the victim's stomach! Wild!" Weatherman members were soon greeting each other with the "sign of the fork," four uplifted fingers. Only about one hundred radicals remained after the meeting to organize into "affinity groups" that would operate as terrorist cells. So began the next phase of the New Left's history, as Weatherman prepared to go underground as a terrorist group.

The counterculture, Black Power movement, and the myriad organizations that fell under the umbrella of the New Left were not alone in responding to the heady atmosphere for change in the late 1960s. The Youth International Party, founded on the final day of 1967, defied definition as a party and lacked any formal organization or leadership, though among its founders, Abbie Hoffman and Jerry Rubin were the most renowned of the group, whose adherents took the name Yippies. Bridging the gap between the counterculture and the New Left, Yippies sought to subvert the establishment by mockery, rejecting any ideology and turning guerrilla theater against the absurdities of the system. Anti-authoritarian and anarchistic, Yippies strove to make protest fun as well as symbolic, perhaps most famously when they nominated the pig "Pigasus" for their

1968 presidential candidate. They were, according to a 1969 American Broadcasting Company piece, "Groucho Marxists." One of the longest-lived protest organizations of the era, the Yippies continued their antics well beyond the 1970s.

The late 1960s also witnessed the birth and growth of numerous organizations dedicated variously to women's rights, gay rights, Native American rights, and environmentalism, all movements that would gain momentum in the 1970s. The National Organization of Women (NOW), founded in 1966 by Betty Friedan, Mary Eastwood, and Catherine East, strove to ensure that NOW did not become associated in the public mind with more radical feminist elements and the lesbian rights movement. NOW's struggle to manage the direction of the women's rights movement was challenged again in the fall of 1968 when feminist Robin Morgan, founder of WITCH (Women's International Terrorist Conspiracy from Hell), organized a protest of the Miss America Pageant in Atlantic City, New Jersey. The action, which did *not* involve bra-burning, was meant to protest the commodification and exploitation of women. More challenges awaited as Friedan fretted that the role of lesbians in the movement would discredit it, and warned younger radicals that the focus should remain on employment equality and education rather than "sexual fantasy." The battle for gender equality, over who should be included in the women's rights movement, and what issues should be foremost continued into the 1970s, a decade that would bring great gains for American women of every orientation.

The issue of sexual orientation arose elsewhere in 1969 as the gay rights movement was born amid battles with New York City police in Greenwich Village. By then, however, as historian David Carter writes, "the subject of homosexuality was more and more in the air." One major focus of anti-gay violence was in Queens, New York, where gay men and women were regularly terrorized by hoodlums and arrested in Greenwich Village gay bars. The pent-up frustration and anger of the victims exploded at the Stonewall Inn on June 28, 1969, as a police squad sought to herd arrested patrons into waiting police wagons. A crowd of about four-hundred onlookers soon gathered, shouting and throwing objects at the police, who were driven back into the bar. Amid all the chaos, there was one shout that captured the moment as well as a movement: "We're not going to take this anymore!" The arrival of a Tactical Patrol Force restored order early the next morning.

The following night, however, a crowd again gathered at the Stonewall Inn, chanting the slogan, "Gay Power!" The arrival of police assured a virtual rerun of the previous night's violent confrontation. The Stonewall Riots brought about the founding of the Gay Liberation Front (GLF), which asserted in its mission statement: "We are a revolutionary group of men and women formed with the realization that complete sexual liberation for all people cannot come about unless existing social institutions are abolished. We reject society's attempt to impose sexual roles and definitions of our nature." The Stonewall riots reverberated well beyond the 1970s and into the next century.

Relentlessly driven from their native lands, defrauded by countless treaties, relegated to areas deemed worthless by whites, and ultimately victimized by nineteenth-century federal policy that was in all but name genocide, Native Americans likewise felt the stirrings of radical change in the 1960s. In November 1969, Richard Oakes, a young Mohawk activist and member of the Indians of All Tribes, led a group of Native Americans ashore on Alcatraz Island in San Francisco Bay, which under an obscure 1868 treaty could be claimed by Native Americans. Though removed from the island by the Coast Guard, Oakes and about eighty others returned the following day. Joined by more than one hundred "Red Power" advocates on Thanksgiving Day, the occupiers gained considerable public and celebrity support but were ultimately compelled to abandon the island due to its lack of water and other necessities. Though the occupation was brief, it inspired members of the recently formed American Indian Movement (AIM), whose leader Russell Means noted, "Before AIM, Indians were dispirited, defeated, and culturally dissolving. People were ashamed to be Indian. . . . Then there was that spark at Alcatraz." Historian Rob Kirkpatrick writes, "Alcatraz did for AIM what Stonewall did for the Gay Rights movement."

By the 1960s, the term "environmentalism," which suggested a philosophy that encompassed conservation and preservation as part of a broader concern for the totality of the planet's health, began to achieve common usage, as series of events focused public attention more intensely on the need to protect the natural environment. Arguably the most extreme example was the polluted Cuyahoga River, which burst into flames on June 22, 1969. It was the twelfth such blaze, a testament to human irresponsibility. Three other rivers had also suffered similar combustions.

Were the interminable smog that engulfed southern California cities not enough warning of the dangers of air pollution, the threat posed by water pollution became reality in January 1969, when a blowout in a Union Oil offshore oil field dumped an estimated three million barrels of crude oil into the Santa Barbara Channel. The damage to the ecosystem was catastrophic. Thousands of oil-soaked birds lay dead or dying on thirty-five miles of beaches. Seals, sea otters, fish, and dolphins also fell victim to the viscous oil, as volunteers made often futile efforts save as many victims as possible. "If there was any event that would mobilize the nascent environmental movement in 1969," writers Ernest Zebrowski and Judith Howard concluded, "that was it." For many Americans, the Santa Barbara oil spill was a clarion call to action in defense of the environment. In 1969, David Brower, long-time activist and former president of the Sierra Club, founded Friends of the Earth, which promotes environmentalism as an international concern. The initial indication of a national awakening to the issue was the first Earth Day, celebrated on April 22, 1970. Some two thousand universities and colleges, as well as tens of thousands of elementary and secondary schools, took part in teach-ins concerning the environment. Subsequently, the environmental movement continually gained momentum and public support in the 1970s.

Even as the counterculture degenerated, the Black Power movement ran up against its limits, and the New Left foundered in factionalism, the Vietnam War was reaching new heights of violence as delegates to the Paris peace talks wrangled over the shape of the conference table. During President Richard Nixon's first month in office, 542 Americans died in Vietnam, even as US troop strength peaked at 543,000 in April. Despite President Nixon's announcement of a program of gradual withdrawal of US forces from Vietnam, there were two massive antiwar demonstrations in the nation's capital that fall. Neither succeeded in moving Nixon, who boasted that he had watched a televised football game instead. By year's end, another 11,616 Americans had died in the conflict.

By 1969, there were undoubtedly numerous weary Americans who found their state of mind summed up in Blind Faith's song "I Can't Find My Way Home." However, not all was horror and despair in 1969. The majority of Americans did not protest, riot, demonstrate, or use drugs. Most went to work, school, tended to family, enjoyed films, theater, concerts, and sports. The New York Mets demonstrated that hope sprang eternal by winning their first World Series. If there was a single event that lifted American spirits out of the morass of fear and despair, it grew out of the accomplishments of the Apollo program, sought to realize President Kennedy's promise to put an American on the moon by the end of the decade. On July 20, 1969, the lunar module *Eagle* carried by *Apollo 11* and manned by Neil Armstrong, Buzz Aldrin, and Michael Collins touched down in the moon's Sea of Tranquility, an event covered by live national television. Few who watched would ever forget the words, "Houston, the *Eagle* has landed," or the blurry video of Armstrong setting foot on the lunar surface and uttering the equally unforgettable words, "That's one small step for man, one giant leap for mankind." The astronauts returned safely to Earth on July 24 to be hailed as national heroes who had demonstrated that the nation could still strive for and achieve greatness, even in the worst of times.

❖

As New Year's 1968 dawned, five activists were celebrating in the New York City apartment of Abbie and Anita Hoffman, smoking grass, reveling in their successful protest activities of the year past, and planning a new form of "protest art" for the coming year. Also there were Jerry Rubin, college drop-out and longtime antiwar activist, together with his girlfriend Nancy Kurshan and Paul Krassner, editor of *The Realist*. A committed activist, having worked in voting rights and civil rights campaigns, community organizing, and antiwar protests, and having planned and engaged in numerous other antiestablishment actions, Abbie and the others struggled to come up with a concept by which they could fuse aspects of the counterculture with radical left politics. It was Krassner who came up with the idea of Yippie! He later remarked, "We needed a name to signify the radicalization of hippies . . . a coalition of psychedelic hippies and political activists." Anita Hoffman suggested that were they to be taken seriously, Yippies needed a more formal name. Thus was born the Youth International Party (YIP), a completely fictional organization in which anyone could claim membership. The group held its first press conference on March 17 at New York's Americana Hotel. Already baffled and disgusted by hippies, Middle America now had to ponder the meaning of a new mutant variant, whose objectives remained obscure.

Abbie Hoffman was born on November 30, 1936, to John and Florence Hoffman in Worcester, Massachusetts. Growing up in a middle-class Jewish family, Hoffman later recalled his childhood as "idyllic," generally doing above-average academic work in junior high. At Classical High School, he established a reputation as a troublemaker, fighting, vandalizing school property, and taunting his teachers. Hoffman's career at Classical High ended during his second year when he attacked a teacher who called him a "communist punk." Graduating from Worcester Academy in 1955, Hoffman gained admission to Brown University, studying psychology under Herbert Marcuse and Abraham Maslow. Graduating with a bachelor's degree in 1959, he completed coursework for a master's degree in psychology at the University of California at Berkeley, where he married Sheila Karklin in May 1960; the couple had two children. It was at Berkeley that two major influences on the trajectory of Hoffman's life become evident. Embracing the Beat scene that was taking root on the West Coast, Hoffman was also drawn to the first glimmerings of New Left activism that were taking shape at the University of California's Berkeley campus. Hoffman claimed to have been among the protestors who disrupted the local hearings of the House Committee on Un-American Activities and were assaulted by city police.

Between 1960 and 1966, having returned to the Worcester, Massachusetts, Hoffman was drawn into a variety of left-wing and civil rights causes. He was moved by Stokely Carmichael's suggestion that white radicals focus on ending the Vietnam War and was involved in organizing Worcester's first antiwar demonstration in October 1965, the year of the nationwide "Teach-In" about the war. The following year, he also tried marijuana and LSD for the first time. His growing focus on radical activities and intrigue with the counterculture widened a growing breach between himself and Sheila, and the couple divorced in 1966. With no further marital ties, Hoffman moved to New York City, where he opened Liberty House, a center of movement activity. There he met Anita Kushner, a volunteer, whom he married in 1967. Hoffman embraced the bohemian lifestyle of the Lower East Side and Greenwich Village but was dismissive of the younger hippies who, he felt, lacked a commitment to the self-actualization, friendship, community, and self-expression that could be found in social commitment. In an article in *WIN* (*Workshop in Nonviolence*) magazine, Hoffman summarized the proto-Yippie perspective, "We as a movement must become more concerned with communication and that involves emotional visual presentations more than factual analysis. . . . I think we should watch more TV than read, [and] listen to music more than lectures." The seeds of Yippie! were sown. On Easter Sunday 1967, Hoffman helped realize the East Coast's first Be-In in Central Park. That same year, as he and Anita celebrated the birth of their son "america," his efforts to help found a Digger "Free Store" in the East Village, which would abjure capitalism and be manned by volunteers, foundered on what biographer Martin Jezer described as "the hippies' nonexistent work habits." Hoffman was convinced that the Village was simply too small a venue for such a revolutionary enterprise and moved on to more ambitious goals. "I was determined," he recalled in his book *Soon to Be a Major Motion Picture*, "to bring the hippie movement into a broader protest." While Hoffman hoped to ally hippies with the Black Power movement, the burgeoning antiwar movement offered the more likely dynamic vehicle.

Hoffman had participated in his first antiwar march in New York City in early November 1966. He became a leader in the Cambridge, Massachusetts, Vietnam Summer project and, aided by activist Jim Fouratt, succeeded in getting a "Flower Brigade" inserted into a New York City "loyalty parade" in early May. Insults and hurled objects from the sidewalk crowds led Hoffman to reconsider his thoughts on nonviolence. "Doctrinaire" nonviolence should be rejected in favor of a new conception of nonviolence as wedded to spontaneity, enthusiasm, and optimism—guerrilla theater, soon to be a major Yippie tactic.

The action that would ever after be associated in the public mind with Hoffman and Yippies, though the latter did not yet exist, was the "assault" on the New York Stock Exchange on August 24, 1967, when Hoffman and a few others made their way into the visitors' gallery, which overlooked the floor of frenetic brokers. The action was simple—the protestors flung wads of dollar bills onto the trading floor, completely disrupting activity as brokers and clerks rushed to get the money while others booed the hippies. Hoffman and his compatriots were quickly removed, but the action had succeeded brilliantly, exposing the crass greed of the capitalists who crawled on their hands and knees for the free money. On the sidewalk outside, where Hoffman and others burned dollar bills in view of baffled New Yorkers, was Jerry Rubin, West Coast antiwar activist who had just arrived to direct a demonstration planned for the nation's capital. Rubin, a sociology graduate student, had been a leader of Berkeley's Vietnam Day Committee, later subpoenaed by the House Un-American Activities Committee (HUAC) as a subversive. Rubin had mocked the proceedings by appearing dressed as a revolutionary war soldier, foreshadowing later Yippie tactics. Deriding Berkeley's Free Speech Movement as "too fucking polite," Rubin found a soulmate in Hoffman, whom he believed could bring hippies into the antiwar movement. What he saw at the Stock Exchange that day confirmed his belief that radical politics could be fused with counterculture.

When Rubin arrived in New York, the Student Mobilization Committee (Mobe) had already formalized plans for an October demonstration at the Pentagon. There was to be a day of draft-card burning, a rally at the Lincoln Memorial, and a march to the Pentagon. Invited to speak at Mobe's press conference, Hoffman unveiled a plan to levitate the Pentagon three hundred feet into the air. When federal authorities warned that mace would be used on demonstrators, Abbie proclaimed that hippies would come equipped with a chemical spray called lace, which would act as an irresistible aphrodisiac, incapacitating Pentagon defenders. The much ballyhooed "levitation" of the Pentagon was, as it turned out, only a sideshow, involving a small percentage of the protestors and lasting less than an hour. Nevertheless, Abbie, costumed as a Native American wearing an Uncle Sam hat, and Anita, decked out in Sgt. Pepper garb, advanced on the building until halted by military police (MPs), where Abbie announced, "We're Mr. and Mrs. America and we declare this liberated territory!" The more dramatic confrontation occurred on the building's main steps, where for two days demonstrators confronted a line of armed soldiers, some conducting a teach-in on Vietnam with the troops, while others goaded them. Many were drive off by bayonet-wielding troops after the media left, with federal marshals intervening to arrest and beat protestors. Abbie and Anita were arrested on Sunday night and jailed, but even given the failure to levitate the Pentagon, organizers considered the event a great success, drawing national attention to the antiwar cause and radicalizing protestors, especially those who were beaten.

It was in the following months that Yippie! was born and the central event on the action agenda was the Democrats' nominating convention, to held in Chicago from August 26 through 29. The Mobe—whose leaders included David Dellinger, Rennie Davis, and Tom Hayden—had been laying plans for a major protest since 1967. Yippies envisioned a "Festival of Life," which would contrast with the Democrats' "Convention of Death." Abbie proclaimed an "American Youth Festival" that would draw 500,000 dope-smoking hippies to rampage through the city. "When [President] Johnson mounts the rostrum," he promised, "we will run naked through the streets." The Yippie leadership drastically underestimated the determination of the city's Democratic boss and mayor, Richard J. Daley, who had no intention of permitting protestors to disrupt the convention. Yippie requests for permits were ignored, leaving any gathering to the mercies of the Chicago police, who were notorious for their insensitivity to protestors of any type. By August, 12,000 Chicago police had been put on alert, backed up by 6,000 Illinois National Guardsmen, with 6,000 army troops in reserve. Some protest organizers began warning their followers not to go, foreseeing a potential bloodbath, though some hardcore radicals came prepared for battle. Groups like the Motherfuckers and some SDS factions planned to provoke the police. Hoffman fanned official paranoia when, at a Yippie meeting, he threated to put LSD in the city water supply. Threats to kidnap convention delegates in fake taxis provoked further concerns, as did a joint press statement by Hoffman and Rubin in which they promised to use "super-hot" hippie women to seduce the delegates as well as hippie "studs" to seduce the delegates' wives. "We will piss and shit and fuck in public," their statement threatened, "we will be constantly stoned or tripping on every drug known to man." Were that not enough to alarm officials and the public, Jack Mabley of the *Chicago American* ran a weekend column in which he claimed, with no evidence, that the Yippies planned various deadly acts of arson, introducing poison gas into the convention hall, blowing up the control tower at O'Hare Airport, and driving gasoline tankers into police stations.

The first Yippie action was far less ominous. On Friday, August 23, Rubin and five Yippies held a "nominating convention" at the Civic Center for their presidential candidate, a pig christened "Pigasus." As Rubin was giving the nominating speech for the squirming pig, numerous police vehicles roared up and officers arrested all present. As Pigasus was hauled off to an animal shelter, one of the Yippies shouted, "They're arresting our candidate!" Meanwhile, as protestors began gathering in Lincoln Park on August 24, it became evident that the expected thousands would not be there. The planned Festival of Life took shape the following day when Mobe protestors joined the hippie crowd, but by evening it became a festival of chaos as police drove the crowd from the park swinging clubs and chanting, "Kill, kill, kill the motherfuckers."

For the next two days, protestors clashed with police, being driven from one park to another. On Tuesday, Abbie spent most of the day attending an "un-birthday party" for Lyndon Johnson at the Chicago Coliseum, where a crowd of six thousand listened and cheered as activists attacked the president, with Abbie leading a chant of "Fuck you, LBJ." The following day a march on the convention hall was to take place, but Hoffman was not among the marchers, as he had been arrested that morning and taken on a round of police stations, being beaten in each. His incarceration prevented his attendance at the rally in Grant Park, where police again attacked peaceful demonstrators, enraging many and setting the stage for the momentous events during Wednesday evening in front of the Hilton Hotel.

The "battle of the Michigan Avenue," as it came to be called, occurred during the expected nomination of Vice President Hubert Humphrey, who was seen by the antiwar crowd as little more than a Johnson puppet. Protestors gathered in front of the Hilton, where the candidates and their staffs were housed, and around 8:00 p.m., in the lights of television camera crews, the simmering rage on all sides broke loose, as police suddenly charged into protestors, journalists, and bystanders, sparing no one. As some protestors fought back with fists, police pushed a group of bystanders through the plate glass window of the Haymarket Inn before pouring inside to beat people sitting peacefully at the bar. Amid the chaos, the crowd took up an unforgettable chant that captured the power of the "cool" though immediate medium of television: "The whole world is watching!" Following his nomination and televised acceptance speech, which some networks interspersed with scenes of the street fighting in front of the Hilton, Humphrey returned to his hotel room and wept, knowing that the violence would likely doom his candidacy. A presidential commission later characterized the event as "a police riot."

1969 brought the Nixon administration and uncertain prospects for the movement. Anti-Nixon protests at his inauguration had been tepid. For Abbie, however, the publication in late 1968 of *Revolution for the Hell of It* made him a national figure just months before his indictment as one of the Chicago Eight indicted for inciting a riot. In his quickly published *Woodstock Nation*, Hoffman argued that there was a political context to the "Three Days of Love and Peace," even though he was booed off the stage at the festival. Otherwise, the book's message was incoherent. Hoffman claimed that, given his upcoming trial, "I want to be tried because . . . I think property eats shit . . . that the schools should be destroyed . . . because I think people should be able to do whatever they want . . . because I think kids should kill their parents." In the face of objections from acquaintances, Hoffman argued that the words were intended for shock value and to compel people to acknowledge the "generational war." For obvious reasons, his 1971 book *Steal This Book* had to be self-published but proved a humorous guide to living free.

Badgered by Mayor Daley and determined to crush the antiwar movement, the Nixon administration supported a federal Chicago court indictment of the perceived leaders of the Chicago protests: Yippies Hoffman and Rubin, ex-SDS leaders Tom Hayden and Rennie Davis, the Black Panther Bobby Seale, pacifist David Dellinger, and antiwar activists

Figure 1.2. Prominent founder of the Youth International Party Abbie Hoffman advocated a guerrilla theater criticism of American values, habits, and politics. Hoffman (center), pictured here visiting University of Oklahoma students in 1969 sans his usual American flag shirt, later delivered an unhinged tirade before an audience of 11,000 students at the University of Texas. Source: Wikimedia Commons / Richard O. Barry

John Froines and Lee Weiner. Among the variety of charges were conspiracy to cross state lines to incite riots and aiding others in doing the same. The trial of the Chicago Eight, later seven after Seale was ordered to be tried separately, was Abbie's final opportunity to achieve national notoriety, and he planned to disrupt the proceedings in every way possible. Movement lawyers William Kunstler and Leonard Weinglass had the unenviable task of defending the assorted radicals when the trial began in late September 1969. Though the trial's most dramatic moment came when Judge Julius Hoffman ordered defendant Bobby Seale bound and gagged due to Seale's persistent insistence that he be permitted to defend himself, it was Abbie who most successfully turned the trial into farce by doing handsprings into the courtroom, wearing outrageous clothing and judicial robes, and capturing both headlines and Judge Hoffman's ire with his irreverent responses to questioning. Asked by Weinglass to identify himself, Hoffman replied that he was "an orphan of America" and resided in "the Woodstock Nation." Baffled, the judge asked what state that was in, only to be told that "it is the state of mind." Asked when he was born, Abbie rejoined, "Psychologically, about 1960." Judge Hoffman's ire was further raised when Abbie accused him of "being a disgrace to the Jews" and mocked him in Yiddish.

The jury began deliberations on February 14, 1970, as Judge Hoffman declared the defendants and their lawyer guilty of 159 instances of contempt of court. Abbie alone was cited on twenty-four counts. Ultimately, the jurors reached a compromise, acquitting all seven of conspiracy but convicting Hoffman, Rubin, Dellinger, Davis, and Hayden of crossing state lines with intent to riot. Judge Hoffman then sentenced them to five years in prison and fines in addition to revoking the bail that had permitted them freedom in previous weeks. In the course of a series of appeals, all were again free on bail, and by November 1972, all the convictions were overturned. The few remaining contempt charges were reduced to time already served. For his part in the Chicago actions, Abbie Hoffman spent two weeks in jail.

The reality was, however, that the 1960s were over. The Yippies, their numbers reduced, journeyed to Miami Beach in the summer of 1972 to protest at both the Democratic and Republican Conventions, but the times were "a-changing," and street actions were minimal. Hoffman and Rubin coauthored *Vote!*—a book calling for political reform from within the system. That year, the Yippies endorsed the presidential candidacy of Democrat George McGovern, and later at the Republican Convention did their best to undercut the Zippies, a small group dedicated to re-creating the Chicago riots.

Now thirty-five, Hoffman, who was prone to depression and had been diagnosed with bipolar disorder, was drawn into a plan to purchase and sell cocaine, leading to his arrest. Skipping bail in 1974, he went underground and began a new life as Barry Freed, living on the St. Lawrence River in the Thousand Islands area of New York and seriously dedicating himself to the new environmentalism. He resurfaced in 1980 and served four months of a one-year sentence before returning to environmental activism. That same year, he published *Soon to Be a Major Motion Picture*, an unsparing examination of movement and counterculture conceits. He could not, however, escape the disease that plagued him, and on April 12, 1989, Abbie Hoffman was found dead in his Pennsylvania apartment, having overdosed on phenobarbital. Yippie! outlived him, as small groups remained into the early 2000s, inspired by his unique blend of political theater and social commitment.

"A DECENT INTERVAL"
America's Exit from Vietnam, 1969–1973

By 1969, the Battle of Ap Bac was long forgotten by most Americans, who were still absorbing the impact of the January 1968 Tet Offensive that had fatally damaged the credibility of the Lyndon Johnson administration's claims that the American war in Vietnam was being won. Worse, the fighting had only intensified in 1969, even as US troop strength reached its peak. But there were those who like former army lieutenant colonel John Paul Vann, now a civilian adviser to US troops in Vietnam, had long ago discerned the flaws in the conduct of the war. One of some 16,000 military advisers sent to aid the Army of the Republic of South Vietnam (ARVN) during the Kennedy administration, Vann, who arrived in 1962, soon became disillusioned with the idea that the South Vietnamese could stave off their communist enemy without extensive US military involvement. The epiphany for the thirty-nine-year-old officer came during the Battle of Ap Bac, almost six years before the Tet Offensive.

In early January 1963, Vann was acting as chief adviser to ARVN's Seventh Division, based in the Mekong delta and headed by ARVN Colonel Bui Dinh Dam, a protégé of South Vietnam's prime minister, Ngo Dinh Diem, notorious for prioritizing palace politics over military victory. The province chief, Lam Quang Tho, whose irregulars supported ARVN, owed political allegiance to Diem. Vann was aware of ARVN's predilection to avoid direct clashes with the Vietcong (VC), preferring to call in artillery and air strikes or simply permit the enemy to escape, thus

Figure 2.1. John Paul Vann in his Saigon office. In the early 1960s, Vann was convinced that the communists could be defeated if the South Vietnamese army was properly trained and led. By the latter years of the war, his optimism faded, and he despaired of the survival of South Vietnam. Source: Wikimedia Commons / USOM/Office of Rural Affairs, Saigon

avoiding casualties. Nevertheless, prior to the Battle of Ap Bac, Vann had been among those US advisers who were convinced that the VC could be defeated "if they would only stand and fight," affording ARVN troops the confidence they needed to take the offensive against the communists. The events at Ap Bac were to prove otherwise.

Vann and ARVN lacked several critical pieces of intelligence prior to their plan to engage a reported Vietcong buildup at Ap Bac. First, nearly three times as many Vietcong soldiers were positioned there as was thought, and second, their superiors knew of the planned ARVN assault. Accordingly, the VC dug in along a canal and were prepared to stand and fight. ARVN Seventh Division's plan of attack, formulated with Vann's help, seemed reasonably conceived: a three-pronged pincer movement consisting of an infantry regiment to be helicoptered in, two regional battalions that would arrive by foot, and a rifle squadron carried by armored personnel carriers (APCs) that would surround the enemy. ARVN and irregulars would command a nearly ten-to-one numerical advantage over their opponents. Nothing went as planned. The VC let three waves of helicopter-borne infantry arrive before they revealed their presence in a fusillade of automatic weapons fire as the fourth wave of airborne troops arrived. As Vann circled overhead in an L-19 spotter plane, it became evident that the ARVN troops were hopelessly pinned down and unable to advance. After several hours of stalemate, it was obvious that the APCs would have to be sent forward to rescue them. The ARVN officer in command of the APCs did so only upon Vann's profane urgings by radio, after which the APCs that were not stuck in the canal began backing out as VC snipers picked off their outriders. Later that afternoon, a mass parachute drop of ARVN troops landed a half-mile away from the target, and the hapless parachutists were quickly taken under fire by the waiting VC. When the Battle of Ap Bac was over, the VC still held most of the ground, five helicopters had been shot down, and sixty-three South Vietnamese troops and three Americans were dead. Vann afterward described the battle as "a miserable fucking performance, just like it always is."

The Battle of Ap Bac, journalist and historian Neil Sheehan recalled, "was the biggest story we had ever encountered." He and journalist David Halberstam were among the few foreign correspondents to witness the disaster, rather than depending on the "five o'clock follies," as the official briefings were known. Most senior American officials claimed that the battle was a South Vietnamese victory, contrary to actual events. American journalists learned that any skeptical questions about the progress of the war were not welcome at press conferences. When Associated Press correspondent Peter Arnett questioned the official account of the Battle of Ap Bac at such a "presser," Pacific area commander Admiral Thomas C. Hart snarled at Arnett to "get on the team." Such official obtuseness ensured that the South Vietnamese and their American allies would refuse to acknowledge the realities of the conflict over the next four years.

Disgusted at the official response to Ap Bac, Vann resigned from his position several months later. An outspoken individual, Vann did not hide his belief that the Diem government was content with letting the conflict proceed inconclusively in order to secure endless American aid. He was not alone in his misgivings about the trajectory of the war. Many mid-level State Department officials and Central Intelligence operatives who had viewed the war firsthand were equally skeptical, believing that no progress was possible unless the Diem regime's corruption, which pervaded the upper ranks of ARVN, was effectively addressed. Frustrated, Vann left the army a few months after completing his Vietnam assignment in March 1963.

In the following months, President Kennedy and his chief civilian and military advisers, notably Secretary of Defense Robert McNamara, concluded that Diem, together with his conniving brother Nhu, were the chief impediments to success in Vietnam. After weeks of discussion and planning, it was agreed that Diem would have to go, hopefully to be replaced by more honest and effective leadership in Vietnam. A *coup d'état* by a cabal of ARVN generals was formulated in October, and when the group was apprised that the US would not intervene, Diem's fate was sealed. On November 1, troops loyal to the plotters arrested Diem and Nhu, who were both executed, much to Kennedy's horror. The new leadership, under ARVN general Duong "Big" Minh, proved no more successful in stabilizing the situation, and Vietnam was governed by a series of revolving-door military juntas until 1967.

Vann's often contentious manner almost seemed to spring from his disjointed childhood. Born out of wedlock on July 2, 1924, to the West Virginia couple John Spry and Myrtle Tripp, the boy took his stepfather's surname when his mother married Aaron Frank Vann. Escaping childhood poverty while attending boarding school, Vann went on to junior college in 1941 and enlisted in the Army Air Force in 1943, where he was trained as a pilot and navigator, winning a second lieutenant's commission in 1945. Vann saw no action in World War II and married Mary Allen shortly after the war ended; the couple had five children.

Forsaking the Army Air Force when it became a separate service branch in 1947, Vann made the army his home until 1963. He first saw action when the Korean War broke out in June 1950, when his unit was posted to the dangerous Pusan Perimeter at the low point of the war for United Nations forces. Later in 1950, Vann was given command of the Eighth Army Ranger Company, leading perilous reconnaissance missions behind enemy, often Chinese, lines. He left the combat zone only after one of his children was stricken with a serious illness. Transferred back to the United States, Vann served as an assistant professor of military science and tactics at Rutgers University, during which time he earned a bachelor's degree with a focus on economics and statistics.

Posted to Schweinfurt, Germany, in 1954, the year of the French defeat in their Indochina War, Vann commanded the Sixteenth Infantry Regiment's Heavy Mortar Company. Major Vann was soon transferred to the army's European headquarters in Heidelberg, before returning stateside, where he attended Leavenworth's Command and General Staff College in 1957, simultaneously earning a master's degree in business administration and a doctorate in public administration from Syracuse University. Those years were not without controversy, however, as in May 1959, he was accused of the statutory rape of a fifteen-year-old girl. Both the army's Criminal Investigation Division and an Article 12 investigation reviewed the evidence at length before concluding that there was insufficient evidence to convict Vann.

Now a lieutenant colonel, Vann assumed his duties as an adviser to ARVN in 1962, until disgust at the advisory mission's evident failure led him to resign his commission. Having returned home, Vann accepted employment with defense contractor Martin Marietta, though he was soon drawn back to Vietnam, where he returned as an official of the Agency for International Development (AID) in March 1965, just as the war was on the verge of being Americanized. For the next three years, Vann served as Deputy for Civilian Operations and Revolutionary Development Support (CORDS). As a senior adviser in the Third Corps Tactical Zone, which included the twelve most crucial provinces to the north and west of Saigon, Vann supervised 243 civilian and 2,138 military advisers. At this point, he became optimistic that the program was a key to success in Vietnam.

One of the most crucial means of defeating the communists in Vietnam was known as "winning hearts and minds," convincing the people of South Vietnam, especially those in rural areas, that their most promising future lay in supporting the government of South Vietnam (GSV). Various permutations of this approach had been attempted prior to the establishment of CORDS in May 1967. The first was the ill-fated "strategic hamlet" program initiated by the Diem government in 1961, in part to counter the Vietcong's land reform program. The concept involved herding villagers into "protected" hamlets, where medical and educational facilities would be made available and, more importantly, the VC would be prevented from contact with the rural population. The effort failed miserably, due in large part to peasant resistance to being forced off ancestral lands, as well as terrorist tactics by the VC. By 1964, it was estimated that the VC controlled most of the nation's 2,600 strategic hamlets. The next effort was undertaken with the direct aid of the Military Assistance Command, Vietnam (MACV), with the intent of gradually "pacifying" rural areas. This program also failed, due largely to the inability of ARVN to provide adequate security to isolated villages.

"Winning hearts and minds" took secondary priority by 1965 as commanding army general William Westmoreland insisted that US resources be directed toward engaging and destroying VC and People's Army of Vietnam (PAVN) units. The intensified combat drove rural Vietnamese into the cities, and, by the end of 1966, the GSV claimed that it controlled 4,700 of the country's 12,000 villages. President Lyndon Johnson supported this pacification program and named Robert Kromer of the CIA and National Security Council to bring together the CIA, AID, the State Department, and the US military in a renewed effort to win hearts and minds. CORDS was soon established in all of South Vietnam's forty-four provinces by 1968. A Vietnamese provincial chief was supported by an American adviser in each, organizing both civilian development programs and military security issues. Even as CORDS focused on strengthening the Regional and Popular Forces (RF/PF) and expanding the National Police, it initiated several other programs. The Chieu Hoi Program sought to encourage communist defectors, while the Phoenix Program sought to identify, capture, try, and even execute VC operatives. CORDS statistics claim that between 1968 and 1972, more than 81,000 VC were "neutralized" by these various means. There was further hope that the 1967 presidential election, which President Johnson had insisted on, would bring greater political stability. Nguyen Van Thieu and Nguyen Cao Ky, both former ARVN generals, were elected, respectively, president and premier in a contest of dubious legitimacy.

During his years in Vietnam as both an army officer and a civilian adviser, Vann had both ruffled feathers and earned the respect and trust of others. His military superiors were often infuriated when he challenged official accounts of the war's progress. An expert at statistics, Vann confronted his superiors with evidence that the GSV grossly inflated VC body counts, which was not welcome information. He also made clear that ARVN troops avoided dangerous search-and-destroy missions, preferring to remain in defensive positions or, even worse, permit enemy troops to escape battle zones unscathed. Because of his honesty and advocacy for a war of smaller and aggressive units, Vann won the admiration of many officers and civilian personnel. This strategy fitted with Vann's belief that the war would be a lengthy conflict of low-level engagement, rather than a short war of major battles.

Though the Tet Offensive temporarily slowed CORDS's successes, relative stability had returned to the countryside by May 1968. Emboldened, American officials urged GSV officials to accelerate the pacification program. The following year, the new Nixon administration ultimately settled upon a policy of Vietnamization, meaning the gradual withdrawal of American troops as South Vietnam's ability to defend itself was strengthened through continuing American aid and intensified bombing both north and south of the Demilitarized Zone (DMZ). As Vann discovered, this inevitably meant a gradual resumption of conventional warfare as ARVN received greater numbers of armored vehicles, artillery, helicopters, and fixed-wing aircraft. As of February 1970, Vann, now CORDS head in the Fourth Corps area south of the Mekong delta, long a VC stronghold, nevertheless delivered an upbeat report to US senators. In his region, Vann claimed, one could now take a daylight drive without any armed escort to any one of the sixteen provincial capitals. The Chieu Hoi Program, he noted, had attracted 30,000 VC defectors, and fewer than 800,000 of the region's 6 million people were still living under VC control. CORDS, it appeared, was a major factor in gaining ground against the VC.

Despite CORDS's successes, the Nixon administration expanded the conflict with an invasion of the "Fishhook" region of Cambodia in late April 1970, with the announced object of destroying VC and PAVN forces staging attacks from neutral Cambodia. Though the operation was hailed as a success, it further destabilized Cambodia. A more ambitious effort, known as Operation Lam Son 719, was launched by ARVN forces in early February 1971, with the intent of defeating PAVN units in Laos as well as demonstrating the ability of South Vietnam to conduct offensive operations. Though aided by US air support, by late March ARVN troops were routed in a debacle in which ARVN troops clung to the skids of helicopters to escape the fighting, accompanied by a massive refugee exodus. Vietnamization, it appeared, had failed.

Vann was posted farther north as senior adviser to the Second Corps Tactical Zone (CTZ) in May 1971. Though a civilian, Vann was given the authority to command the small number of US troops still present and in the spring of 1972, as it was becoming evident that a major engagement was in the offing as North Vietnamese Army (NVA) commanders planned an offensive aimed at Kontum, with the goal of taking Pleiku.

To reach their goal, NVA forces would have to take the outpost of Tan Canh, which Vann played a major role in defending. On April 23, Tan Canh was attacked by a large NVA force supported by Russian-built T-54 tanks. Vann took a helicopter into the beleaguered post, where he aided in evacuating civilians, and ultimately fifty were wounded. The outpost fell the following day. Vann was awarded the Distinguished Service Cross, one of few civilians to earn the award.

Ultimately, US airpower foiled the NVA's plans to take Kontum and Pleiku, as more than three hundred B-52 airstrikes halted the communists. By early June, Kontum was saved, but time had run out for Vann. In one of the war's many ironies, Vann died not in battle, but as a result of an accident, when on June 9 his helicopter crashed into a copse of trees during a night flight. Buried in Arlington National Cemetery, Vann was posthumously awarded the Presidential Medal of Freedom. Less than three years later, North Vietnamese troops rolled into Saigon, as select South Vietnamese and the few remaining Americans fled by air and sea. In his *A Bright Shining Lie*, Neil Sheehan offered the most fitting epitaph for Vann: "John Vann was not meant to flee to a ship at sea, and he did not miss his exit. He died believing he had won his war."

❖

During the 1968 presidential campaign, Republican candidate Richard Nixon made two chief promises—he would "bring us together" at home and would secure "peace with honor" in Vietnam. The second phrase was masterfully crafted—polls indicated that many Americans wanted out of the Vietnam War but also desired an honorable exit. The devil, of course, was in the details. Reaching political maturity in an era in which "containing" communism was an unchallenged component of American foreign policy embraced by Republicans and Democrats alike, Nixon, like his two Democratic predecessors, was determined "not to be the first American president to lose a war." Earlier that year, there was a worrisome indication that some communist powers felt emboldened to challenge the United States, which was distracted by the southeast Asian war. That January, North Korean naval forces had attacked and seized the USS *Pueblo*, an electronic-intelligence-gathering vessel that was operating offshore. North Korean officials claimed the vessel had violated their territorial waters, and seized both ship and crew, starving and torturing them until they were released eleven months later. The lesson for many was clear—the United States had to demonstrate that it would not back down in the face of communist aggression.

When Richard Nixon took office, the Vietnam war was the outstanding public issue. By the end of 1968, 16,592 Americans had died in Vietnam, and the Tet Offensive of late January that year had badly undercut support for the war. As Nixon assumed the presidency, some three hundred Americans were dying in Vietnam every week and it was now "Nixon's War." Nixon believed that the war was directly tied to ongoing, often violent domestic dissent, making ending the American role all the more imperative. In setting up his foreign policy team, Nixon designated Melvin Laird as secretary of defense and William P. Rogers as secretary of state. Both, however, would take a back seat to Nixon's new national security adviser, Henry Kissinger. Kissinger, who immigrated to the United States in 1938, was educated at Harvard University, earning a doctoral degree and writing a dissertation about the diplomacy of Austrian foreign minister Klemens von Metternich, stressing an international order based on legitimacy. Seeking influence by courting both Democrats and Republicans, Kissinger ingratiated himself with the Nixon campaign in 1968 and was later hired as national security adviser. He left an indelible imprint on the negotiations with the North Vietnamese and on the 1973 Paris Peace Accords.

From the outset of his presidency, Nixon and Kissinger accepted that the war, which had become "a bone in the nation's throat," in the words of a Nixon speechwriter, had to be ended. "I'm not going to end up like LBJ," Nixon had huffed, "holed up in the White House and afraid to show my face on the street." In 1969, Nixon was determined to formulate Vietnam policy chiefly with Kissinger, sidelining both the State and Defense Departments. On January 25, the National Security Council (NSC) was presented with a range of options that grew out of a study that Kissinger had asked the RAND Corporation to undertake in December 1968. Kissinger was impressed with RAND's top analyst, former marine Daniel Ellsberg, but inquired as to why the study produced no "win" option among the other contingencies. Ellsberg responded flatly, "I don't believe there is a win option in Vietnam." The alternatives discussed at the NSC meeting ranged from a harsh military escalation to the unilateral withdrawal of American forces. Somewhere in between was the suggestion of a gradual reduction of US forces while seeking a compromise settlement. These solutions had been either tried or considered by the previous administration.

The meeting concluded with Nixon forgoing any final decision, though subsequently his administration would meld military escalation with simultaneous troop withdrawals, while continuing negotiations with the North Vietnamese in Paris. At another meeting on January 28, Laird confronted Nixon with a proposal for a unilateral US withdrawal from Vietnam, citing domestic opposition to the war and some glibly hopeful military reports citing notable improvement in South Vietnam's armed forces. Nixon warmed to the plan, noting that the "sense of urgency" in training ARVN forces was crucial. It was at this point that Laird interjected that the plan be called "Vietnamizing." Nixon saw much appeal in the concept, as it would pull the rug out from under the antiwar movement while at the same time satisfying hawks. Kissinger, perceiving the basic flaw in the strategy, warned, "Our main asset is the presence of troops in South Vietnam," and insisted that even their gradual withdrawal would deprive the US of any significant diplomatic leverage. Unmoved, Nixon replied, "Our liabilities are the domestic opposition . . . and the continuing weak base of the Saigon government." The debate between the president and his national security adviser over the implementation of Vietnamization as the central American policy continued for several months. In a strikingly Orwellian comment, Nixon declared, "It is a war for peace."

At this juncture, Nixon and Kissinger agreed that the Paris negotiations would go nowhere unless additional military pressure was applied while the United States worked to strengthen the ARVN. Nixon always viewed the Vietnam war as an impediment to *détente* and improved relations with the Soviet Union (USSR) and the People's Republic of China (PRC), which were crucial to creating a stable international order. Convinced that overtures to both communist powers would work to reduce their support of North Vietnam (Democratic Republic of Vietnam, DRV), Nixon had considerable confidence in the concept of "linkage" in ending the war. The president also felt that his reputation as an anti-communist hardliner would potentially help to soften Hanoi's bargaining position. "I call it the Madman Theory, Bob," Nixon told chief of staff H. R. Haldeman. "I want the North Vietnamese to believe . . . I might do anything to stop the war. We'll just slip the word to them that 'for God's sake, you know Nixon's obsessed about communism. We can't restrain him when he's angry—and he has his hand on the nuclear button.' And Ho Chi Minh himself will be in Paris in two days begging for peace." Kissinger likewise believed that "a fourth-rate power like North Vietnam" must have a "breaking point." The United States, Kissinger insisted, must be prepared to use maximum force. Both men were fundamentally wrong in their assessment of the enemy's determination. North Vietnam was driven by a decades-old revolutionary, anticolonial, and nationalist ideology that embraced sacrifice and endurance far beyond what any American administration had been willing to acknowledge. Time, the DRV leadership knew, was on their side.

With the intention of impressing the DRV, the USSR, and the PRC of American determination to ensure the survival of South Vietnam, and as a prelude to Vietnamization, Nixon ordered an aerial bombing campaign known as Operation Menu on March 15. The operation, which was aimed at destroying communist headquarters (COSVN) and staging areas just across the Cambodian border, was to be kept secret, even from the secretary of the Air Force. To maintain secrecy, participating B-52 bombers would be guided to their targets by radar-directed computers, their crews unaware that they were hitting targets in Cambodia, a neutral nation. Post-mission, the officer in charge would destroy all evidence as to what the actual targets were. A falsified report about striking a target in South Vietnam would then be submitted. Nixon was adamant about the operation's secrecy, as he feared the public would perceive it as an expansion of the war and that it might constitute an illegal act. (Indeed, one of the articles of impeachment considered but not pursued in 1974 alleged that Nixon had illegally warred against a neutral nation.) Thus, on March 18, there began a fourteen-month secret nighttime bombing campaign comprised of 3,875 sorties that dropped more than 108,000 tons of ordnance. The American public remained unaware of this for the next five years. As historian Greg Grandin wrote, "That's how an illegal, covert war came to be waged on a neutral country, a war run out of a basement by a presidential appointee who a few months earlier was a Harvard professor."

Menu failed in its primary mission of destroying the southern communist command headquarters on the Cambodian border. The bombing killed thousands of communist troops, but drove others deeper into Cambodia, which some scholars argue destabilized that nation's government and allowed for the takeover by the murderous Khmer Rouge regime. On March 20, however, Kissinger informed Nixon that the show of force seemed to have worked. "Hanoi has agreed to bilateral private talks," he enthused. The leadership in Hanoi, however, was less motivated by the bombings than by knowledge that the United States would soon begin withdrawing troops. The announcement of a gradual reduction in American troop strength on April 1 was generally well received by war-weary Americans. Nixon's assurance that this would be coordinated with the strengthening of South Vietnamese forces seemed evidence that this might indeed assure "peace with honor."

On its face, Vietnamization seemed a brilliant political move on Nixon's part. The troop withdrawals would take time, especially given that the first announced reduction was to include only 20,000 troops. This policy bought precious time for the Nixon administration, quieting domestic anxieties, partially disarming the antiwar movement, and allowing space for the Paris negotiations to produce desirable results. To further bolster his Vietnam policy, Nixon gave free rein to his vice president, former Maryland governor Spiro Agnew, to denounce and demonize the antiwar movement and the national media, accusing the former of giving aid and comfort to the enemy and the latter of being unpatriotic through "negative coverage" of the war. When no progress in negotiations was evident by July, Nixon was determined to force an end to the conflict either through diplomacy or enhanced military actions. In an ill-considered move, Nixon sent a message to Ho Chi Minh expressing his desire for a "just peace" but warning that, if there was no progress by November 1, the United States would have no option but to resort to "measures of great consequence and force." On Nixon's orders, Kissinger convened an NSC study group to ponder what "savage, punishing blows" might be unleashed against the DRV, including massive bombing of cities, blockading ports, and even the use of tactical nuclear weapons.

As had been the case in the past, Hanoi was unmoved by the threats but agreed to secret peace talks between Kissinger and DRV diplomat Xuan Thuy. Thuy stuck to the position that the United States would have to withdraw all troops and abandon the Saigon government if any agreement were to be reached. For the next three years, the peace talks stalled as Kissinger and his North Vietnamese counterpart danced around seemingly intractable positions. Bereft of any plan to end the war quickly,

Nixon was drawn to the theories of British counterinsurgency expert Sir Robert Thompson, who convinced the president that the Saigon regime could be preserved as long as the United States continued massive military and economic assistance. Nixon seized on this concept, believing that if he could muster American public opinion behind him, convince Hanoi that the United States would not abandon the Thieu government in Saigon and build up RSVN military strength, the North Vietnamese would conclude that it was better to negotiate with the United States now than with Saigon later. Given these certainties, the United States could, he believed, wrest the necessary concessions from the DRV to achieve peace with honor.

To secure public support, Nixon received network television time on November 3 for what would come to be called his "Great Silent Majority" speech. Nixon's plan to end the war was to strengthen the Saigon regime, compromise with the DRV if they agreed to recognize the Saigon government, and respond with "strong and effective measures" if the communists increased hostilities. Meanwhile, US troops would be gradually withdrawn as GSV forces demonstrated an ability to defend the country. The most memorable portion of the speech came at its conclusion as Nixon intoned: "And so tonight—to you, the silent great majority of my fellow Americans—I ask for your support. . . . Let us be united for peace. . . . Because let us understand: North Vietnam cannot defeat or humiliate the United States. Only Americans can do that." The speech drew massive public and congressional support, though antiwar activists, who were preparing for the November 15 Vietnam Moratorium, were outraged at being characterized as impediments to peace, if not outright traitors.

American advisors were working nonstop to realize Vietnamization, building GSV forces up from 850,000 to more than 1 million. Massive amounts of arms and ammunition flowed into the country, supplemented by ships, planes, and helicopters. This was accompanied by an Accelerated Pacification Campaign, designed to extend government control over South Vietnamese villages. Yet public support was shaken on November 13 when journalist Seymour Hersh revealed that American troops, some under the command of army Lieutenant William Calley, had massacred between 347 and 504 Vietnamese civilians while conducting operations around the village of My Lai. Gang rapes and mutilations had also taken place. The only saving grace was that the pilot of a helicopter who witnessed the atrocities warned that he ordered his door gunner to open fire on any Americans he saw shooting civilians. There would be more horrors to come when the atrocities of the Tiger Force, which operated from 1965 to 1967, came to light. The unit was later discovered to have killed at least one thousand Vietnamese, some completely innocent, in addition to committing unspeakable atrocities.

The year ended with Congress concluding that a move to an all-volunteer military force was feasible, and a lottery system was established by which inductees would be selected randomly by birth date. The new system deprived the antiwar movement of one of its chief criticisms, that being that the poor, the uneducated, and minorities were regularly inducted, while wealthy whites were routinely granted deferments. The New Year, however, brought little in the way of good news about the war. Against the strenuous objections of General Creighton Abrams, who had taken over command of the war from General William Westmoreland in 1968, Nixon announced the withdrawal of another 150,000 troops, in hopes of defusing any springtime antiwar activities. But then on April 30, 1970, Nixon went on television to announce an offensive that was guaranteed to reignite the antiwar movement. The overthrow of the neutralist Cambodian government of Prince Sihanouk by General Lon Nol presented the opportunity to conduct an offensive in Cambodia against the so-called Parrot's Beak, Cambodian territory near Saigon, as well as the Fishhook, a PAVN base northwest of Saigon. In his speech, Nixon again cited the need to destroy COSVN and justified the extension of the war on American credibility, "If when the chips are down," he warned, "the world's most powerful nation acts like a pitiful helpless giant, the forces of totalitarianism and anarchy will threaten the free nations and free institutions throughout the world."

Nixon's Cambodia speech touched off the most widespread and violent demonstrations against the war to date. Thousands of colleges and universities went on strike or were shut down; antiwar demonstrators clashed with police in the streets of numerous cities. The tense situation was not helped by the president's characterization of the protestors as "bums." Demonstrations and violence only intensified in May after National Guardsmen fired into a crowd of student protestors at Kent State, Ohio, killing four, and state police fired on a girls' dormitory at all-black Jackson State in Mississippi, killing six. The Cambodian invasion also provoked the Democratic-controlled Senate to revoke the 1964 Tonkin Gulf Resolution. Amendments put forward to cut off all funds for US operations in Cambodia on June 30 failed, as did the Hatfield-McGovern amendment that would have required the withdrawal of all US forces from Vietnam by the end of 1971. Clearly, congressional patience was growing thin.

Nixon kept his pledge that all US forces would be out of Cambodia by the end of June, but the invasion produced limited results. COSVN was found to be little more than a few huts. Thousands of PAVN and VC troops were killed and weapons seized, but the DRV's timetable was only set back temporarily. Seeking to wring some gain out the dubious invasion, Nixon again turned to television, promising a "major new initiative for peace," including a call to put "a cease-fire in place." DRV leaders rejected this latest proposal, leaving Nixon with no policy other than more bombing in both the DMZ and the Hanoi-Haiphong area as withdrawals proceeded. Meanwhile in Paris, Kissinger alternately threatened and cajoled the North Vietnamese delegation as the terms offered by each side remained mutually unacceptable.

By 1971, there was growing pressure on the GSV to demonstrate its supposedly improved military capabilities, which would be crucial to American withdrawal. The recently modified Cooper-Church amendment, which cut off funding for US operations in Cambodia, prevented the United States from providing anything other than air support. On February 8, President Thieu announced that ARVN had begun Operation Lam Son 719, an offensive into Laos to attack PAVN forces positioned there. Within two weeks, it was obvious that the ARVN offensive had stalled badly due to heavy troop and helicopter losses. "Our material losses are shocking," Westmoreland informed Kissinger as network broadcasts featured scenes of ARVN troops desperately clinging to the skids of helicopters in their haste to flee the battle zone. In truth, some ARVN units had fought well, but the overall impression was that Vietnamization was, at best, a forlorn hope. Undeterred, Nixon used a television address on April 7 to declare, "Tonight, I can report that Vietnamization has succeeded." Hailing the "achievements" of ARVN in Laos, Nixon announced an increase in the rate of troop withdrawals, despite the worsened circumstances in Vietnam.

Pressure on the Nixon administration to end the war was building in 1971, as the "Winter Soldier Investigation" conducted by Vietnam Veterans Against the War took place in January, providing first-person testimony of atrocities by US troops in Vietnam. Another massive antiwar demonstration took place in Washington in April. Kissinger returned to Paris in late May to present the DRV delegation with "the most sweeping plan we have offered yet." Kissinger proposed a cease-fire, the withdrawal of all US troops in exchange for American POWs, and an offer to permit North Vietnamese troops to remain in the south, all of this to be accomplished under international supervision. What went unsaid was that Kissinger and Nixon agreed that the United States would continue the bombing while providing South Vietnam with "everything it needs in the way of helicopters, planes, artillery, and supplies." Some historians contend that it was at this point that Kissinger and Nixon had both accepted the "decent interval" option, in which the US objective would be to assure that there was a decent interval of time between the final withdrawal of US forces and the inevitable defeat of the Saigon regime. Both Kissinger and Nixon remained convinced that Hanoi might yield if China and Russia lessened or withdrew their support. No word of these negotiations was shared with President Thieu.

Events of the spring and summer brought little in the way of positive news regarding the war. In April, a court-martial found Lieutenant William Calley guilty of at least twenty-two murders during the My Lai Massacre. On May 31, Hanoi rejected Kissinger's latest proposals and submitted its own, the most notable being that the United States stop supporting the Saigon government, but otherwise hinting at continuing negotiations. Making matter worse, however, in June the *New York Times* began publishing what came to be known as the *Pentagon Papers*, a classified history of the American war in Vietnam ordered by Robert McNamara and later released by his subordinate Daniel Ellsberg. In sum, the document revealed that the Johnson administration had regularly lied to the American people about the war. Nixon's fear was that secret undertakings of his government might likewise be revealed. That same month, the Senate passed the Mansfield amendment, calling for a mandatory withdrawal of all US forces within nine months and an end to military operations after the release of all POWs. Public approval of Nixon's handling of the war fell to 31 percent. Congressional legislation mandating a deadline for US withdrawal failed only because of objections by House members. On October 3, the voters of South Vietnam reelected president Thieu with 94.3 percent of the vote, an event that was greeted with considerable skepticism in the United States. Hopes raised in May that some peace agreement might be reached faded. There were no further Paris negotiations in 1971.

By 1972, as more US troops withdrew from Vietnam, the rationale for continuing the war seemed more questionable, and the effect on troop morale was notable. The US command estimated that some 65,000 troops were using drugs, with many being drawn to hard drugs like heroin, which was readily available and inexpensive. Racial antipathies erupted into the open. Discipline began to collapse as some enlisted men simply refused to obey orders that they deemed pointless or suicidal, and officers deemed to be overly enthusiastic about dangerous missions ran the risk of being "fragged" with grenades; some two thousand such incidents were reported as early as 1970.

As this was a presidential election year, Nixon was determined to achieve some breakthrough. Summit meetings had been arranged in both Peking and Moscow and the Nixon administration placed its hopes on some agreements that would leave North Vietnam isolated and more willing to negotiate. North Vietnam meanwhile strove for military victory, launching a massive invasion of the South through the DMZ in March with troops and armor. Only about six thousand American combat troops remained in South Vietnam, so ARVN was compelled to depend upon American air support. The initial success of the North Vietnamese was slowed by B-52 strikes and hampered by attacks on fuel depots in the Hanoi-Haiphong area. Meanwhile, Kissinger met with Soviet Premier Leonid Brezhnev, hinting that in future negotiations the United States would be willing to allow DRV forces to remain in the South, a message that was forwarded to Le Duc Tho. Hanoi's rejection of the offer led Nixon to pledge that "the bastards have never been bombed like they're going to be bombed this time." True to his word, Nixon ordered the mining of Haiphong Harbor and a naval blockade of North Vietnam, complemented with Operation Linebacker, a massive aerial bombing campaign of North Vietnam. The North's invasion faltered by summer, with little accomplished other than, as historian George Herring put it, raising "the stalemate to a new level of violence."

Nixon's major concern in 1972 was his reelection, which he feared might be in jeopardy as long as the war continued, hence his unsparing use of military power against the DRV between March and June. In Paris, Kissinger and Le Duc Tho seemed to be moving toward an agreement, the most crucial component being the implication that the United States would no longer insist on the survival of the Thieu government. The United States was agreeable to a post-cease-fire political settlement that would be decided by a tripartite electoral commission including representatives of the GSV, the VC, and "neutralists." The predictable sticking point was Thieu, who quickly perceived that he would likely be thrown overboard were this agreement to go into effect. Nevertheless, Kissinger prematurely proclaimed that "peace is at hand" on October 26, one week before the presidential election. Meanwhile, Nixon's fears about losing the election proved unfounded. He easily defeated Democratic candidate Senator George McGovern of South Dakota, who was derided as a "peacenik," winning forty-nine states and 60.7 percent of the popular vote.

Throughout the fall, Thieu's continued objections again stalled the talks, as did perceptions in Hanoi that Nixon's bargaining position would be further weakened when a new, heavily Democratic Congress was sworn in in early 1973, which would likely cut off funding for the war. November was taken up with Kissinger and Tho striving to close the distance between the two nations, and by early December, the only remaining obstacles were Hanoi's insistence that the Provisional Revolutionary Government be mentioned in the treaty's text and that language about the DMZ be clarified. Kissinger nevertheless accused the DRV delegates of "equal parts of insolence, guile, and stalling" as well as "cock-sure insolence." The bespectacled former professor fumed that unless Hanoi failed to respond positively to the most recent US terms, "we start bombing the bejeezus out of them." After another aerial pummeling, Kissinger declared, the United States should offer withdrawal in exchange for POWs and "let them settle their problems among each other." The United States was washing its hands of Vietnam.

Thus began Operation Linebacker II, during which US aircraft dropped around 15,000 to 20,000 tons of bombs during eleven days. The "Christmas bombings" were disastrous for both nations. Nearly 2,000 North Vietnamese civilians died, and much of Hanoi was destroyed. American losses amounted to fifteen B-52s and eleven other aircraft. The public relations blowback was disastrous for Nixon, as opinion polls showed two-thirds of the public opposed the bombings, while the president's approval rating fell to 39 percent. International condemnation was universal. On December 22, Nixon notified Hanoi that he would halt bombing above the twentieth parallel if Le Duc Tho would return to Paris. Four days later, Hanoi was heavily bombed again. That afternoon, Hanoi indicated that Tho would meet Kissinger in Paris on January 8, 1973.

Both sides by now were determined to finalize an agreement and, during the second week of January 1973, peace terms were finalized: the DMZ would be deemed a provisional demarcation line; the Provisional Revolutionary Government (PRG) would be recognized only in the treaty's preamble; the phrase "South Vietnamese parties" would replace "South Vietnam"; remaining US troops would be withdrawn within sixty days and all prisoners returned; and 150,000 PAVN troops would remain in South Vietnam. There was no mention of securing Thieu's government or South Vietnam from North Vietnamese aggression. Nixon privately promised Thieu that the United States would come to his aid if necessary. A signing ceremony was scheduled for January 27. On January 23, one day after Lyndon Johnson's death, Nixon informed Americans that the treaty would "ensure peace in Vietnam" and contribute to "lasting peace in Indochina and Southeast Asia." Neither were to prove true.

By January 1973, most Americans were simply weary of the war and were willing to credit Nixon with achieving "peace with honor," though there is ample evidence that what was sought in the end was a "decent interval" between the final withdrawal of American troops and the inevitable unification of Vietnam under communist rule, a cynical solution that cost untold numbers of lives for the appearance of an "honorable" American exit. The costs for the United States were staggering: 58,318 deaths, some 20,553 who died in the final four years of the war; 153,372 were wounded; and 1,586 remain missing in action. Tens of thousands were seriously wounded, losing limbs or suffering mutilations. The POWs returned numbered 587, and 114 to 116 died in captivity. Material losses included 10,000 aircraft. The long-term consequences were equally devastating. The US Army had to be virtually rebuilt, given sagging morale and losses. The war shattered the social contract that had bound the nation together since World War II. For the next quarter century, the nation would be haunted by the "Vietnam Syndrome," which spoke to a US hesitancy to resort to military force in future situations. Nixon's presidency, events would soon prove, had been as fatally wounded by the war as Johnson's. On November 7, 1973, both houses of Congress approved the War Powers Resolution, which placed restrictions on presidential authority to wage war indefinitely. Congress overrode Nixon's veto of the act.

Nor was there peace in Southeast Asia. Estimates of Vietnamese dead are only that; some go as high as 4 million. The country itself was left scarred by unprecedented bombing and poisoned by herbicides. North Vietnam invaded across the DMZ in April 1975; as President Nixon had been forced to resign the previous year, there would be no further American aid for the Saigon regime, which quickly collapsed. The homicidal Khmer Rouge regime seized Cambodia that same spring, killing millions. Vietnam went to war against both Cambodia and China in the late 1970s even as fighting spread through Laos. For Indochina, peace remained elusive through the 1970s.

❖

On April 22, 1971, recently discharged Navy lieutenant John F. Kerry took his seat at a table before a panel of the Senate Foreign Relations Committee in the nation's capital, prepared to testify about the conduct of American service personnel in the Vietnam War, much of which had been given voice at the recent Operation Winter Soldier, which brought together 125 veterans and civilians in Detroit to give witness to the horrors that they had seen committed by US forces in Vietnam. Kerry was well chosen to present the thoughts of those in the Vietnam Veterans Against the War (VVAW). Commander of two Swift (Shallow Water Inshore Fast Tactical) Boats between 1968 and 1969, thrice wounded in combat, recipient of three Purple Hearts, the Bronze Star, and Silver Star, Kerry's patriotism and courage were as unquestionable as his forcefulness as an articulate spokesman for his cause.

"I would like to talk," Kerry told the senators and gallery, "representing all those veterans, and say that several months ago in Detroit, we had an investigation in which over 150 honorably discharged and many very highly decorated veterans testified to war crimes committed in Southeast Asia, not isolated crimes but crimes committed on a day-to-day basis with the full awareness of officers at all levels of command." Kerry's shocking testimony was even more relevant, given the ongoing public controversy about the charges that Lieutenant William F. Calley had led a massacre of Vietnamese civilians at My Lai in 1968. The veterans at the Winter Soldier meeting, Kerry testified, had recounted how "they had personally raped, cut off ears, cut off heads, taped wires from portable generators to human genitals . . . cut off limbs, blown up bodies, randomly shot at civilians, razed villages in a fashion reminiscent of Genghis Khan, shot cattle and dogs for fun, poisoned food stocks, and generally ravaged the countryside of South Vietnam."

Kerry continued to note that it was not communism that threatened the nation but the crimes committed in its name. "In our opinion, and from our experience," the young veteran continued, "there is nothing in South Vietnam, nothing which could happen that realistically threatens the United States of America." Most Vietnamese, Kerry noted, "didn't even know the difference between communism and democracy." They just wanted all sides to "leave them alone in peace." "We rationalized destroying villages to save them. . . . We learned the meaning of free fire zones, shooting anything that moves. . . . We watched the US falsification of body counts." Kerry spoke to the pointlessness of sending men to their deaths to capture hills "because a general said that hill has to be taken," only to then abandon the same hill. The war went on only "so that we can't say that we have made a mistake. Someone has to die," he emphasized, "so that President Nixon won't be, and these are his words, 'the first president to lose a war.'" Kerry's most memorable words followed as he calmly posed a haunting question: "How do you ask a man to be the last man to die in Vietnam? How do you ask a man to be the last man to die for a mistake?"

Kerry continued his testimony, noting high veteran unemployment, the unacceptable care offered in Veterans Administration facilities before asking pointedly, "Where are the leaders of our country? Where is the leadership?" Referencing Robert McNamara, Walt Rostow, McGeorge Bundy, and "so many others," Kerry charged, "these are commanders who have deserted their troops, and there is no more serious crime in the law of war." Asked as to his solution for ending the war, Kerry answered "immediately and unilaterally" at "the earliest possible date." Responding to additional queries, Kerry asserted that ARVN troops often "refused to come in and help us, point blank." Asked about the Calley issue, Kerry denounced it as "a horrible, horrible thing" but went on to affirm that "you have to separate guilt from responsibility, and I think clearly the responsibility for what happened there lies elsewhere." The responsibility rested, Kerry asserted, "with the men who designed free fire zones. I think it lies with the men who encourage body counts."

Kerry's testimony that day was riveting, horrifying, and often drew applause from the galleries. Kerry had earlier made clear that he had chosen to address a Senate committee, as nothing could be gained from discussions with Nixon administration officials. Following his testimony, Kerry joined nearly one thousand VVAW members in a protest that included tossing service medals and ribbons over a fence erected at the front steps of the US Capitol.

On May 30, Kerry was among more than four hundred demonstrators arrested during a peaceful VVAW march in Massachusetts. The mass arrests, which conformed to the Nixon administration's aim of crushing the antiwar movement, only served to heighten public support for the marchers and the VVAW.

John Forbes Kerry, born to Richard and Rosemary on December 11, 1943, remembered childhood as a series of frequent moves from his childhood home in Massachusetts, as his lawyer father took work in the nation's capital, first for the Navy Department and then for the State Department. Overseas assignments gave John and his two sisters a broad perspective on the world at an early age prior to John's attendance at boarding schools in Massachusetts and New Hampshire. Attending Yale from 1962 to 1966, Kerry later recalled that there was some discussion of the Vietnam War among himself and his friends, but they often raised more questions than answers, the rationale for the conflict being uncertain. For a graduation present, Kerry requested flying lessons, which his parents funded. Kerry applied to Officer Candidate School (OCS) and, in February 1966, enlisted in the Naval Reserve. That summer, he attended OCS in California and, upon graduation, was assigned to duties aboard the USS *Gridley*, a guided missile destroyer.

What the young lieutenant really desired, however, was the opportunity to command and, in February 1968, requested that the chief of naval personnel assign him to duty in Vietnam aboard Swift Boats, one of two types of coastal craft that the United States used in Vietnam, the other being the Patrol Boat River (PBR). The Swift Boats, originally intended for use as water taxis to offshore oil rigs, were not well suited to the

Figure 2.2. Former Navy lieutenant, Purple Heart recipient, and Vietnam veteran John Kerry, who commanded Swift Boats on dangerous river patrols, leads an antiwar protest in 1971. Testifying before a Senate committee during the Winter Soldier campaign, Kerry posed the haunting question, "How do you ask a man to be the last man to die for a mistake?"

Source: Library of Congress / Leffler, Warren K.

often shallow and mudbank-ridden waters of the Mekong delta. The fifty-foot-long aluminum-hulled craft drew nearly three feet of water and, as Kerry complained, produced so much noise that surprising the enemy was impossible. These boats, powered by twin 480 horsepower engines, carried six-man crews, twin .50 caliber machine guns atop the pilot house, an 81mm mortar on the stern, and a variety of small arms.

Having completed the necessary training for this duty, Kerry arrived at Cam Ranh Bay in November 1968 only to find that the Swift Boat coastal division he was assigned to was derided as the "Fun in the Surf and Sand Division." Desirous of seeing the war firsthand, Kerry asked to be assigned to a squadron at Cat Lo, on the mouth of the Saigon River, or to Da Nang. He was refused. Before being assigned his own command, Kerry took part in several patrol missions, which produced only nighttime fishermen, prisoners of dubious utility, and sometimes brief firefights. It was during one of these operations that Kerry received a piece of shrapnel in his arm. About two weeks later, Kerry was given his own command, PCF-44, and ordered to report to the Swift base at An Thoi, near the Cambodian border, where he and his crew became part of Operation Sealord in late 1968, which involved runs through the treacherous Mekong delta waterways, the object being to engage VC units. About the time his boat was ordered to Cat Lo, which was often the target of VC mortar attacks, Kerry began to silently doubt the trajectory of a war in which "it even seemed we cared more about winning than our South Vietnamese allies." Kerry was aghast at the environmental damage done along the Soai Rap River, where "the banks of the river looked like an atomic wasteland" due to aerial Agent Orange spraying. Kerry recalled discussing the situation with a Marine at the Nha Be Base on the same river. Asked, "What's it been like?" the Marine, standing in PCF-44's pilothouse, responded, "I can't say it's really been worthwhile. . . . We've torn up a lot of villages . . . killed a lot of people that probably shouldn't have been killed. We've lost a lot of good men too. I dunno. . . . I sure as hell know that we can't ever win over here."

As a Swift Boat commander, Kerry recalled that "it was almost impossible to patrol effectively" at night. Trying to effectively police Vietnamese river traffic, he remembered, was equally pointless, given the large number of junks and sampans. Kerry had little positive to say about his South Vietnamese counterparts. "I rarely saw them go out on patrol," he observed.

"They spent most of the time painting the boats. . . . Generally, however, they were anchored and everybody aboard was asleep. . . . When they weren't asleep, they were usually fishing." Beginning in 1969, Kerry returned to An Thoi, where he took over command of PCF-94 and, over the next several weeks, "engaged in the highest operational tempo to date." It was during this time that his actions earned him the Bronze Star and the Silver Star. Operation U-Haul involved ferrying Vietnamese forces up narrow rivers, setting up ambushes, and working in conjunction with SEAL missions. It was on the Bay Hap River that Kerry's boat, along with two others, took considerable fire from the bank and Kerry ordered all boats to "head into the beach," a position from which they could deliver optimum firepower. The maneuver surprised the VC ambushers, who were either killed or driven off.

On another upriver mission a few weeks later, Kerry's was one of five boats that took considerable punishment from VC mines, rockets, and small-arms fire at the same place on the river. This action left one of the boats badly damaged, sailors blown overboard, and Kerry with another wound. Four days later, on March 17, 1969, Kerry was informed that he was now qualified under the "three times wounded and you're home rule." During his remaining days "in country," Kerry concluded that the average Vietnamese "just wanted to be left alone." "We were losing hearts and minds," he concluded. "I began to see Vietnam with the vision of the critical observer rather than the participant. . . . I was heading home with truths to share, if anyone would listen."

Upon returning home, Kerry was assigned as an admiral's aide, but the war intruded again when he learned that one of his closest friends had been killed. That death, he recalled, "was the spark. . . . I felt a fundamental responsibility to do something." His path became clearer when the opportunity arose to serve as private pilot to peace activist Adam Walinsky, which kept him in touch with the antiwar movement. Kerry also began writing down his wartime reminiscences, still uncertain as to how to put them to use. Discharged in early 1970, Kerry ran for a Massachusetts congressional seat, but withdrew from the race when Father Robert Drinan seemed more likely to defeat the prowar Republican candidate. Kerry's association with VVAW came as a result of a VVAW advertisement he saw in *Life* magazine, and he subsequently joined the group for a weekend march to Valley Forge, where he addressed other Vietnam vets and antiwar activists. Speaking invitations came frequently following this appearance, culminating with an invitation to speak at the three-day-long January 1971 Operation Winter Soldier meeting. "What I heard and saw in Detroit was disturbing, raw, and human," Kerry remembered. "Grown men breaking down in anguish, describing terrible, terrible things that they'd seen and done, actions they said had robbed them of their youth and their innocence. . . . We all knew terrible things had happened."

Kerry proposed to his fellow vets that they take their fight directly to Congress, demand meetings, and march on the capital. Operation Dewey Canyon III was planned for the third week of 1971, when the vets would gather in Washington. In the following days, the vets sought to meet with legislators, with varying success. The strategy paid off—Senator William Fulbright, chair of the Senate Foreign Relations Committee, phoned Kerry and invited him to testify before the committee. Kerry kept up his speaking for the VVAW after the hearing, but eventually decided that he could accomplish more as a congressman, though he lost his first race for a House seat.

Kerry's future life included a law degree from Boston College, work as an assistant district attorney, and election as lieutenant governor of Massachusetts in 1982. In 1984, he was elected to the Senate, and twenty years later, when he was running as the Democratic nominee for the presidency, the war came back to haunt him. Running partly on the strength of his military service, Kerry found himself under attack by a group called "Swift Boat Veterans for the Truth." Some 250 Swift Boat veterans, most of whom had not served with or at the same time as Kerry, came together to claim that he had exaggerated his combat experience and was "unfit to serve" as president. There was considerable conjecture that the group was formed to offset any criticism of President George Bush, who was running for reelection. Bush, like many, had avoided combat duty in Vietnam, in his case by joining the Texas Air National Guard. Investigative journalists found that more than half of the anti-Kerry group's funding came from just three wealthy Republican donors. Only one sailor who served on Kerry's boats joined the group; all the others supported Kerry. Republican Senator John McCain, himself a Vietnam veteran and former prisoner of war, denounced the smears as "dishonest and dishonorable." The Swift Boat controversy was not the sole or even primary cause of Kerry's loss that year, but it was testament to the power of even spurious allegations in a close election. Kerry remained in the Senate until early 2013, when he succeeded Hillary Clinton as secretary of state and in 2021 was named "climate czar" by President Joe Biden, for whom he had worked.

Kerry's 1971 Senate testimony, perhaps the most moving moment in a full life, is most often remembered for the haunting question he posed: "How do you ask a man to be the last man to die for a mistake?" Fewer remember what he sought for his fellow veterans. It was the Vietnam veterans' "one last mission," Kerry asserted, "to pacify our own hearts, to conquer the hate and the fear that have driven this country these last ten years . . . so when, in thirty years from now, our brothers go down the street without a leg, without an arm or a face, and small boys ask why, we will be able to say 'Vietnam' and not mean a desert, not a filthy obscene memory, but mean instead the place where America finally turned and where soldiers like us helped it in the turning."

"SHOULD HAVE DESTROYED THE TAPES"
The Collapse of the Nixon Presidency

In 1970, historian Garry Wills published *Nixon Agonistes: The Crisis of the Self-Made Man*, one of the earliest assessments of the newly elected president Richard M. Nixon. More an analytical and psychological evaluation than a standard biography, the book dug deep into Nixon's early roots as well as followed him through his successful 1968 presidential campaign. Wills sought to discover, within the broader context of modern America, what sort of man this new president was and the nature of his appeal. His conclusions were insightful, troubling, and memorable. Will found Nixon to be "the least 'authentic' man alive, the late mover, tester of responses, submissive to 'the discipline of consent.'" Nixon's hope and appeal, Wills theorized, was to "resurrect a lost world," the Middle America of decades past. Few modern presidents have been the subject of scholarly inquiry as often as has Nixon, who is often credited with forging the electoral strategy that the Republican Party followed in future decades. Yet Nixon seems in retrospect to have been peculiarly unfit for combat in the political arena. An extraordinarily complex man whose political genius was matched only by myriad resentments, neuroses, and inexplicable self-destructive impulses, Nixon remained at core a man who preferred isolation and solitude. As presidential historian Richard Reeves writes, Nixon was "a strange man of uncomfortable shyness, who functioned best alone with his thoughts and the yellow legal pads he favored." Nixon's biographers concur that he manifested some egregious defects of character; some are simply more unsparing than others. As Rick Perlstein writes, "Nixon would lie about anything."

Some of the answers may lie in his early life, experienced in the context of the deprived, if not impoverished, circumstances of the Quaker family of Francis (Frank) A. and Hannah Nixon. Born on January 9, 1913, Richard was the second of five children to share a small farmhouse in Yorba Linda, California. His was a strict upbringing, as Quaker beliefs forbade alcohol, dancing, and swearing; his father was an unhappy, often belligerent man who withheld any sign of affection from his children. The family lived on an isolated section of land where the lemon grove Frank tended failed to thrive. In 1922, the family moved to Whittier, where Richard's father opened a grocery store and gas station. Hardship was joined by tragedy in 1925 when Richard's brother Arthur died of tubercular meningitis; Harold died in 1933 from tuberculosis.

Frank, who never completed elementary school, turned a modest profit from his store, which provided the family with some stability, though it did little to ameliorate his chronic ill temper. On the other hand, Hannah, as Nixon often reminisced, was "a saint," gentle but emotionally distant. Given to lonely contemplation and reading, Richard only gradually overcame his early shyness, even becoming president of his eighth grade class at East Whittier Elementary School. By the time of his years at Fullerton Union High School, Richard demonstrated success as a debater, played junior varsity football, and maintained superior grades. Having transferred to Whittier High School in 1928, Nixon was offered a tuition grant to attend Harvard upon graduation, but family finances kept him in Whittier.

Some of Nixon's lifetime resentments of the entitled likely stem from his years at Whittier College, where he was refused admission to the Franklins, a student group drawn from prominent families. Rather than sulk, Nixon founded the Orthogonian Society, a club that would welcome students of his socioeconomic status. He graduated with a bachelor's degree in history in 1934, whereafter a full scholarship took him to the Duke University School of Law, from which he graduated in 1937. He began practicing law with the firm of Wingert and Bewley, opening up a branch in La Habra in early 1938. It was there that he met Thelma "Pat" Ryan, whom he married in June 1940. The couple produced two daughters, Tricia and Julie, both born shortly after World War II. The war took Nixon and his wife to Washington, DC, where he briefly worked for the Office of Price Administration before joining the US Naval Reserve in June

1942. Eventually assigned to the South Pacific Combat Air Transport Command, Lieutenant Nixon carried out logistical assignments. Returning to the United States in early 1945, Nixon remained on active duty until March 1946 and in the Naval Reserve until 1966.

Nixon was drawn into national politics by a group of California Republicans seeking a challenger to Democratic representative Jerry Voorhis in that state's Twelfth Congressional District. A Nixon family friend recommended the young veteran, and he and Pat returned to Whittier. It was in this campaign that Nixon's lifelong embrace of anti-communism came to the fore, and he soon joined other successful candidates in the Republican-dominated Congress that sat in early 1947. Nixon was quickly brought into the House Un-American Activities Committee (HUAC) as the second Red Scare took shape and gained national renowned for his part in the 1948 Alger Hiss spy case. Hiss, a former federal employee, was accused of being a Soviet spy, which he vigorously denied. Nixon insisted that congressional investigators pursue the case further, and in 1950, evidence proved that Hiss had indeed perjured himself. Nixon's reputation as a red hunter was firmly established by the affair, which aided in his victory over Helen Gahagan Douglas in the 1950 US Senate race in California. His questionable assaults on his opponent's patriotism, however, had a price—it was in this race that he earned the moniker "Tricky Dick" that followed him throughout his career.

What he later characterized as the second of the "six crises" that marked his early political life grew out of his acceptance of the Republican vice presidential nomination in 1952, running with the highly respected war hero and former general Dwight D. Eisenhower. "Ike" was content to let Nixon take the low road and left to him most of the negative campaigning. A crisis erupted in September when newspapers alleged that Nixon had personally benefited from a campaign "slush fund"; one rumor held that he had purchased a mink coat for his wife, Pat, with the donations from wealthy Californians; another held that the money was used to hire a maid for Pat. The overall impression was raised that the Nixons were living in grand style because of these cash "gifts." As one of Eisenhower's campaign themes was corruption in the Truman administration, the Nixon story had to be quashed quickly. Many notable Republicans began distancing themselves from Nixon and Eisenhower's position as not clarified until a few days later in a phone call in which Nixon told his waffling running mate to "shit or get off the pot." Nixon offered to step down, but Ike instead suggested that Nixon buy television time and explain the contretemps to a national audience.

What followed on September 23, 1952, changed American political history. Faced with the humiliating prospect of laying out his personal finances before the nation on live television on NBC, Nixon appeared in a sparsely furnished set featuring only a desk and chair, a bookcase, and, to one side, his seated wife, Pat. In a thirty-minute broadcast, Nixon painstakingly revealed his family's debts and income, insisting that "every dime we've got is honestly ours" and that his wife "doesn't have a mink coat," but only a "respectable Republican cloth coat." Finally, Nixon noted that there was "one other thing I probably should tell you." The family did get a gift, which he felt compelled to mention or "they'll probably be saying this about me, too." Summoned to the Baltimore station, the Nixons found a crate waiting for them. "You know what it was?" Nixon asked his audience. "It was a little cocker spaniel . . . black and white, spotted. And our little girl Tricia, the six-year-old, named it 'Checkers.' And you know, the kids, like all kids, love the dog." Stiffening, he declared, "Regardless of what they say about it, we're gonna keep it." Refusing to be bullied by liberal elitists, Nixon asserted that he was "not a quitter" and would leave it up to the public whether he should step down.

The "Checkers Speech" salvaged Nixon's candidacy, and Ike greeted him with a hug and the assurance, "You're my boy." Republicans easily defeated the Democrat Adlai Stevenson in both 1952 and 1956, giving Nixon the opportunity to acquire considerable experience in both domestic and international affairs during two terms. Though he often felt that Eisenhower sought to avoid him and thought little of his abilities, Nixon was one of the most active vice presidents up to that time. Yet other crises awaited him. His television experience failed to help him in a series of debates with Democratic presidential candidate John F. Kennedy in 1960, and he lost the election by a margin of less than two-tenths of 1 percent of the popular vote. Returning to California, Nixon sought to unseat incumbent Democratic Governor Pat Brown in 1962 but lost by a substantial margin. He seemed to write his own political obituary when he angrily confronted a group of reporters and told them, "You won't have Nixon to kick around anymore because, gentlemen, this is my last press conference," words that spoke volumes about Nixon's enduring disdain for the press. The Nixon family moved to New York City, where he began work in a law firm, little knowing that his absence from national politics for six years would prove tremendously advantageous in 1968.

Between 1962 and 1968, Nixon kept a low political profile, emerging only in 1964 to support the presidential candidacy of Arizona Senator Barry Goldwater. Though he believed that Goldwater's radically conservative positions would preclude his victory, Nixon introduced him at the San Francisco convention and campaigned for him. The year 1964 brought electoral disaster for Republicans, as Goldwater carried only Arizona and five Deep South states, garnering a humiliating 38 percent of the popular vote. Democrat Lyndon Johnson was elected with 486 electoral votes. Goldwater's defeat also devastated downballot Republican candidates, leaving the party in shambles. Few could have guessed that Goldwater conservatism would become a foundation of Republican policies in future years.

When the 1968 presidential election year took shape, the nation had changed beyond recognition in only four short years. The hopes and promises of the early 1960s had turned to ashes as Lyndon Johnson's Americanization of the Vietnam War in 1965 produced immense domestic discord and fractured the Democratic Party even as the war's cost threatened the funding of Great Society programs. Johnson's presidency foundered on the war, intensifying racial tensions, urban riots, white backlash, and a burgeoning willingness to blame the nation's ills on Democratic liberalism. Challenged by antiwar candidates within his own party, Johnson announced in March that he would not run again. Largely absent from politics during the years in which the turmoil shaking the nation took shape, Nixon was well positioned to step forth as the "New Nixon," mature in judgment and capable of healing the nation's wounds. Though George Romney, Nelson Rockefeller, and Ronald Reagan all sought the Republican nomination at the Miami Beach convention, Nixon won the nomination on the first ballot, naming Maryland Governor Spiro Agnew as his running mate.

Aided by deep fissures in the Democratic Party, which became manifest in the riotous Chicago convention that nominated Vice President Hubert Humphrey, Nixon left the most virulent negative campaigning to Agnew and presented himself as a responsible statesman and spokesman for Middle America. This time, Nixon proclaimed to aides, "We're going to build this whole thing around television." Nixon had already taken aboard young producer Roger Ailes, who would later head Fox News, and employed a team of professionals whose talents would hopefully prevent the disasters that had blemished his 1960 debates, crafting the image of a practiced and seasoned leader. This phenomenon of "packaging" a candidate was later the subject of Joe McGinniss's *The Selling of the President, 1968.* Additional direction came from a memo written by the young Republican activist Kevin Phillips. His "Middle America and the Emerging Republican Majority" argued that electoral victories came from pandering to popular resentments and that ordinary Americans resented the prominence of a cultural elite comprised of condescending liberals whose social theories, when realized in policy, were the root cause of the nation's ills. Republicans, Phillips contended, should strive to appeal to the "great, ordinary, Lawrence Welkish mass of Americans." Nixon fit the bill perfectly—he took great pride in being a "square" who enjoyed Lawrence Welk and embraced middle-brow culture. In a May 1968 radio address, Nixon proclaimed his solidarity with "the millions of people . . . who do not demonstrate, who do not picket or protest loudly." This "silent center," Nixon declared, was the new majority. The great majority of working- and middle-class Americans, he knew, despised the dope-smoking hippies, campus radicals, and urban rioters who garnered the bulk of media attention.

In addition to these new directions, Nixon had begun to formulate a "Southern strategy" before 1968, carefully straddling a political fence by endorsing federal civil rights acts while regularly denouncing "mob rule," which he knew many whites interpreted as meaning black demonstrators and student protestors. He cultivated friendships with Southern Republicans like South Carolina Senator Strom Thurmond, who switched to the Republican Party in 1964. These positions proved useful in 1968, when Nixon hoped he could derail the third-party candidacy of segregationist former Alabama governor George Wallace, who was capitalizing on the resentments of "the angry white man." Wallace's "law and order" theme, a thinly veiled appeal to racists, was co-opted by Nixon, who made it more palatable by applying it to crime in general, rioters, and campus disturbances, while avoiding the crude language and threats of violence that Wallace thrived on.

As to the central issue of the Vietnam War, Nixon was a master of vagueness, declaring that "under no circumstances should a man say what he will do in January," thus immunizing himself against demands for specifics. This same approach served him well in his acceptance speech at the Miami Beach convention on August 8. After painting a portrait of unprecedented domestic turmoil, Nixon declared that the solution to the crisis lay with "the great majority of Americans, the forgotten Americans . . . the non-shouters, the non-demonstrators," a people who were not "racists or sick" or "guilty of the crime that plagues the land," though he offered no specifics as to how the current apocalypse might be resolved. Rather, Nixon ended with a typical bit of schmaltz, proclaiming that "the time has come for us to leave the valley of despair and climb the mountain so that we may see the glory of the dawn."

The greatest surprise of the fall campaign was the surge in voter support for the Democratic candidate in October. Humphrey's chances had always been captive to his vindictive president, who belatedly declared a bombing halt in late October, suggesting the possibility of successful

Figure 3.1. Republicans Richard Nixon and Spiro Agnew accept the presidential and vice presidential nominations of their party at the 1968 convention. Nixon promised to "bring us together" but pursued the politics of division. Both Nixon and Agnew were driven from office due to criminal activities. Source: Wikimedia Commons / National Archives Catalog

peace negotiations that might draw antiwar Democrats into Humphrey's camp. Nixon was not above persuading the Thieu government, through Anna Chennault, that better peace terms would come with a Republican administration. He wrapped up his campaign promising "peace with honor in Vietnam" and a pledge to "bring us together" at home. As in 1960, the election was close, with Nixon's winning popular margin of 43.4 percent besting Humphrey's 42.7 percent, with the remaining 13.5 percent going to Wallace. One close election loss and one close election win left Nixon determined to win reelection by a wide margin, whatever the cost.

Nixon faced an unenviable task upon assuming office in January 1969. Clearly, the chief challenges facing the nation were ending the Vietnam War in an acceptable manner and quieting domestic discord, much of which was related to the war. While admitting privately to an aide that the Vietnam War was lost, Nixon looked to address the two related issues as quickly as possible, as he wanted to focus on foreign policy achievements that required ending the Southeast Asian quagmire. With inflation and unemployment low, most domestic issues were of secondary concern to the new president. To address the two outstanding issues simultaneously, Nixon proposed Vietnamization, which promised fewer American casualties as troops were brought home. Hopefully, this would calm public concerns about record US deaths in the war and quiet the antiwar movement. The second arm of this strategy was "positive polarization," a conscious effort to pit Nixon's "Silent Majority" against the minority of radicals and protestors who were believed to be at the root of domestic unrest. This job was turned over to Vice President Agnew, who was unleashed to denounce any who challenged the president's policies. Nixon aide Thomas Huston also proposed the "Huston Plan," which sought to coordinate national security, law enforcement, and investigatory agencies to undermine the activities of targeted antiwar, radical, and counterculture groups, often through illegal means. Astonishingly, FBI director J. Edgar Hoover, never a champion of civil liberties, objected to the plan, which Nixon rescinded in 1970. The Nixon administration also targeted the three national news networks, which were to be intimidated with threats to their FCC (Federal Communications Commission) licensure if they continued to report negative stories about the war in Vietnam.

To understand Nixon's domestic agenda, it must be understood that he was no ideologue, but a moderate conservative focused more on achieving his agenda rather than fitting into any ideological mold. While some deemed this approach pragmatic, detractors often castigated Nixon as an opportunist. His chief domestic innovation was the "New Federalism," which proposed federal grants to the states, strengthening state power and lessening that of Washington. Few of these proposed grants were realized. In 1970, with inflation rising in part because of borrowing for the Vietnam War, Congress authorized Nixon to implement wage and price freezes, which Nixon did briefly in the summer of 1971, when he also ended the convertibility of the dollar into gold. Neither were conservative actions.

Perhaps Nixon's most surprising innovations came in the area of environmentalism, as he established the new Environmental Protection Agency in 1970 and signed the Clean Air Act (1970), the National Environmental Policy Act (1970), and established the Occupational Safety and Health Administration (1970). Nixon believed that Middle America supported most environmental and workplace protections, which he endorsed "for defensive [meaning political] reasons." In 1971, he told Chief of Staff H. R. Haldeman that the administration had done enough for the environment at that point, clarifying that his interests were not born of convictions but were the product of political calculations.

Nixon proposed a broad overhaul of the nation's welfare system in 1969 with the Family Assistance Plan (FAP), which would have provided a guaranteed annual income that would ostensibly ameliorate some of the defects in the Aid to Families with Dependent Children program, a New Deal innovation condemned by conservatives for discouraging employment and encouraging single mothers to have illegitimate children. Racists promoted the belief that this "welfare" went mainly to black Americans, which is statistically false. Though Democrat Daniel Patrick Moynihan was drawn to the idea and sought to work with the administration to reform the welfare system, after three years of congressional debate, the FAP withered away. In August 1970, Massachusetts Senator Ted Kennedy proposed a single-payer health care plan, which was countered in February of the next year by Nixon's plan for employee-mandated health care and support for health maintenance organizations. After months of debate, both proposals were dropped. Democrats were not about to let Nixon get credit for any national health care program, and Southerners and conservatives opposed many of the provisions of the Democratic plan.

Given his focus on foreign policy, it is not surprising that Nixon steered away from some of the most controversial social issues. Although he believed abortion should be a state issue, Nixon worried that it encouraged permissiveness, but confided to aide Chuck Colson that "there are times when abortions are necessary. I know that. When you a black and a white." The square from Whittier once condemned an episode of the television comedy *All in the Family* that counseled toleration of gay people because, as he ranted to aide John Ehrlichman, "Goddamn, I don't think you glorify it on public television, homosexuality, even more than you glorify whores." This was followed by a lengthy discourse as to how homosexuality had destroyed ancient societies: "You know what happened to the Greeks. Homosexuality destroyed them. Sure, Aristotle was a homo, we all know that, so was Socrates. Do you know what happened to the Romans? The last six Roman emperors were fags."

As to gay marriage, Nixon predicted, "Maybe in the year 2000."

As a traditionalist when it came to gender roles, Nixon was wary of the impact of Title IX of the 1964 Civil Rights Act, which banned gender discrimination in education and, thus, collegiate sports, but signed the higher education act, which provided equal funding for women athletes, despite his misgivings. As to women's rights in general, Nixon supported the passage of the Equal Rights Amendment as early as 1968, though he devoted little energy to the issue. His civil rights policies were aimed at charting a path between racist Wallace voters and liberal Democrats, whose integrationist policies angered whites in the North and South. Hoping to divest himself of the troublesome issue of federally mandated integration, he appointed Vice President Agnew to chair a task force to work with local black and white leaders as to how to integrate schools. Hopes for defusing racial tensions faded as often violent protests of school desegregation spread into the North.

Bolstered by multiple viewings of the film *Patton*, Nixon ordered assaults on the Vietcong (VC) and the People's Army of Vietnam (PAVN), enclaves on the border of Cambodia and South Vietnam in late April 1970. That invasion reinvigorated the antiwar movement that now denounced "Nixon's War." It also presented Nixon with the opportunity to begin building a new political coalition based on working-class ethnic whites and labor, two crucial components of the long-lived New Deal coalition. Within two years, Nixon had shifted the political dialogue away from the "bread and butter" issues that had served the Democratic Party and toward cultural and social issues, as well as laying claim to patriotism. "He gloried in cultural warfare," writes Richard Reeves, "dividing the nation geographically, generationally, religiously." "When we need support on tough problems," Nixon told his inner circle, "the uneducated are the ones that are with us." Nixon meant those without college degrees, the innately patriotic Americans, who fought the nation's wars, who disdained the cultural elites, the liberals, the know-it-all academics, the spoiled student brats who dodged service in Vietnam and waved Vietcong flags. These Americans would rally against the elites "who want to take their money and give it to people who don't work."

May 1970 brought the first indications that this strategy was working. Following a late-night May 9 impromptu meeting with antiwar protestors at the Lincoln Memorial, where Nixon sought to engage baffled protestors with an incoherent monologue on football and surfing, the president solidified support from a more traditional constituency. Earlier that month, construction workers in New York City poured into the streets for several weeks to shout their disdain for antiwar protestors and liberal Mayor John Lindsay while proclaiming their support for winning the Vietnam War. During the first protests, construction workers beat youthful protestors and raised back to full staff a city hall flag that had been lowered in mourning for the students killed at Kent State. The laborers then stormed the steps of city hall before chasing and beating protestors through the financial district. The blue-collar revolt culminated on May 20 when a rally sponsored by a labor union drew 150,000 participants. A jubilant Nixon held several meetings with labor leaders with mixed success, winning over the Teamsters (and releasing Jimmy Hoffa from prison), though he was never able to win over the American Federation of Labor and Congress of Industrial Organizations' (AFL-CIO) George Meay. Nevertheless, Nixon knew that he had the support of blue-collar workers, which was essential to forging his New Majority.

Long before 1972, Nixon was giving thought to reelection. He authorized multiple illegal activities to assure this in 1971, all relating to the one issue that Nixon feared had the most chance of preventing a second term. Nixon had defused some of the public concern about the Vietnam War by ending the draft and bringing the troops home, but the conflict continued despite intensified US military activity against North Vietnam and extensive negotiations. If he was unable to achieve the "peace with honor" that he had promised, his electoral fortunes were problematic. It was this fear that led Richard Nixon down the path to criminality and disgrace. By 1972, Nixon's 1968 election slogan "Nixon's the One" would take on a much more ominous meaning.

Like some of his predecessors, Lyndon Johnson had installed a taping system in the Oval Office, which Richard Nixon ordered dismantled and replaced with a more comprehensive system including five microphones embedded in the Oval Office's executive desk, as well as more microphones in Nixon's office in the Executive Office Building, the Cabinet Room, and in the presidential lodge at Camp David in Maryland. Numerous phone taps were also installed. The system recorded more than three thousand hours of conversation between 1971 and 1973, when it was turned off following its disclosure by presidential aide Alexander Butterfield. Unlike earlier systems, Nixon's recording system was voice-activated—all conversations were automatically recorded once someone began speaking. This aspect of the system provided House investigators with the "smoking gun" that would bring down the Nixon presidency in August 1974.

In February 1971, RAND Corporation employee Daniel Ellsberg handed Neil Sheehan of the *New York Times* a thick bundle of photocopied documents that would soon be known as the *Pentagon Papers*. Authorized by Robert McNamara, *The Report of the Office of the Secretary of Defense Vietnam Task Force* was meant to be an "encyclopedic history of the war." Most damagingly, the contents chronicled the Kennedy and Johnson administrations' deceptions about the conflict. The *New York Times* published three articles drawn from the study before it was halted by a federal injunction sought by the Nixon administration. However, the *Washington Post* had also been given portions of the study and began publishing them only days after the injunction against the *Times* went into effect, and in late June the US Supreme Court ruled that the publication of the study could not be halted, as that would constitute prior restraint. One of the most damning revelations in the study was that the United States remained at war in Vietnam not chiefly to assure the freedom of the South Vietnamese but to "avoid a humiliating defeat" and damage to the national reputation. Though the *Pentagon Papers* directly damaged only two Democratic administrations, Nixon's concern was that similar leaks might impact his administration. In a recorded conversation on

June 17 with Henry Kissinger, Bob Haldeman, and John Ehrlichman present, Nixon urged burglarizing the Brookings Institution, a liberal Washington think tank that he believed might hold damaging documents about Johnson's bombing halt. The president ordered Haldeman, "Goddamnit, get in and get those files. Blow the safe and get it." On June 30, Nixon reiterated his demand to Haldeman, Kissinger, Attorney General John Mitchell, Defense Secretary Melvin Laird, and Press Secretary Ron Ziegler: "They have a lot of material. . . . I want Brookings. I want them [White House operatives] just to break in and take it. . . . Go in around eight or nine o'clock."

In response to the publication of the *Pentagon Papers*, the scope of illegal activities run out of the White House accelerated rapidly. In August, Nixon aides Egil Krogh and David Young met with Haldeman to establish the Special Investigations Unit, later known as the "Plumbers Squad," to prevent future leaks and to go after Ellsberg. Krogh and Young soon met with former FBI agent G. Gordon Liddy and ex-CIA officer E. Howard Hunt to plan a covert operation that would hopefully reveal damaging information about Ellsberg's mental state. On September 3, Hunt, Liddy, and three former CIA employees broke into the office of Lewis Fielding, Ellsberg's psychiatrist, with the intent of rifling through Ellsberg's file. The group found nothing of use and attempted to cover up the black bag job by trashing Fielding's office so that it would appear that drug addicts had been the culprits. The public was unaware that the event had any connection to the Nixon White House until April 1973.

Though Nixon's obsession with political intelligence remained intense throughout his presidency, foreign affairs remained a major focus. Working closely with National Security Adviser Henry Kissinger, Nixon strove to carve out the reputation of peacemaker that he so dearly desired, though with mixed results. Nixon's commitment to anti-communism defined his Cuba policy, and he maintained close relationships with Cuban Americans in south Florida and authorized covert operations against the Castro regime. In 1970, Nixon reassured the Soviets, with whom he hoped to improve ties, that the United States would not attack Cuba. Elsewhere in Latin America, the US trod more heavily. The election of the Marxist Salvador Allende as Chilean president in September 1970 led Nixon and Kissinger to plot to undermine his government by supporting crippling strikes and Allende opponents. "I don't see why we need to stand by and watch a country go communist due to the irresponsibility of its people," Kissinger arrogantly opined. "The issues are much too important for the Chilean voters to be left to decide for themselves." By 1973, the economic and political situation in Chile had become so destabilized that Allende was ousted and murdered in a violent military coup. Subsequently, Chilean general Augusto Pinochet imposed a military dictatorship that murdered more than three thousand opponents and imprisoned and tortured thousands more.

In the Middle East, the Nixon administration strongly supported Israel but was insistent that the Israeli government seek a peace accord with the nation's Arab neighbors. This came to naught in October 1973, when Egyptian and Syrian forces attacked Israel. Initial heavy Israeli losses spurred Nixon to order an airlift of military supplies to the beleaguered nation. The crisis passed, though Arab oil-producing nations imposed an oil embargo, which lasted into early 1974. Following the Yom Kippur War, the Nixon administration restarted regional peace negotiations, reestablishing relations with Egypt in 1973.

The greatest achievement, Nixon believed, would be strengthening *détente* by smoothing relations with the two major communist powers, the People's Republic of China (PRC) and the Soviet Union. The 1971 opening to China occurred when the aging Mao Tse-tung invited a team of US table tennis players to Peking to engage their Chinese counterparts. Nixon seized the opportunity to send Kissinger to the PRC for secret meetings with Communist Party officials. The gambit paid off, and in February 1972 Nixon visited China, where he seemed to get along well with Mao. This visit set in train events that would lead to the US recognition of the PRC in 1979. Nixon hoped that this new Sino-American alliance would make the Soviets more amenable to improved relations, and that May, he flew to Moscow to meet with Soviet leaders to discuss arms reduction. While some new trade agreements were reached, the more significant breakthrough came with two major arms control treaties. The Strategic Arms Limitation Talks (SALT I) reduced the number of strategic intercontinental ballistic missile (ICBM) launchers, while the Anti-Ballistic Missile Treaty prohibited the development of systems designed to intercept incoming ICBMs. These were accomplishments of which Nixon could be legitimately proud.

Even as these foreign policy initiatives were solidifying Nixon's image as a capable world leader, much more sordid activities were underway in the United States. The 1972 general election season was well underway when Nixon undertook his China and Russia trips, and his subordinates did not let the moment pass to work on ensuring the president's reelection. One of the chief objectives of Nixon's reelection committee, now headed by former Nixon attorney general John N. Mitchell and bearing the unfortunate acronym CREEP (Committee for the Re-Election of the President), was to undermine his most likely Democratic challengers. At a January meeting, Liddy proposed Operation Gemstone to a group of campaign operatives. The bizarre plan involved kidnapping key "radical" leaders and holding them in Mexico so they could not disrupt the Republican Convention. In March, Liddy proposed a more convoluted plan that involved drugging and kidnapping key Democrats during their convention, taking them to yachts offshore, and taking compromising photos of the victims with women hired for that purpose. Some campaign officials were alarmed by Liddy's advocacy of brazenly illegal acts, which were rejected; Nixon privately referred to Liddy as "nuts."

Early in the primary season, it appeared that Maine Senator Edmund Muskie might be the greatest electoral threat. On March 24, White House staffers Donald Segretti and Ken Clawson forged a letter to the *Manchester Union-Leader* alleging that Muskie had demeaned French Canadians with the epithet "Canuck." The following day, the Republican-leaning paper published a false story that Muskie's wife was a drunkard and a racist. Enraged, Muskie responded in a speech outside the newspaper's offices, delivered from a flatbed trailer during a snowstorm. White House operatives spread the story that Muskie had begun weeping during the address, though the reality was that he was wiping melting snowflakes from his face. The baseless accusations seriously wounded the senator's candidacy.

Nixon was comfortable with his Southern strategy of slowing court-ordered busing and cynically nominating two questionably qualified Southerners for Supreme Court positions; when a Democratic senate rejected them, Nixon proclaimed that it was because they were Southerners. Yet he feared that this strategy would be short-circuited by a third-party run by George Wallace. The solution was to get Wallace to agree to run as a Democrat. Controversy still swirls around a Nixon phone call to Wallace, with some suggesting that he convinced the Alabaman to run in the Democratic primaries. Wallace's decision to run as a Democrat was the Democratic National Committee's worst nightmare, as the fiery Alabaman, who now downplayed overt racism and instead focused on "law and order" and federal overreach, would likely win over the "angry white man" vote. Wallace had pulled off wins in Florida, Tennessee, and North Carolina and was scoring high in national polls when, on May 15, the nation was once again witness to the horror of the politics of the gun. Wallace was campaigning in a shopping center in Laurel, Maryland, when a gunman thrust his arm through the crowd of Wallace supporters and fired five .38 caliber bullets at the candidate at close range. Arthur Bremer had earlier planned to assassinate Nixon in a gambit for fame but, for unclear reasons, settled upon Wallace as the target. Critically wounded, Wallace survived but was partially paralyzed for the remainder of his life. His appeal was not diminished; he won two more primaries, one in Michigan. Hoping to capitalize on the tragedy, Nixon wondered aloud if Democratic campaign literature might not be planted in Bremer's residence. The FBI, however, had sealed it off as part of the investigation. Bremer was sentenced to a lengthy prison term and released in 2007.

When FBI director Hoover died in 1972, Nixon appointed L. Patrick Gray as the new FBI director, with Mark Felt serving as his deputy. Nixon would later voice fears that Gray was "not under control," and Felt would become the mysterious "Deep Throat" in months to come. More immediately, Nixon's chief concern absent a vibrant Wallace candidacy was who his most likely Democratic challenger would be. By June, Senator George McGovern was the last man standing. The South Dakotan's campaign was immediately wounded by its own organizational ineptitude. McGovern's campaign staff failed to fully vet his vice presidential choice, Thomas Eagleton of Missouri, who was revealed to have undergone electroshock treatments for depression. Desperately seeking a new running mate after the July convention, McGovern was turned down by six prominent Democrats before bringing aboard Sargent Shriver, a Kennedy family friend. Despite the president's enormous lead in the polls, the Nixon campaign characterized McGovern as the candidate of "amnesty (for draft dodgers), abortion, and acid." McGovern's ill-considered promise to give every American $1,000 further wounded his candidacy. Running chiefly as president, Nixon seemed destined for certain victory.

Nixon's hopes for an uncontroversial campaign began to unravel on June 17, the night that a security guard at the capital's Watergate Complex discovered a taped-over lock on a basement door and called police. Responding officers soon discovered an open door at the Democratic National Headquarters and held five men at gunpoint. They included E. Howard Hunt and four others, all operatives of the "Plumbers," who were there to replace a defective telephone bug installed during an initial break-in on May 28. Watching from a hotel window across the street, "Plumbers" Liddy and Bernard Barker realized that Hunt and his Cuban American accomplices had been arrested. The two quickly abandoned their post, leaving behind $3,200 in new $100 bills and two address books containing Hunt's name and a White House telephone number. These items were discovered by police the following day.

Inexplicably, the Watergate break-in produced little interest by either the media or the public during the 1972 campaign period, much to the frustration of Democrats. Press Secretary Ron Ziegler breezily dismissed the incident as "a third-rate burglary." On August 29, Nixon stated "categorically" that no one associated with the White House was involved. Dismissing the incident proved the best strategy. In November, Nixon won a landslide victory, claiming the electoral votes of forty-nine states and 60 percent of the popular vote. The simmering scandal, however, played a role in Nixon's oddly depressed mood following his landslide electoral victory, as did the burglars' continued demands for "hush" money. Though the January 1973 Paris Peace Accords and the return of American POWs briefly lifted the president's spirits, the year brought indications that suppressing the scandal would not be easy.

Though the national media generally seemed uninterested or incapable of perceiving the wider implications of the Watergate burglary, two investigative reporters for the *Washington Post*, Bob Woodward and Carl Bernstein, were among the few who believed there was more to be seen than had been revealed. Their investigations, aided by an anonymous source referred to as "Deep Throat" (revealed only in 2005 to have been Mark Felt), pointed to a broad cover-up aided by some in the upper echelons of the Department of Justice, the FBI, the CIA, and the White House. It would later be determined that since 1969, the White House had ordered taps on reporters' phones as well as IRS tax audits against perceived media opponents. More suspicions were raised in December

1972 when E. Howard Hunt's wife was among the forty-five people who died in an airliner crash in Chicago. Police discovered $10,000 in her purse; it was hush money that was to be distributed to the burglars. The conviction of the Watergate burglars on January 30, 1973, did not end discussion of the scandal but rather renewed it, especially when Judge John Sirica released a letter from burglar James McCord that alleged perjury among the defendants and revealed that they were being pressured to remain silent.

On April 13, Jeb Magruder told US attorneys that he had perjured himself during the burglars' trial and implicated John Dean and John Mitchell in a cover-up. In a March 21 meeting, Dean informed Nixon of "a cancer growing on the presidency" and that there was an immediate need for more hush money for the burglars. When Dean told Nixon that "these people are going to cost over a million dollars over the next two years," the president casually responded, "We could get that. What I mean is, you could get a million dollars. And you could get it in cash. I, I know where it could be gotten." Dean then began to suspect that their conversations were being recorded. When Nixon later asked him to compose a history of the administration's response to the break-in, Dean suspected that he was being set up as a patsy. Since March, Nixon had been pondering throwing his inner circle under the bus in order to exculpate himself. On April 30, Nixon announced Haldeman and Ehrlichman's resignations, quickly followed by demands that Attorney General Richard Kleindienst and White House Counsel Dean also resign. Elliot Richardson was appointed as the new US attorney general, and in May, due to growing public pressure, Nixon authorized Richardson to name Archibald Cox as special counsel to investigate the Watergate affair. Nixon was cleaning house with the intent of cutting all ties with any of those who were aware of the conspiracy.

From May 17 to August 7, a Senate committee began hearings about the Watergate affair that were covered live by the three national networks. Some of the most dramatic testimony came in June, when John Dean read a 245-page statement that took most of the day, in which he acknowledged Nixon's involvement and described a litany of "White House horrors," criminal acts aimed at political opponents and to maintain the cover-up. On June 27, Dean provided the committee with a Nixon "Enemies List," naming well over a hundred Americans, ranging from elected officials to academics, media personalities, actors, and business figures, who were to be targeted so federal agencies like the IRS could "screw them." Another jaw-dropping revelation that surfaced during the hearings was that there was a White House connection to the break-in at Ellsberg's psychiatrist's office. Only days later, White House assistant Alexander Butterfield dropped an even bigger bomb when he acknowledged the existence of Nixon's taping system. The committee's chief counsel Samuel Dash set the stage for the final battle when he asked, "If one were therefore to reconstruct the conversations on any particular date, what would be the best way to reconstruct those conversations?" With no evident emotion, Butterfield responded, "Well, in the obvious manner, Mr. Dash. To obtain the tape and play it." On July 19, confined to bed at Bethesda Hospital with pneumonia, Nixon scribbled on a bedside pad, "Should have destroyed the tapes after April 30, 1973."

Butterfield's revelation completely altered the course of the investigation. Both the Senate and Cox's office immediately sought access to the "White House Tapes," as they were quickly dubbed, but Nixon ignored a Cox subpoena, claiming executive privilege. Even as this stand-off gained the status of a constitutional crisis, more shocking news emerged on October 10 when Vice President Agnew pleaded *nolo contendere* to charges of tax evasion in a Maryland federal court and resigned. Only pretrial agreements had saved Agnew from facing much more serious charges of bribery and extortion. Nixon quickly named the popular Michigan congressman Gerald Ford as the new vice president. The potential for Nixon's removal from office grew exponentially, as Ford, unlike Agnew, was broadly viewed as an acceptable alternative to Nixon.

A desperate Nixon took a dangerous gamble on October 20 when he ordered Richardson to fire the relentless Cox "in the national interest." In a tense confrontation, the attorney general informed Nixon that he and the president had "very different understandings of the national interest" and resigned in protest. Deputy attorney general William Ruckelshaus likewise refused to carry out the dismissal and resigned. The solicitor general, Robert Bork, third in line in the Justice Department, agreed to fire Cox. This "Saturday Night Massacre" led the news throughout the nation's media, touching off a storm of protest and fears that the nation faced an unprecedented constitutional crisis. At best, Nixon had bought some time—but little else. Investigations into his private finances and the use of government funds to improve his Miami and San Clemente properties were underway, as well as questions about his tax filings. On November 18, speaking before a New Orleans audience, Nixon insisted that he had never profited from public office, had never obstructed justice, and proclaimed, "People have got to know whether or not their president is a crook. Well, I am not a crook." Most listeners quickly drew the opposite conclusion. Nixon's regular declarations that the nation was tired of "wallowing in Watergate" bore less and less force.

The new special prosecutor, Leon Jaworski, took over in November and his office again requested the tapes. The White House responded that two of the tapes were "missing" and the June 20, 1972, tape was found to have an eighteen-and-a-half-minute gap in the recording. Nixon's secretary, Rosemary Woods, explained to a skeptical public that she might have accidentally erased that section while transcribing it, while others conjectured that Nixon himself edited the tape. The year 1974 brought little in the way of good news for Nixon. On March 1, Haldeman, Ehrlichman, Mitchell, and Colson were all indicted on charges of conspiracy and obstruction of justice. Still looking for a means of batting down Jaworski's demands for the tapes, Nixon took to television on the evening of April 29, sitting at a desk stacked with thirty-eight binders containing 1,300 pages of transcripts from forty-six of the tapes. He gambled that by releasing these selections, which he had edited to include just enough profane and derogatory material to make them appear representative but not damning, the public uproar over the tapes would subside and Jaworski would back off.

The gamble backfired catastrophically. The "White House Tapes" transcripts, soon available in bookstores, were rife with profanities, blasphemies, and vulgarities, as well as racial, ethnic, and religious slurs. The president frequently chortled with his inner circle as to how they would "screw" their political enemies. Worse than this meanness of spirit, these edited transcripts revealed a president deeply involved in numerous criminal abuses of power. The general public reaction was one of disgust. Republican Senator Hugh Scott described the presidential conversations as "shabby, disgusting, and immoral." Conservative columnist William Safire read in the transcripts a man "guilty of conduct unbecoming a president." Longtime friend Billy Graham said he could only "deplore the moral tone implied" and was appalled at the "situational ethics" of the president.

On February 6, the House authorized the Judiciary Committee to investigate impeaching the president, as Nixon continued to resist turning the tapes over to Jaworski despite a court order. The Supreme Court began hearing arguments on July 8 in the case of *United States v. Richard Nixon*. Although Nixon tried to invest the summer months with some sense of normality, a growing sense of impending doom settled over the White House. Stories began to circulate about the president's unbalanced mental state and heavy drinking. Having long since abandoned those in his original inner circle, he was increasingly a man alone, with the only major support coming from his family.

Nixon's fate now rested on the outcome of the Supreme Court case, in which his lawyers argued that the tapes were protected under executive privilege. With Justice William Rehnquist having recused himself, the court issued its finding on July 24. In a unanimous 8 to 0 vote, the justices found against Nixon, writing that executive privilege was not absolute and did not extend to materials subpoenaed in a criminal case. In essence, the president was not above the law. The White House complied six days later, releasing the tapes to the public and to the House Judiciary Committee. The damage to Nixon was devastating, especially from the "smoking gun" tape of June 23, 1972, in which the president discussed with Haldeman how the Watergate break-in investigation might be halted. Fearing that the FBI was "not under control," Nixon suggested approaching the CIA and warning them that any further investigation into the break-in "is going to open up the whole Bay of Pigs thing . . . and that they should call the FBI in and say that we wish for the country, don't go any further into this case, period." It was damning evidence of obstruction of justice, an impeachable offense.

The "smoking gun" tape and other conversations, which were made public on August 5, quickly turned the public against the president. The House Judiciary Committee, chaired by Peter Rodino, had rapidly approved three articles of impeachment between July 27 and July 30 that would go to the full house for consideration: obstruction of justice, abuse of power, and contempt of Congress. A proposed article concerning the secret bombing of Cambodia and one dealing with emoluments and tax fraud did not advance. Though Nixon continued to plead innocence and pondered fighting impeachment, by August 7 it was clear that the game was up. With most congressional Republicans having abandoned Nixon,

Figure 3.2. Ex-president Nixon proffers a final iconic goodbye as he departs the White House in August 1974 after resigning from the presidency rather than face impeachment and conviction. Nixon never conceded any crime, but rather only "bad judgment." Source: Wikimedia Commons / Nixon White House Photographs, 1/20/1969–8/9/1974

Senators Barry Goldwater, Hugh Scott, and Congressman James Rhodes met with Nixon in the Oval Office to inform him that impeachment and conviction were a certainty, with Goldwater stressing that he would vote to convict for abuse of power.

On the evening of August 8, 1974, Nixon announced his resignation during a live television broadcast, padding the announcement with considerable self-serving verbiage and his assertion that "I have never been a quitter." The following morning, Nixon delivered a maudlin and bizarre farewell speech to his staff before boarding *Marine One* for the flight to Andrews Air Force Base before heading back to California.

Though he absented himself from the national spotlight, Nixon remained busy writing numerous books calculated to exculpate himself while noting his achievements and offering thoughts on American global diplomacy. In 1977, Nixon agreed to a series of televised interviews with British journalist David Frost, during which he perhaps inadvertently offered some crucial insight into his thinking. "Well, when the president does it, that means it is not illegal." Nixon never came close to conceding any guilt for his crimes, conceding at most only mistakes in judgment.

President Gerald Ford granted Nixon an unqualified pardon on September 8, sparing him any further prosecution for crimes known or yet undiscovered. For others in the Nixon White House, the future was not as rosy. Of the sixty-nine officials charged because of the Watergate investigation, forty-eight were found guilty and twenty served prison terms, including two attorneys general and eighteen others associated with the break-ins at the Watergate and Fielding's office. There was much for the American public to ponder in the wake of Nixon's resignation; both the president and vice president had been driven from office because of criminal acts. In the end, the system had worked, due in large part to honest and dedicated public servants and elected officials who were committed to protecting the nation's fundamental institutions, as well as government and journalistic investigators who struggled against heavy odds to root out the truth. But the disheartening realization was that an American president was proved to be a criminal, having lied to the public on numerous occasions and ordered clearly illegal acts to punish his perceived enemies and maintain his position of power. This was to be Nixon's most damaging legacy, feeding a growing public cynicism in subsequent years as to the efficacy and trustworthiness of government.

❖❖❖

One of the most notable political television ads in 1968 was a Democratic production that featured a close-up shot of a television set, the only sound being muffled laughter in the background. As the camera pulled back, slowly revealing the entirety of the television's screen, the laughter ramped up to unbridled hilarity as the words "Agnew for Vice President?" were revealed together with a text reading, "This would be funny if it weren't so serious." Spiro Agnew, Republican governor of Maryland, had been selected by 1968 presidential candidate Richard Nixon to serve as his vice presidential running mate. Few in Nixon's circle supported the choice, and Agnew himself was evidently stunned, even acknowledging at the Republican Convention that he had "a deep sense of the improbability of this moment."

Nixon saw in Agnew, as someone put it, "Nixon's Nixon," who could play the role of attack dog while Nixon took the high road. Agnew had a reputation as a no-nonsense supporter of "law and order" who advocated harsh measures for rioters and chastised black community leaders. On the campaign trial that fall, Agnew showed little restraint in his public remarks, referring to Polish Americans as "Polacks" and describing a Japanese American reporter as "a fat Jap." Dismissing questions as to why he did not visit impoverished urban areas, he opined that "if you've seen one slum, you've seen them all." The Marylander's inflammatory remarks scored points with many conservatives and bolstered Nixon's Southern strategy. Despite reports in the *New York Times* of numerous shady financial dealings that involved Agnew, there was little consequence, and in November, the Nixon/Agnew ticket squeaked out a narrow win over Democrats Humphrey and Muskie.

Like many of his generation, Agnew was the son of an immigrant father, Theophrastos Anagnostopoulos, who married Margaret Pollard. Born in Baltimore on November 9, 1918, Spiro climbed the American ladder, attending Johns Hopkins University prior to earning a degree at the Univeristy of Baltimore School of Law. He married Elinor "Judy" Judefind in 1942, and the couple had four children. Agnew was elected Baltimore County Executive in 1962 and proved moderately progressive in his support of education and city improvements. However, his racial views were formed in a county that was 97 percent white, and in 1963 he denounced protests of the Birmingham, Alabama, bombing that killed four young black girls. Although there were already rumors about cronyism at this point, his political ascension was steep, as he won the state's governorship in 1966. As governor, he drew kudos for supporting tax reform and clean water regulations and repealing a law against interracial marriage.

Agnew's initial support of civil rights earned him the support of NAACP leader Roy Wilkins in 1966, but as racial tensions and inner-city rebellions increased after the mid-1960s, Agnew's intolerance of black protests became more manifest. Following the Cambridge riot of July 1976, which many blamed on the inflammatory rhetoric of black militant H. Rap Brown, Agnew declared that authorities should "put him away and throw away the key." Agnew also derided the conclusions of the Kerner Report, which found the roots of urban riots in years of black rage and discontent, blaming instead "a permissive climate." Agnew insisted instead that "lawbreaking has become a socially acceptable and occasionally stylish form of dissent." In March 1968, he shut down historically black Bowie State College when unrest led to the arrest of two hundred students. In the wake of Martin Luther King Jr.'s assassination on April 4, when rioting spread across Baltimore and continued for three nights, Agnew declared a state of emergency and called out the National Guard; the disorder ended with six dead and more than four thousand arrested. Seeking to capitalize on the tragedy, Agnew summoned more than one hundred black leaders to the state capital, where he chastised them for not stopping the riots. Agnew's crude tirade proved a turning point with Baltimore's black community. "He has sold us out," remarked one black state senator, "he thinks like George Wallace, he talks like George Wallace."

Whatever hopes Agnew might have had for his vice presidency, he was quickly sidelined by Nixon's inner circle and appointed as nominal head of several insignificant commissions. His chief job was to serve as Nixon's bulldog, verbally attacking hippies, protestors, and Democrats. Agnew introduced into the American political lexicon a lengthy series of unforgettable and sometimes hilariously alliterative phrases, often in speeches written by White House aide Patrick Buchanan. In an October 19, 1969, speech in New Orleans, Agnew proclaimed that "a spirit of national masochism prevails, encouraged by an effete corps of impudent intellectual snobs who characterize themselves as intellectuals." Less than a month later in Des Moines,

Iowa, Agnew launched an attack on the media, complaining that the president's remarks were "subjected to instant analysis and querulous criticism . . . by a small band of network commentators and self-appointed analysts." Surprisingly, Nixon asked him to tone down his vitriolic attacks on the national media in view of the upcoming 1970 elections.

Rhetorical attacks on elites, intellectuals, and political opponents were still approved, however, and in a Chicago speech, Agnew castigated "supercilious sophisticates." Events in Vietnam in early 1970 led the vice president to direct more attacks at antiwar protestors and liberal educators, demanding in late April the resignation of Yale University president Kingman Brewster Jr. following antiwar protests there. The May deaths of students at Kent State and Jackson State brought Agnew's denunciation of a "general malaise that argues for violent confrontation instead of debate." Later that fall, Agnew turned his blasts against Democratic liberals, blaming the ills of working-class Americans on the "pusillanimous pussyfooting" of Democratic congressmen. Speaking to Republicans in San Diego in September, the vice president blamed the state of the nation on "the nattering nabobs of negativism" who had "formed their own 4-H Club—the hopeless, hysterical hypochondriacs of history." As entertaining as his verbiage was, it proved of limited value at the ballot box. The fall elections brought Republicans only two new seats in the Senate, while they lost twelve seats in the House and eleven governorships.

As the election of 1972 approached, Nixon gave some thought to replacing Agnew with Treasury Secretary John Connally. However, Agnew's reception by delegates at the Miami Beach convention made clear that his popularity with the party rank and file remained high. There, Agnew attacked McGovern's support for busing and claimed that if elected, McGovern would humiliate the nation by begging the North Vietnamese to return American POWs. On the campaign trail, Agnew defended Nixon against early Watergate allegations, and when McGovern attacked the Nixon administration as the most corrupt in history, he countered that McGovern was a "desperate candidate who can't seem to understand that the American people don't want a philosophy of defeat and self-hate put upon them." Election day seemed to bear him out, as the Nixon/Agnew ticket, running on the slogan "Now More Than Ever," won a landslide victory, though the Democrats retained control of Congress.

For both Agnew and Nixon, 1973 proved to be a fraught year. In February, Agnew learned of an investigation headed by George Beall, the US attorney for the District of Maryland, that targeted rampant corruption in Baltimore, including engineering firms, architects, paving contractors, and the public officials they were alleged to have been paying off for years. Though Agnew was assured by George White, his personal attorney, that he was not under investigation, events soon proved otherwise. In June, Beall learned of evidence that Agnew had accepted bribes for contracts during his governorship and his vice presidency. There was no statute of limitations that would shield Agnew from prosecution.

Apprised of Agnew's dilemma, Nixon immediately fell back on the same sort of tactics that would bring down his presidency. Ultimately, he and Agnew decided to pressure Beall to shut down the investigation by going through his brother, who was a senator. In early July, Beall informed Attorney General Richardson that Agnew was in fact a target of the probe and later informed Agnew's attorney that the allegations involved tax fraud and corruption. Lenny Matz, who headed an engineering firm, was willing to testify that he had handed Agnew $10,000 in cash in the White House. Jerome Wolff, head of Maryland's Roads Commission, claimed that he could document every bribe he ever paid to then-governor Agnew.

Throughout August, both Nixon and Agnew denied the vice president's culpability, but as more evidence arose, Nixon began to recognize the need to distance himself from Agnew. Agnew and his lawyer eventually settled upon a defense strategy that would have enormous repercussions nearly fifty years later. A sitting vice president, they maintained, could not be indicted but could face criminal indictments only after having been impeached and convicted in Congress. Nixon was aware that an adverse Supreme Court ruling on this issue could well affect his own perilous position. A memo from the Office of Legal Counsel, however, maintained that as the presidency was a unique position with duties that went far beyond the essentially minor duties of the vice president, a president could not be indicted while in office. Nixon breathed a temporary sigh of relief, even as Agnew's legal peril grew.

Maryland's federal prosecutors had already drawn up a lengthy list of offenses to be levied against Agnew, including bribery, extortion, graft, tax evasion, and conspiracy to defraud the United States. In early September, Agnew's attorney, Marty London, told the involved parties that his client was ready to make a deal—Agnew would resign if he could do so without any fear of incarceration, would plead guilty only to tax evasion, and would be permitted to enter a plea of *nolo contendere*. This deal was accepted by a Baltimore federal court on October 10, 1973, and Agnew resigned the vice presidency, being fined $10,000 and placed on three years' unsupervised probation. Unrepentant to the end, Agnew maintained that he passively took part in multifarious crimes in Baltimore because he thought it was just part of a historical tradition.

Agnew's post-vice-presidential career was peripatetic. He was disbarred in Maryland and borrowed $200,000 from his friend Frank Sinatra. To support himself and his family, he established Pathlite, an international business consultancy. He turned author in 1976, publishing *The Canfield Decision*, a novel that contained some troubling references to "Jewish cabals" and "Zionist lobbies." In 1980, Agnew asked for a two-million-dollar loan from the Crown Prince of Saudi Arabia while congratulating the prince on his call for a *jihad* against Israel. In 1983, Agnew acceded to a court order to repay Maryland $268,482, the total of the kickbacks he received plus interest. Having moved to Rancho Mirage, California, in 1977, Agnew published the controversial memoir *Go Quietly . . . or Else*, which implied that he had been threatened with assassination. Subsequently, he dropped out of the public spotlight until 1994, when he attended the funeral of Richard Nixon and the dedication of a bust of himself in the Capitol rotunda, which had been delayed for years because of his criminal reputation. Agnew died on September 17, 1996.

BRINGING THE WAR HOME
Last Spasms of the Radical Left

On May 21, 1970, select radio stations received a tape-recorded message from the Weatherman Underground, the radicalized remnants of Students for a Democratic Society (SDS), as the *New York Times* received a transcript of the same communiqué. On the tape, a calm female voice announced, "Hello, this is Bernardine Dohrn. I'm going to read a declaration of war." Anyone familiar with New Left radicalism and SDS knew who she was. Addressing the "destruction of the empire," Dohrn noted that "black people have been fighting almost alone for years" and proclaimed that "our job is to lead white kids into armed revolution. . . . Tens of thousands have learned that protest and marches don't do it. Revolutionary violence is the only way." The revolution would be brought about, Dohrn continued, by "adapting the classic guerrilla strategy of the Viet Cong and the urban guerrilla strategy of the Tupamaros to our own situation." Peaceful reform was impossible: "The war and racism of this society show that it is too fucked-up. We will never live peaceably under this system." She proclaimed a fusion of left radicals with the counterculture, proclaiming, "Guns and grass are united in the youth underground. Freaks are revolutionaries and revolutionaries are freaks." "We will never go back," Dohrn promised, before concluding with an ominous threat: "Within the next fourteen days we will attack a symbol or institution of Amerikan [sic] injustice" as homage to "all the black revolutionaries who first inspired us. . . . Never again will they fight alone." The Weather Underground would soon make good on its threat.

Few would have guessed that the "declaration of war" was composed by a former high school cheerleader, Dance Club treasurer, National Honor Society member, and school newspaper editor. Or that in just a few years, the girl from Whitefish Bay, Wisconsin, would be exhorting SDS's Women's Militia during the October 1969 "Days of Rage" in Chicago's Grant Park not to falter in the face of police violence as they prepared to assault an army induction center, assuring her compatriots that "a few buckshot wounds, a few pellets, mean we're doing the right thing here." Dohrn led the six dozen helmeted and stick-bearing militant women in an enthusiastic charge against a line of three hundred Chicago police, and the ensuing wild melee ended when the Women's Militia was allowed to walk away, nursing numerous contusions from police batons.

The journey to militant radicalism would not have been discernible during Dohrn's early years. Dohrn was born to a middle-class family in Milwaukee, Wisconsin, on January 12, 1942, and grew up in Whitefish Bay. Daughter of Bernard Ohrnstein, who "Americanized" the family name due to anti-Semitism, and Dorothy Soderberg, Bernardine was an exceptional student at Whitefish Bay High School and later graduated from the University of Chicago with a bachelor's degree in political science in 1963. While attending the university's School of Law, she was drawn into community activism, spending a summer in New York City working for an anti-poverty program before returning to Chicago to support Martin Luther King Jr.'s efforts to desegregate the city's all-white suburbs. As a law student, she provided legal services to rent strikers in Chicago's ghettos, where she was introduced to JOIN (Jobs or Income Now), a community organizing effort begun by SDS. Completing a juris doctorate in 1967, Dohrn immediately went to work for the National Lawyers Guild (NLG), which offered legal services to the poor and unpopular radical groups and individuals.

Thus began Dohrn's commitment to the "Movement," a generic term encompassing a variety of leftist radical causes. Undergoing a rapid political evolution, Dohrn abandoned her earlier liberalism for radical activism. In 1968, she joined SDS, destined to become one of its best-known and most notorious leaders. Working as an NLG assistant executive director, Dohrn educated law students on counseling draft resistors. She made an indelible impression on that group, as a coworker recalled: "First of all, there was her sex appeal. . . . People would come from miles around just to *see* her. But she was regarded as a good 'political person' at a time when other women in the movement weren't given any responsibility at all. Students really turned on to her." While working at the NLG's New York office, Dohrn developed friendships with local SDS activists and was asked to participate in a women's liberation conference. In late March, she attended the SDS National Council meeting in Lexington, Kentucky. Nineteen new SDS chapters were recognized as the organization grew to about three hundred chapters nationally. A resolution stated the group's strategy: "We must see our job as one of moving the white population into a position of rebellion which joins the black struggle of liberation to make the American revolution."

It was the assassination of Martin Luther King Jr. on April 4, 1968, that drove Dohrn to take to the streets. "She was really stunned," recalled a friend. "She cried for a while and she talked about Chicago, when she had worked for King. . . . Then she went home and changed her clothes. . . . She said she was changing into her riot clothes: pants." Dohrn and her friend went to Times Square, where they joined a crowd in "trashing" property. Afterward, her friend remembered, she spoke of the need for "urban guerrilla warfare" and declared her adherence to the Malcolm X slogan "By any means necessary." It was the birth of a committed radical.

Dohrn was not alone in that spring of 1968 in believing that revolution was in the offing. Global youth uprisings, most spectacularly in Paris, seemed to signal the dawn of a new age. The student strike at Columbia University in April not only radicalized many who were beaten by police but also established SDS as the dominant leftist radical organization. Dohrn joined SDS in the summer of 1968 and quickly achieved prominence there and within the radical movement. As Bryan Burrough writes, "Dohrn was destined to become the glamorous leading lady of the American underground, unquestionably brilliant, cool, focused, militant, and highly sexual." As SDSer Susan Stern commented years later, "She possessed a splendor all her own, like a queen . . . a high priestess, a mythological silhouette." The stodgy J. Edgar Hoover characterized Dohrn as "La Pasionaria of the Lunatic Left."

Dohrn's journey from left radicalism to underground terrorism was a rapid one. Elected as interorganizational secretary at the June 1968 SDS convention, after declaring that she considered herself "a revolutionary communist," she became part of the National Office leadership in Chicago and played a major role in the December 1968 National Council meeting. There the attendees voted to endorse the position paper "Toward a Revolutionary Youth Movement," which advocated fusing students with working-class youth. Dohrn and the proponents of RYM I, as the position paper was known, proved the dominant faction at the June 1969 SDS convention in Chicago when Progressive Labor (PL), a Maoist faction, was ousted. The RYM I group seized the national office and its files and assumed the name Weatherman, now the sole remaining fragment of SDS. Rigidly disciplined Weatherman "collectives" were organized that summer, even as Dohrn and a select group journeyed to Castro's Cuba for five weeks of ideological discussion, sugarcane harvesting, and meeting with representatives from North Vietnam and the Vietcong.

The major event on the calendar, however, was the planned National Action in October, which was to incite working-class youth and radicals for a revolutionary action. The "Days of Rage" drew much media at-

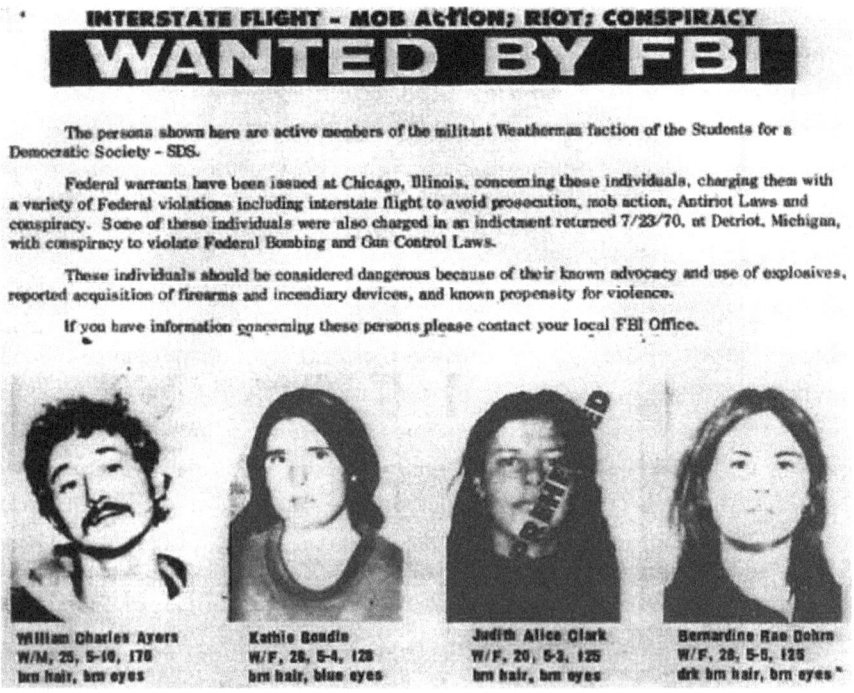

Figure 4.1. FBI wanted poster of Weatherman leadership, including Bernardine Dohrn, who led the remnants of the organization into ever-more violent actions in the 1970s. Source: Wikimedia Commons / FBI

tention, but the expected masses of radicalized youth failed to show for street battles with police, and the action was deemed a failure. Dohrn was arrested three times in subsequent months, once for drug possession and later for her involvement with the 1968 Chicago riots and the later "Days of Rage." Her convictions were overturned in 1972. Dohrn's final and most notorious public appearance was at the National War Council in Flint, Michigan, in December 1969, where speakers attacked "white skin privilege" and urged "the destruction of the mother country." Dohrn's lasting infamy grew out of her praise for the Manson Family's heinous deeds, which she later admitted regretting.

Weatherman's disappearance into the underground began in 1970, where it took the name Weatherman Underground. A planned campaign of bombings went awry on March 6 when a bomb being constructed in the basement of a Greenwich Village townhouse was accidentally detonated, killing three radicals and totally gutting the townhouse. Though stunned by this horrible setback and loss of life, Weatherman made good on Dohrn's tape-recorded promise to "attack a symbol or institution of Amerikan [sic] injustice." A few weeks later, the group set off a bomb at New York City police headquarters, presaging a wave of bombings in future months. The group also helped spring incarcerated Timothy Leary from a California prison in September. On October 14, Dohrn was added to the FBI's "Ten Most Wanted" list. From 1970 through the late 1970s, Weatherman, together with its leaders, underwent a number of changes in name, strategy, tactics, and ideology. Rejecting the indiscriminate bombing of earlier months, Dohrn and the leadership released the December 1970 communiqué "New Morning—Changing Weather," in which Dohrn announced that future bombings would target property and abjure killing, kidnappings, and assassination. In recognition of its commitment to feminism, the group now took the name Weather Underground Organization (WUO).

Indeed, under the leadership of Dohrn and fellow radical Bill Ayers, who were now married, the WUO carried out a variety of bombings, including one in the Senate wing of the US Capitol. Life underground was difficult for the perhaps three dozen members who remained active. Names and addresses had to be changed frequently, as did residences. Yet Dohrn and Ayers were increasingly convinced that armed struggle was unproductive. The apocalyptic end of the Symbionese Liberation Army

(SLA) in 1974, in which six members died in a wild gunfight with Los Angeles Police, indicated that a new direction was again necessary. The final permutation of the WUO now occurred, as Clayton Van Lydegraf, a former American Communist Party member, gained growing influence, leading the group back to orthodox Marxism. The result was the publication of *Prairie Fire: The Politics of Revolutionary Anti-Imperialism*, to which Dohrn was a major contributor, arguing for both clandestine actions and a new mass revolutionary base. A new joint organization, the Prairie Fire Organizing Committee (PFOC), arose. Shortly after, Dohrn and the original founders of Weatherman were expelled at Van Lydegraf's insistence.

With the original membership of Weatherman now whittled to a dedicated few, the PFOC carried out a few bombings, but by the late 1970s, it was evident that the radical tide of the late 1960s had long since ebbed. Now living in Chicago with their two sons, Dohrn and Ayers decided to turn themselves in to federal authorities in December 1980. After making themselves available for a press conference, the couple boarded a plane for Chicago. Dohrn's long career as perhaps the best-known radical refugee from the 1960s ended as she was sentenced to three years' probation and fined $1,500. Refusing to testify against former Weatherman Susan Rosenberg, Dohrn was held in contempt and served seven months in prison. Charges against Ayers had already been dropped. Bernardine Dohrn had remained true to her commitment to radical change for more than a decade, before surfacing to begin a new life with husband Bill Ayers and their children.

Denied a law license, Dohrn nonetheless found work with the Chicago law firm of Sidley Austin, where she worked from 1984 to 1988. Her controversial past reemerged as an issue when she was hired as an adjunct professor by the Northwestern University School of Law; she also helped found the Children and Family Justice Center at the Bluhm Legal Clinic at the same university. The university defended the hire when confronted with protests from conservatives, stating: "While many would take issue with the views Ms. Dohrn espoused during the 1960s, her career at the law school is an example of a person's ability to make a difference in the legal system." Dohrn retired from the position in 2013, proudly declaring the following year, "I still see myself as a radical."

·:·:·

The Beatles had warned as early as 1968 with the release of their *White Album* in the song "Revolution" that "if you go carrying pictures of Chairman Mao / You ain't gonna make it with anyone anyhow," and Gil Scott-Heron had concluded in a 1971 song that "the revolution will not be televised." Thunderclap Newman's "Something in the Air" in 1969 nonetheless held out the promise of continued revolutionary activism, and domestic radicalism endured in a number of forms and well into the new decade. The remnants of SDS and the Black Panthers, though fragmented and smaller in number, still fomented plans for revolution. They were joined by newer organizations, often equally small in number but equally willing to endorse violence as a tool for combating American injustice. The 1970s did not escape the radical violence of the 1960s.

For law enforcement agencies in New York, one of the most daunting questions of the 1970s was "What is the Black Liberation Army?" Journalist Bryan Burrough writes that many police officers considered the Black Liberation Army (BLA), which evolved out of remnants of the BPP, as "a murderous black counterpart to the Weathermen." If the comparison lacked accuracy, it was chiefly because of the BLA's alarmingly frequent murder of police officers in the early 1970s, spanning cities from New York to San Francisco to Atlanta, often through planned ambushes and with weapons ranging from handguns to submachine guns and even hand grenades. Far more ambitious and violent than the WUO, BLA members hijacked a Delta Airlines flight in 1972, collecting one million dollars in ransom and diverting the aircraft to Algeria. BLA members even cooperated with WUO members in a 1981 robbery of a Brinks armored truck, which left one Brinks security guard and two law enforcement officers dead. A Justice Department report on BLA actions listed the group as suspected in over seventy incidents of violence between 1970 and 1976. The Fraternal Order of Police holds the BLA responsible for the murder of thirteen police officers. Regardless of its small numbers and loose organization, the BLA was a deadly organization that had police in multiple cities nervous and often trigger-happy. As of 2015, six former BLA members remained incarcerated.

The Weather Underground Organization began the 1970s by organizing its internal structure and formulating a strategy of violence to be aimed at police and military personnel. With three remaining collectives established in San Francisco, the Midwest, and New York, Weatherman leadership decided to strike at the police with bombs and Molotov cocktails, but the early attacks in Berkeley, Cleveland, Detroit, and New York were poorly executed with minimal property damage, though a bombing in San Francisco's Haight district killed one policeman. Led by Terry Robbins, the New York collective launched a similarly unproductive assault on the house of the judge overseeing the Panther 21 trial; though the firebombs went off, they did little more than blow out windows. The embarrassing and amateurish action set Robbins on a path that would lead to death, destruction, and a shock wave that rippled through the whole organization.

On Tuesday February 24, 1970, Cathy Wilkerson arrived at the Greenwich Village townhouse that her parents had reluctantly given her permission to use while they were away on vacation. By the following day, five Weathermen had moved into their temporary headquarters: Wilkerson, Teddy Gold, Diana Oughton, Terry Robbins, and Kathy Boudin. At a strategy meeting, it was agreed that the group would have to move beyond firebombings, which Wilkerson felt "had become routine." Robbins proposed using dynamite bombs; according to Wilkerson, Robbins extolled an "existential belief in the power of the will" and often praised the film *Butch Cassidy and the Sundance Kid*, in which the two antiheroes dynamite train cars and later die in a blaze of glory in a gunfight against overwhelmingly superior forces. On February 28, the collective decided that their target would be a dance at Fort Dix; two fifty-pound cases of dynamite were purchased and unloaded at the townhouse, where Robbins would assemble the bombs in the basement. Having gleaned some basic information about bomb-making, Robbins met with the group on March 5 to review details of the planned attack. It soon became evident that Robbins's understanding of bomb-making was marginal at best. No one had any idea how many sticks of dynamite should be used. Queried as to a safety switch to test the device's circuits, Robbins dismissively waved off the question. The bombs, he stated, would be packed with roofing nails to inflict maximum casualties.

The following day, Robbins and Oughton descended to the basement to finish construction of the explosive devices. Wilkerson later offered a harrowing firsthand description of what followed. Shortly after noon, as she ironed sheets in the kitchen, prefatory to her parents return, Wilkerson "felt a shock wave ripple through the house, along with a deep rumbling from below. . . . A second, louder explosion came, then the floor gave way."

Falling through the floor before landing in a pile of wreckage, Wilkerson was blinded by dust and smoke but located Boudin, and the two women stumbled out of the flaming, smoking remains of the townhouse just as a third explosion blew a hole in an adjoining building. Wilkerson was left nude from the waist up by the blast; Boudin was completely unclothed by the blast force. After being helped to a nearby house by a neighbor, who gave them an opportunity to shower and put on some clothes, the two women fled the scene.

Robbins's inexperience had resulted in a cataclysmic series of blasts that blew off the entire front of the townhouse, leaving upper floors hanging precipitously as debris fell into the basement; windows were shattered up and down the street. Over the next several days, as authorities sorted through the debris, the fragmentary remains of three human bodies were discovered—Ted Gold, Diana Oughton, and Terry Robbins were dead. Dohrn and Jeff Jones were in San Francisco when they learned of the disaster. As scattered Weatherman collectives and individuals struggled to come to grips with the disaster, the common feeling was that Weatherman was finished. Wilkerson remembered that the event left the leadership "completely unresponsive for two or three weeks. Hundreds of people just disappeared. They were gone. Weather evaporated. It basically ceased to exist." The Midwestern tribes in Cleveland, Pittsburgh, and Buffalo simply disintegrated. Susan Stern, who would shortly go underground, remembered her shock upon learning of the explosion in which her compatriots had "blown themselves to smithereens." She was especially shaken by the death of Diana Oughton, whose "sweet shadow" had often warmed her life, her anguish evident in her lament, "A finger. They found her fucking finger."

Some were determined to reconstruct the organization, despite this horrendous setback. In Sausalito, California, Dohrn and Jones quickly assumed leadership of a rejuvenated Weatherman, now numbering only about thirty. In mid-May, the remnants of Weatherman leadership met at a beach house rented by Dohrn and Jones, where the initial discussion focused on the townhouse debacle. It was Dohrn who laid out the new direction, noting that the movement had changed substantially in the previous three months, with hundreds of thousands of hippies and "freaks" being drawn in. As one historian put it, "What remained of the New Left was being lost in a sea of tie-dye and LSD." Sensing the need to fit in with the Bay Area scene, something more of a "hippie" look became fashionable, as Ayers and Jones grew beards and Dohrn took to fishnet tops and went braless, which, as one wit put it, served the strategic purpose of keeping "men from staring at her face." Weatherman would no longer focus on killing the oppressors, Dohrn proclaimed; the organization had to become more "life affirming," restricting its bombings to buildings and symbols of the establishment. It was this meeting that set the stage for Dohrn's May 21 tape-recorded "Declaration of War."

If terrorist bombings were to be central to Weatherman's new direction, Dohrn and the others were painfully aware that they had to learn how to build a safe bomb. Wilkerson and others began poring over explosive manuals, but it was Ron Fliegelman, something of a drifter until he found a home in Weatherman, who became Weatherman's "bomb guru" and dedicated himself to the study of dynamite, quickly developing his skills and confidence in constructing workable bombs. In the years after the townhouse fiasco, between 1970 and 1975, Weatherman bombed or attempted to bomb dozens of governmental and commercial targets, usually citing the bombing as retaliation for some perceived injustice. Perhaps most notably, the radicals set off a bomb in the US Capitol in March 1971. Efforts were always made to alert the staff at the target to be bombed. Weatherman activists often chose restrooms in public buildings to plant their bombs, because they afforded some privacy as well as many hiding places above ceiling tiles. Every bombing was declared to be retaliation for some official act of injustice. The US Capitol bombing, for example, was in retaliation for the US-backed invasion of Laos. It was in response to these bombings that the Nixon administration formulated the Huston Plan in June 1971, which proposed empowering the CIA as well as the FBI and other federal agencies to engage in illegal break-ins, unlimited wiretapping, opening mail, and placing informants on college campuses. Surprisingly, FBI director Hoover effectively killed the plan.

Weatherman also became involved in the escape of LSD guru Timothy Leary, who was serving a ten-year sentence at the California Men's Colony in San Luis Obispo. Aided by Bay area Weathermen, Leary easily escaped on the night of September 12. Communist Clayton Van Lydegraf and others helped Leary change clothes and dye his hair, and drove him to a meeting with Dohrn, Ayers, and Jones, after which he was spirited out of the country to Paris. Though Weatherman seemed to have regained national attention with Leary's escape, an episode in Madison,

Wisconsin, brought bombing into further disrepute when four radicals blew up the Army Mathematical Research Center at the University of Wisconsin. The blast was the worst act of terrorism in US history as of that date, completely destroying a six-story building and killing a graduate student. Though Weatherman's bombing continued on schedule, public outrage grew. In 1970 alone, the nation experienced 330 bombings, three times as many as in 1969, though not all were Weather Underground actions. Dohrn, Katherine Ann Power, and Susan Edith Saxe were now on the FBI's Ten Most Wanted list and Weatherman was down to somewhere between thirty and fifty members. A new direction was needed.

On December 6, 1970, Weatherman, in yet another nod to Bob Dylan, released the manifesto "New Morning—Changing Weather." The statement acknowledged previous failure and proclaimed that "the future of our revolution has changed decisively." The townhouse disaster, the manifesto read, "forever destroyed our belief that armed struggle is the only real revolutionary struggle." The new "weapons of revolution" were to be "grass and organic consciousness-expanding drugs." Dohrn also announced that Weatherman was a sexist term and the group would now be known as the Weather Underground Organization. The WUO leadership left San Francisco in the spring of 1971 and began a rather peripatetic existence. Dohrn ended her relationship with Jeff Jones and took up with Bill Ayers, whom she eventually married. Jones moved to rural New York, married Eleanor Stein, and settled into a tranquil life. These personal changes paralleled national events; the antiwar movement was becoming less dynamic as the Vietnam war wound down and campuses cooled. The WUO continued its campaign of bombing, but now almost entirely in response to specific events.

By 1972, the WUO was a fading organization, though Dohrn still traveled the country attempting to revive radical alliances. The alliance with the revolutionary counterculture youth had proved a dead end. A "transformative moment" arrived with the July 1974 publication of *Prairie Fire: The Politics of Revolutionary Anti-Imperialism*, to which Dohrn was a major contributor. It was a cynical effort to surreptitiously regain control of the Movement by having the leadership resurface and gather the remnants of the radical left into an organization that they would control. This led to the publication of *Osawatomie*, which presented left-wing position papers and the creation of the Prairie Fire Distribution

Committee, which was to play a leading role in rounding up straggling leftists. Only the leadership knew that this was merely a front for a reinvigorated Weather Underground, which would be brought together by the Prairie Fire Organizing Committee (PFOC). Things went from bad to worse as Clayton Van Lydegraf reemerged to seize control of the PFOC, redirect it toward orthodox Marxism-Leninism, and have Dohrn, Ayers, and other former leaders expelled for "deviationism." Jones, Boudin, and the rest of the longtime WUO leadership were also purged or simply left. All remnants of 1969's Weatherman were now gone. To sum up, as Burrough aptly writes, "in every conceivable way, the young intellectuals who had come together in 1969 to form Weatherman had utterly failed."

As PFOC continued to conduct sporadic bombings, it was revealed in 1976 that the FBI had infiltrated the group; Van Lydegraf and his few followers were arrested in 1977. Dohrn and Ayers continued their underground life in Manhattan, producing two sons, Zayd Shakur and Malik. As the decade wore on, arrests and surrenders further thinned Weatherman ranks. Mark Rudd surfaced to face charges in 1977, and three years later Cathy Wilkerson, one of the townhouse explosion survivors, gave up and went to prison for three years. Dohrn and Ayers emerged in December 1980, Dohrn serving time for contempt of a grand jury and facing other minor penalties. Jeff Jones, arrested in October 1981, faced only probation. However, only days later, Kathy Boudin, the other townhouse survivor, joined BLA members in the attempted robbery of a Brinks armored truck; in the ensuing gun battle, two police officers and a Brinks guard were killed. Boudin was sentenced to twenty years to life and released in 2003. Born in a moment of liberal hope, the vestiges of SDS disappeared into prison, anonymity, and bourgeois life, leaving behind a legacy of leftist radicalism that has yet to be eclipsed.

The Black Panther leadership responded to the "New Morning—Changing Weather" manifesto with clear disdain, scoffing at Weatherman's abandonment of revolutionary fervor. The BPP did not voice similar objection to the support offered by sympathetic white liberals such as conductor/composer Leonard Bernstein, who held a fundraiser for the group in January 1970, an event mocked in Tom Wolfe's *Radical Chic and Mau-Mauing the Flak Catchers*. The year 1970 saw the BPP continue its assaults on police, wounding two in a gunfight and with fragmentation bombs that spring. That same year, Huey Newton's conviction was overturned and he was freed just as a fundamental split fractured the BPP, as one faction headed by Cleaver advocated an international stance with "revolutionary" and "socialist" regimes, with Panther delegations making trips to North Vietnam, North Korea, and China. Both Cleaver and Bobby Seale attended that year's Pan-African Cultural Festival in Algeria, leading to the establishment of an international section of the BPP. Newton, however, insisted that the focus should be on seeking justice and improvement in America's black communities, notably in his Oakland base. In 1971, the two leaders issued mutual expulsion decrees. In subsequent months, the two ordered retaliatory assassinations against the other's followers, leading hundreds of members to quit the BPP. With reduced membership, Newton and David Hilliard dedicated their energies to community services, while Cleaver continued to endorse a more confrontational strategy.

Between 1972 and 1974, Newton focused his energies on Oakland, closing chapters elsewhere in the nation and stressing winning local electoral offices, with few victories other than in local commissions. In early 1974, Newton purged a number of Panthers whose loyalties remained with Seale, including Seale himself, Hilliard, and numerous others. Further resignations from the party followed. That same year, Newton was again arrested and charged with assaulting policemen and murdering prostitute Kathleen Smith. Out on bail, he fled to Cuba.

Newton had appointed Panther Elaine Brown as chairwoman of the Oakland chapter in his absence, although she lost two elections for a seat on the Oakland City Council in 1973 and 1975. Brown's initiative of giving women a greater role in the party was greeted with skepticism by many male Panthers, and more troubles arose following the mysterious death of BPP bookkeeper Betty Van Patter after she discovered irregularities in party bookkeeping. Newton later admitted taking part in the torture, rape, and murder of the woman. He returned from Cuba in 1977 to stand trial for Smith's murder and to find a shrinking party divided by Brown's inclusion of women.

The sordid final years of the BPP now unfolded as Panther Flores Forbes led a failed attempt to assassinate a prosecution witness, attacking the wrong house and being wounded by gunfire. Newton was acquitted of ordering the murder of Panther Nelson Malloy because the testimony of the witness was impeached, but the BPP leader was convicted for illegal firearms possession and incarcerated. After brief freedom, Newton was sentenced to six months in prison for misappropriation of funds intended for an Oakland school founded by the BPP in 1989. Free for only a short period, Newton was shot to death on August 22, 1989, by drug dealer Tyrone Robinson, a member of the small Black Guerrilla Family, who claimed self-defense but was convicted of murder. The motive for the murder remains unclear. Once hailed as a martyred revolutionary by the New Left, Huey Newton died leaving a legacy besmirched by violence and criminality. With the advent of a conservative era in 1980, the BPP officially disbanded in 1982, though in 1989, a New Black Panther Party was established in Dallas, Texas. Bobby Seale and numerous former Panthers denounced the organization as a fraud. In the opinion of Purdue University's Judson Jeffries, the BPP was "the most effective black revolutionary organization in the twentieth century."

Long before the BPP dissolved, one of its most infamous affiliates was involved in an especially gruesome and deadly courtroom drama that grew out of the incarceration of the "Soledad Brothers," George Jackson, Fleeta Drumgo, and John Clutchette, who were charged with the murder of Soledad State Prison guard John Mills. Mills's murder followed a prison yard incident in which a fistfight led Officer Opie Miller to open fire on the prisoners, killing three black inmates. On January 16, 1970, a grand jury exonerated Miller on the basis of "justifiable homicide." Thirty minutes after inmates heard the verdict, John Mills's badly beaten body was found thrown from a third-floor tier. In mid-February, the "Soledad Brothers" were indicted for the murder.

On August 7, George Jackson's younger brother Jonathan arrived at the Marin County courtroom of Judge Harold Haley heavily armed and determined to take hostages as a prelude to demanding the freeing the Soledad Brothers charged with Mills's murder. Drawing an automatic weapon, Jackson surprised and disarmed the bailiffs before arming the three black defendants present, two of whom were Black Panthers, and seizing the judge, the prosecutor, and three female jurors. The event climaxed in a wild shoot-out with police as Jackson sought to escape in a waiting van. When the gunfire ceased, Jackson, the judge, and the three black defendants lay dead, with one of the jurors and the prosecutor wounded. UCLA professor Angela Davis's problems began when it was discovered that she had purchased several of the firearms. Davis was subsequently charged with aggravated kidnapping and first-degree murder, which soon put her on the FBI's Ten Most Wanted list. She was captured by the FBI on October 13, 1970.

While Davis awaited trial, the final act in George Jackson's saga began, on August 17, 1971, when he allegedly led a riot at San Quentin, where he had been moved. Armed with a 9mm automatic, Jackson released an entire floor of inmates from the maximum-security area, initiating a wild melee in which three guards were killed, as were two inmates suspected of being snitches. Rushing into the prison yard, Jackson was immediately shot and killed. Debate continues over where he obtained the handgun, with some claiming that it was provided by his attorney. The two surviving Soledad Brothers were acquitted of Mills's death in March 1972. Months later, an all-white jury found Davis not guilty. Once free, she continued to tread the path of radical activism, receiving accolades and awards in the Soviet Union and Eastern Bloc nations. Even returning to academia, she taught and lectured at a number of universities while still devoting time to crusades for prison reform, feminism, and environmentalism and remains an activist scholar to the present.

Black Americans were not the only Americans seeking redress for injustices during the 1970s. Mexican Americans began to feel the same urge to challenge the status quo, the chief vehicle being the Brown Berets. Growing out of the Young Chicanos for Community Action in Los Angeles County, the Brown Berets became a national organization in 1967, with an agenda including fighting police harassment, inadequate health care and job opportunities, poor public education, the lack of political representation, and the Vietnam War, in which Mexican Americans disproportionately served. "La Causa," as the struggle was known, supported the United Farm Workers and the New Mexico Land Grant Movement and organized a Chicano Moratorium against the Vietnam War in 1970. The peaceful protest was attacked by Los Angeles County Sheriff's deputies, who killed two of the marchers and a journalist. Nevertheless, the Brown Berets eschewed the revolutionary rhetoric and violence of the BPP, though members of the group did occupy Santa Catalina Island for several days in 1972. That November, Brown Beret prime minister David Sanchez disbanded the organization due to heavy police infiltration and to avoid the internecine strife. In 1970, La Raza Unida Party was formed, but it proved short lived due to internal factionalism and had collapsed as of 1978. The Chicano organization did not end by the mid-1970s, but tended to be local in origin, emerging largely in response to perceived police brutality and injustice.

The same cannot be said of the Fuerzas Armadas de Liberación Nacionale (FALN), a Puerto Rican paramilitary group that sought Puerto Rican independence through direct, often violent actions. Puerto Rico, a territory acquired by the United States subsequent to the 1898 Spanish-American War, had long fostered inhabitants unreconciled to their status, as while they were US citizens, they could not vote in presidential elections. The Puerto Rican Nationalist Party (PRNP) organized in 1922 to gain independence and proved willing to resort to violence. In November 1950, PRNP gunmen attempted to assassinate President Truman at Blair House. On March 1, 1954, four nationalists opened fire on members of the House of Representatives with automatic pistols, shouting, "Puerto Rico libré!" and wounding five. Their imprisonment marked the virtual suppression of the nationalist movement in the 1950s.

The FALN was established in about 1974 with the stated objective of gaining Puerto Rican independence through direct action. Founded by Filiberto Ojeda Rios and drawing from Marxist ideology, the FALN considered their struggle part of a global effort to end colonialism and establish a socialist society in Puerto Rico. Bombings were the chief weapon of FALN and the group claimed responsibility for more than 130 bombings in the United States between 1974 and 1983, the most notorious being the January 1975 bombing of New York City's Fraunces Tavern, killing four. Their activities expanded beyond bombing when armed FALN members invaded the Chicago headquarters of the Carter-Mondale campaign in March 1980 threatening staff and vandalizing the offices. Despite numerous arrests and trials, the FALN remained operative until 1981. It was briefly superseded by the Boricua Popular Army, also known ominously as "The Machete Wielders," led by FALN founder Rios, who was killed by the FBI in 2005.

A few small, often ephemeral radical groups continued to emerge throughout the decade. One of the most unusual was the M19, also known as the May 19th Communist organization, described as "America's first female terrorist group." Operative from 1978 to 1985, M19 consisted of ten regular members and about a dozen affiliated individuals but was capable of carrying out actions far beyond what its small membership might indicate. M19, which derived its name from the birthdays of Malcolm X and Ho Chi Minh (May 19), was created and led by women, most of whom were lesbians as well as feminists. The group's 1979 manifesto announced their creed as "revolutionary anti-imperialism" and proclaimed, "Our science is Marxism-Leninism." This small group of middle-class intellectuals vowed to reject their "white skin privilege" and to "ensure that all the shooting didn't come from one side."

At the core of the movement were Judy Clark and Susan Lisa Rosenberg. Clark was a classic "red-diaper baby" whose leftist parents prepared her for a life of activism. She joined SDS in high school and moved to the Weather Underground when the former fragmented. Arrested for her role in 1969's "Days of Rage," she served seven months in jail. Upon her release, she joined WITCH (Women's International Terrorist Conspiracy from Hell). Her compatriot, Susan Rosenberg, likewise joined SDS in high school and, while at Barnard, joined the Venceremos Brigade in Cuba. Three other women completed this core group: Silvia Bardini, another SDS alumnus, Donna Borup, and Susan Tipograph. Tipograph was a "movement" lawyer, described by an associate as "a bad sister, a woman totally about the get-down for the struggle." Marilyn Jean Buck was also a founder and ex-SDS member and established ties with some Black Panthers, some of whom were drawn into M19. By the 1980s, M19 had gained some notoriety by freeing the BLA's Assata Shakur and the FALN's William Morales. Former WUO member Kathy Boudin was identified as a member of the M19 following her arrest for the Brink's robbery, as was Judy Clark. Between 1982 and 1985, M19 was committed to bombing targets of "imperialist oppression," and had built up an impressive list of achievements in that time, but by May 1985, most M19 members had been arrested except for one, Elizabeth Duke..

Lesser known though equally short-lived was the Sojourner Truth Organization (SJO), a communist group founded in the Midwest in the winter of 1969–1970 with the intent of organizing factories. With a membership of about fifty, the group was active chiefly in the Chicago area, agitating for "mass revolutionary independent workers' organizations" and sought alliances with black and Latino radicals, making the fight against white supremacy central. The organization foundered in the 1970s as the nation entered a postindustrial era in which there were fewer sites to proselytize and organize. Ideological and strategic squabbles, much like those that had destroyed the New Left, led to a gradual contraction of the SJO back to the Chicago area. By the end of 1983, SJO was little more than a memory.

Karl Marx once remarked, "History repeats itself, first as tragedy, second as farce." Many of the groups that reiterated the history of the New Left under new names in the 1970s qualify as a tragic repeat of history. One group, however, as tragic as the fate of some of its members were, more accurately falls into the category of farce. There remained one final cataclysmic death spasm of the New Left, some remnants of which began to celebrate black prison inmates not as potentially dangerous criminals but, rather, as the victims of an oppressive society. The combination of naive radicalism and violent criminality led to a violent spectacle that gripped the nation's attention for eighteen months at mid-decade.

❖❖❖

The influence of Soledad Brother George Jackson did not end with his death in the San Quentin prison yard. In *Soledad Brother: The Prison Letters of George Jackson*, Jackson wrote, "You will find no class or category more aware, more embittered, desperate or dedicated to the ultimate remedy—revolution." In *Blood in My Eye*, published three years after Jackson's death, the vitriol was evident. "We must accept the eventuality of bringing the U.S.A. to its knees; accept the closing off of critical sections of the city with barbed wire, armored pig carriers crisscrossing the streets, soldiers everywhere . . . the smell of cordite, house-to-house-searches, doors being kicked in, the commonness of death." These grim visions of rebellion and death were spewed forth by a man who had begun establishing a criminal record as a child, including arson, muggings, robbery, pimping, and assaults. He spent his adult life in California's prisons, establishing a reputation as a violent, sullen, and mean-spirited debt collector for a prison gang. Nevertheless, George Jackson's writings spoke truth to other black inmates. Donald DeFreeze, serving some of his time at the California Medical Facility at Vacaville in a psychiatric treatment center, was spellbound by Jackson's posthumous writings. He was to become the leader of one of the most bizarre and notorious radical groups of the mid-1970s, the Symbionese Liberation Army.

Born to Louis and Mary DeFreeze in Cleveland, Ohio, on November 15, 1943, Donald was the eldest of eight children in a household that could only be described as dysfunctional. He was, as one historian writes, "a frequent punching bag for his father." The family moved often between Cleveland, Newark, and Buffalo. DeFreeze dropped out of school at fourteen and ran away, later drifting around New York and New Jersey. Arrested for breaking into parking meters and stealing a car, he was sent to a reformatory. Having moved back to Newark in 1963, he married Gloria Thomas and the family soon boasted six children. DeFreeze moved the family to Los Angeles, in hopes of earning a living adequate to providing them with decent care, but the situation overcame him. "I just couldn't take it anymore," he later conceded. "I was slowly becoming a nothing."

Working periodically painting houses, DeFreeze's marriage began to disintegrate as he developed a lifelong taste for plum wine and "playing around with guns and fireworks and dogs and cars," an eclectic and puzzling mix of entertainments. Author Jeffrey Toobin writes that DeFreeze was "almost the opposite of a master criminal" and "was most inventive in finding ways to get caught." "Guns and bombs," Toobin writes, "were his obsession and his downfall." Following a 1968 arrest, a court-appointed psychiatrist noted that DeFreeze exhibited "a strong schizophrenic potential" and concluded ominously that "his fascination with firearms and explosives makes him dangerous." Almost constant arrests between 1967 and 1969 convinced his wife to leave him. In 1969, having assaulted a Hawaiian tourist and stolen a check from her, DeFreeze began serving a five-years-to-life sentence at Vacaville.

The years 1970 to 1973 were critical to DeFreeze's thinking, as he became politically aware after encountering the works of Jackson, Mao Tse-tung, Frantz Fanon, and Régis Debray. Though his comprehension of Marxist ideology was at best simplistic, it did seem to offer an explanation for the injustices that plagued his life. In 1970, DeFreeze joined the Black Culture Association (BCA), which offered lectures, films, music, and poetry about Africa. Like most BCA members, DeFreeze adopted an African name, Cinque M'tume. "Cin," as he was sometimes called, began developing friendships with some of the leftist radicals who did volunteer work at the prison. Eventually DeFreeze established a separate group, Unisight, through which he met radicals Willie Wolfe and Russ Little as well as former Black Panther Thero Wheeler. These individuals not only provided DeFreeze with outside connections but also served as the core of the future Symbionese Liberation Army (SLA).

Transferred to Soledad Prison in late 1972, DeFreeze was reclassi-fied as a minimum-security risk, which afforded him the opportunity to work outside the prison complex. On March 5, 1973, DeFreeze fled from a worksite. With the help of an acquaintance, he obtained new clothes and was dropped off at a commune in Berkeley. Little and Wolfe located a "safe house" for the escaped convict at the residence of Patricia "Mizmoon" Soltysik, with whom DeFreeze established an intimate relationship. Within a month of his escape, DeFreeze was collaborating with Little, now "Osceola," and Wolfe, who was to become "Cujo," together with Nancy Ling "Fahizah" Perry and Joe "Bo" Remiro, on what was to be a manifesto for the SLA. Eventually the core group would be joined by Bill "General Teko" Harris and his wife Emily ("Yolanda"), Angela "General Gelina" Atwood, and Camilla "Gabi" Hall, who had been "Mizmoon's" neighbor and lover.

Journalists Vin McLellan and Paul Avery in *The Voices of Guns* cap-tured the bizarre character of the newborn SLA, describing it as "the inevitable marriage of Charles Manson's insane dune-buggy fascism and the arrogant proto-Marxist terrorism of the early Weathermen." Without question, the tiny organization "had a virtual genius for public theater." An early SLA leaflet claimed that their seven-headed cobra symbol was derived from a 170,000-year-old image "used by people to signify god and life." Several paragraphs explained that the seven heads represented the seven principles of Kwanzaa and thus represented "a revolutionary unity of all people against a common oppressor enemy of the people," a symbiosis of separate entities coming together to serve a single purpose. SLA members proclaimed their leader General Field Marshal Cinque to be "not only a military genius to lead us but a spiritual prophet to save us," as his name meant "the Fifth Prophet."

Having promised "the most devastating revolutionary violence ever unleashed," the SLA's army of eight and their General Field Marshal were off to an uncertain start. They assisted in the escape of Thero Wheeler from Vacaville in August 1973, but Wheeler departed after quarreling with DeFreeze. Other early actions seem almost comic. In September 1973, Soltysik and Perry robbed Seifert's Floral Company in Oakland of less than $600 but had to abandon their getaway van when they noticed bystanders taking down the license number. Aside from a subsequent carjacking, none of the SLA's activities met the definition of "devastating revolutionary violence." Just on the horizon, however, was an action that would provoke broad public condemnation as well as bring the SLA to the attention of the authorities.

In what became a disastrous public relations move, DeFreeze announced his intention to assassinate Marcus Foster, the black superintendent of Oakland schools, in October 1973 because of his advocacy of student identification cards to ensure school security. "We are gonna off that nigger," DeFreeze was said to have promised. Having surveilled Foster's movements for some weeks, on November 6, 1973, DeFreeze, Perry, and Soltysik waited in ambush in a dark parking lot at the school administration building as Foster and deputy superintendent Robert Blackburn emerged and headed toward the latter's car. Perry opened fire on Foster with a .380 handgun, hitting him in the leg. Blackburn was struck by two blasts from DeFreeze's 12-gauge shotgun. Soltysik finished off Foster with repeated close-range shots from a .38 caliber revolver. Foster died on the scene, though Blackburn survived. Forensic experts soon discovered that the SLA bullets had been carefully injected with cyanide.

The SLA could not have been ready for the negative reaction that ensued. Oakland's mayor stood beside Black Panther Bobby Seale at Foster's memorial, and Oakland's BPP denounced the murder as "brutal and senseless." Even the Weather Underground's Bernardine Dohrn commented, "We do not understand the execution of Marcus Foster," who "is not a recognized enemy of the people." The hunt for Foster's killers unnerved the SLA, but they nonetheless issued a constant stream of communiqués that threatened the targeting of specific policemen, the president of the T. A. White Candy Company (damned as a subsidiary of ITT), and the Oakland warehouse director for Colgate Palmolive Company (for ostensible "genocide, murder, and robbery" in a number of Third World countries), well as other targets. The group sought a new safe house following the January 1974 arrests of Remiro and Russell, after the house in Clayton was discovered, revealing documents outlining future actions. Police ignored the listing of Patty Hearst's name, beside which was written "arrest warrant issued." Finding temporary haven in the suburbs of Concord, the SLA began a furious routine of calisthenics, weapons training, and bomb building in preparation for their next mission: freeing their imprisoned comrades by kidnapping newspaper heiress Patty Hearst. In January 1974, ultimately settling in at a new safe house in Daly City, the group made renovations in preparation for kidnapping Hearst. Heavy-duty locks were installed on all outside doors;

windows were covered with heavy paper. Most importantly, the four-by-six-foot closet in the master bedroom was fitted with doorknobs that could only be opened from the outside.

On February 4, 1974, nineteen-year-old Patty Hearst was studying art history at UC Berkeley, living in a five-room duplex with her fiancé Steven Weed, a graduate student of philosophy. Hearst's life changed forever that evening shortly after nine when Weed answered a knock on the door. DeFreeze, Bill Harris, and Angela Atwood pushed into the room, pushing Weed to the floor as Atwood grabbed Hearst. DeFreeze struck Weed three times with a rifle butt as a screaming Patty, carried over Harris's shoulders, was taken downstairs. Someone fired a volley of gunfire to discourage gawking neighbors. Stuffing the gagged and blindfolded heiress into the trunk of a stolen 1964 Chevy, the trio headed for the Berkeley Hills with the car's owner still bound in the vehicle's rear floorboards. Switching vehicles in the hills, they returned to the Daly City house, where Patty was locked in a closet. Weed informed Berkeley police of the abduction from his bed at Cowell Hospital. In short order the FBI and Patty's family were notified of the crime. Astonishingly the perpetrators had inadvertently left an indisputable clue as to their identity in the duplex—a box of cyanide-tipped .38 caliber bullets.

Not until February 7 did the SLA claim responsibility, when a staffer at KPFA radio opened an envelope containing a communiqué from the "Symbionese Liberation Army Western Regional Adult Unit." The message declared Patty a "prisoner of war," denounced her father, Randolph Hearst, as a "corporate enemy of the people," and demanded that the communiqué be disseminated in the media, warning that failure to do so and any effort to rescue the hostage would result in her death. These were not the standard demands of kidnappers. They were not after money—they wanted media attention, and they got it. As one writer noted, the Hearst kidnapping was "probably the greatest media event of the 1970s." Hearst made the cover of *Newsweek* seven times, and, ironically, most of the media coverage focused on her rather than the SLA. Perhaps inured by the activities of the numerous radical organizations that preceded it, the SLA received little in the way of analysis but was more often mocked in the media as a bunch of lunatic misfits who communicated in stilted, time-worn, radical phraseology and dreamed up silly symbols.

Five days later, the next communication sought to clarify to scoffers that the SLA meant business. KPFA was again the chosen medium, receiving eight pages of overblown revolutionary rhetoric together with two audiotapes. One, recorded by Patty, asserted, "These people aren't just a bunch of nuts. They've been really honest with me, but they're perfectly willing to die for what they're doing." Hearst ascribed her capture to the fact that "I'm a member of a ruling class family." DeFreeze, who identified himself on the second tape as "a black man . . . [who holds] the rank of General Field Marshal in the United Federated Forces of the SLA," stated that the Hearst family needed to make a "good faith" gesture before the SLA "court" could consider negotiations. The demand was both bizarre and specific—the Hearsts were to organize a food giveaway, with at least $70 in food going to anyone who presented a welfare card, parole or probation papers, or jail or bail release papers. The giveaway was to begin on February 19 and held on Tuesdays, Thursdays, and Saturdays in poor areas of San Francisco, Oakland, East Los Angeles, Compton, and Watts. A major miscalculation on the part of the SLA was that the Hearst fortune was much diminished from earlier decades, probably down to about $1.4 million in 1974. DeFreeze's giveaway scheme would likely cost about $400,000. The SLA calculated that Patty's release would require donations of about $2 million. Randolph Hearst donated $500,000 to the People in Need (PIN) program and the Hearst Foundation placed $1.5 million in escrow. DeFreeze now demanded an additional $4 million.

The five food distributions were undertaken from February 22 to March 25, with varying degrees of incompetence, rowdiness, and chaos. That same day, Hearst made it clear to the SLA that its demands exceeded his financial resources. He would support PIN with $2 million in return for his daughter's release. Baffled by this resistance, the SLA did not respond. The food giveaway had been a media lure all along. What they really wanted was their comrades freed from prison, but Hearst had no control over that.

On March 9 another SLA tape was received, the first portion voiced by Angela "General Gelina" Atwood, who denounced her leftist brethren for failing to stand by the SLA. The second part of the audio recording moved the Hearst kidnapping into an entirely new context. An emotional and angry Patty denounced her family, asserting that her father had lied about his finances. More importantly, she announced that through reading revolutionary literature, especially Jackson's *Blood in My Eye*, she had developed a greater understanding of "fascism in America." In order that she might defend herself from FBI assassins, she stated, the SLA had provided her with a shotgun. The nature of Patty's captivity and her subsequent conversion to SLA radicalism has long been a topic of controversy. One indisputable fact is that she was kept in a walk-in closet from February 4, 1974, to March 20 or 21. The closet was soundproofed with shag carpeting and she was initially bound for a period and always blindfolded. She claimed that she was raped by both DeFreeze and Wolfe but later developed an intimate relationship with the latter. She was bombarded daily with DeFreeze's deluded rants as well as being relentlessly interrogated and lectured, released from the closet to go to the restroom and later to take meals with the group, though she remained blindfolded. At one point, DeFreeze told her that she would have the choice of joining the SLA or being executed. In late March, she was informed by DeFreeze that "the War Council has decided that you can join us, if you want to, or you can be released and go home again." Patty later said that she did not believe DeFreeze's claim that she could choose release, so she was left with only one choice. Only after she had proclaimed her enthusiasm for joining the group was her blindfold finally removed.

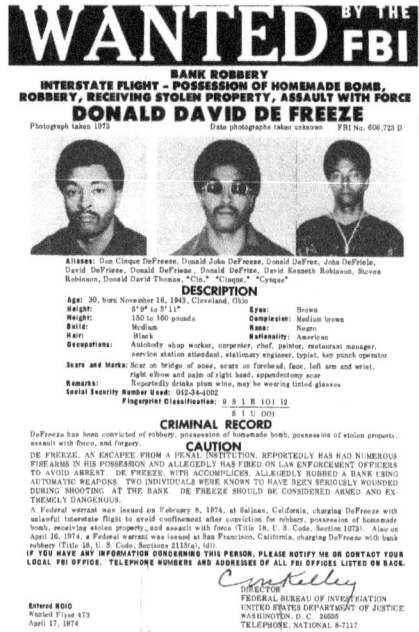

Figure 4.2. FBI wanted poster of escaped criminal Donald DeFreeze, who organized the Symbionese Liberation Army that kidnapped Patty Hearst and precipitated the most violent shoot-out with police in the nation's history.
Source: Wikimedia Commons

There had been no word from the SLA since March 9. Then the editor of the San Francisco *Phoenix* received a birthday card, roses, and a piece of Patty's driver's license on April 2, with the promise that negotiations for her release would begin the following day. It was soon discovered to be a cruel hoax. Delayed in the mail, the package was to have arrived on April Fool's Day. On April 3, another audiotape arrived at San Francisco's KSAN, carrying new revelations. In it, Patty announced that she was never "brainwashed, drugged, tortured, or hypnotized" and had become a member of the SLA, soon to bear the name "Tania." Along with the tape was a photo of the heiress wearing a beret and crouched in combat position with a sawed-off M1 carbine. She was posed in front of the SLA's flag bearing the multiheaded cobra. Reproductions of the photo were soon universal, provoking a firestorm of controversy as to the authenticity of her conversion.

Hearst soon got a chance to prove her commitment to the SLA. Having identified the Hibernia Bank as their target, on April 15, five SLA members arrived at the bank in two rented cars. DeFreeze, Patty, and Gabi entered first, followed by Soltysik and Perry. Wielding a submachine gun, DeFreeze shouted, "The first motherfucker who don't lay down on the floor gets shot in the head!" Shouting, "SLA!" as they went about their appointed tasks, the group quickly completed the robbery and pushed through the front doors just as two customers attempted to enter. Panicked, Perry shot and wounded both of them. On the street, DeFreeze unleashed a wild burst of fire to scatter bystanders. The group arrived back at their hideout with $10,000. Security camera photos of the robbery convinced most that Patty was a willing participant.

Convinced that the SLA needed more "soldiers" that were unknown, DeFreeze came up with the bizarre idea of knocking on neighboring apartment doors to see who might be interested. When this proved unsuccessful, he and Bill Harris went into a neighborhood to try again, locating a black Muslim woman, who gave them food and helped them find a new apartment in a black neighborhood. To safely establish themselves in their new quarters, the whites in the group donned blackface and Afro wigs; DeFreeze actually dressed in drag. When the apartment proved unavailable, the group holed up in a nearby hotel until DeFreeze, who heard that Hearst was offering a $50,000 reward for Patty's safe return, decided to move the group to the Los Angeles area, where they took up residence in a dilapidated shack at 833 West 84th Street in Compton.

The events that marked the beginning of the end of the SLA began on the afternoon of May 16 when Bill and Emily Harris entered Mel's Sporting Goods in Inglewood. Challenged for shoplifting a pair of socks, the Harrises wrestled with two store employees on the sidewalk outside. The struggle ended abruptly when Patty, waiting in a VW van across the street, opened fire with a submachine gun and an M1 carbine, peppering the storefront and allowing the Harrises to scurry to safety in the van. Though fired on several times by one of the employees, the group escaped, stealing another car. What alerted police and the FBI to the SLA's presence in Los Angeles was a parking ticket left in the van, indicating an address next door to their safe house. Having stolen yet another car, the trio waited at a drive-in that had been chosen as a meeting site should the group be separated.

Near 4:00 a.m., having avoided the 84th Street house, DeFreeze, Wolfe, Atwood, Soltysik, and Perry spotted a house on East 54th Street, where six people were drinking and playing cards. DeFreeze gave one of the occupants $100 to let the group stay "for just a little while." The SLA members unloaded piles of luggage from their van, which included nineteen rifles, shotguns, and pistols as well as more than four thousand rounds of ammunition. DeFreeze carelessly introduced his companions as "soldiers of the SLA" and word of their presence made its way around the neighborhood. Shortly after noon, two police officers discovered the SLA van in the alleyway, and at 2:00 p.m., a woman phoned the FBI with word that the SLA was at a hideout on East 54th. Slowly, the residents began to find reasons to leave the house. By 4:20 p.m., 218 LAPD officers and 127 FBI agents had established a perimeter around the house. At 5:44 the first of eighteen police bullhorn requests for the occupants of the residence to surrender was made. With darkness approaching, the decision was made to end the stand-off. The most violent shoot-out in American history was about to take place as Los Angeles media broadcast it live.

At 5:53, the battle began as tear-gas rockets were fired into the house, provoking a barrage of machine gun and rifle fire from within. A hurricane of lead was exchanged for the next hour, lessening only when reloading took place. The situation deteriorated after 6:40 when riot-gas canisters were fired into a window; moments later, smoke and fire began pouring from the house, engulfing the structure in four minutes, possibly due to gasoline bombs stored inside. One final civilian fled the house as an LAPD special weapons team arrived with automatic weapons. As their situation worsened, SLA members chopped a hole in the floor and sheltered in the crawl space under the house, firing from air vents. Perry and Hall charged out of a hole in the foundation; Hall was immediately shot in the head and pulled back inside. Perry died later from two gunshot wounds. A cease-fire was called at 6:58 when all firing had stopped. Exploding pipe bombs and ammunition had previously kept fire equipment at bay; by now most of the home had collapsed.

During the one-hour shoot-out, the two sides expended around nine thousand rounds as transfixed viewers, including the Harrises and Hearst, who watched on television in their motel room, followed the carnage on television. Astonishingly, no police, FBI, or bystanders were wounded. After the fire was extinguished and the wreckage searched, DeFreeze, Soltysik, and Wolfe were found together in a corner of the crawl space. Atwood died just inside the foundation hole from which Perry and Hall had briefly emerged. Perry and Hall had both been buried in the debris. DeFreeze had died of a head wound. The biggest news was that Patty Hearst was not among the dead. After a three-week absence, the surviving SLA members, who were joined by new recruits Wendy Yoshimura, Steve and Kathleen Soliah, James Kilgore, and Michael Bortin, released a message from the "Malcolm X Combat Unit," offering their version of the LA event and expressing rage and grief at their comrades' fate. In addition to special praise for "Cinque," Hearst declared, "I would never choose to live the rest of my life surrounded by pigs like the Hearsts." Bill "General Teko" Harris announced that, henceforth, the group would be known as the New World Liberation Front (NWLF). Eighteen months elapsed before the final arrests of the fugitives.

Donald "Cinque M'tume" DeFreeze's sad and savage life story effectively ended on that mid-May day in 1974, but the three surviving remnants of the SLA sought to continue their revolution, moving frantically from West to East Coast and back again as they sought to rebuild the group's membership and formulate a new strategy. A series of seventeen bombings in California were attributed to affiliates of the loosely organized NWLF, but could not be tied directly to the core group, which proved elusive. Meanwhile, aspiring actress and outspoken SLA fan Kathy Soliah helped recruit new members including her brother Steve and Jim Kilgore. As Patty's "lost year" began to play out, the group debated their next moves. Bill Harris's advocacy of bombings lost out to bank robbery, which could be deemed revolutionary as well as providing operating cash. That enterprise began on February 24, 1975, when Kilgore and Bortin robbed Sacramento's Guild Savings and Loan of more than $10,000 in cash and money orders. As of this time, Patty's assigned role was as a driver. On April 21, Bortin, Kilgore, Soliah, and Emily Harris entered the Crocker National Bank in Carmichael. Harris, taking the lead and wielding a shotgun, had barely ordered everyone down when bystander Myrna Opsahl moved in a manner that panicked Harris, who fired a load of buckshot into the woman's abdomen. Unnerved, the team ran from the bank with little to show for their efforts. With Emily Harris now wanted for murder, the group moved back to the Bay Area.

By summer 1975, it was becoming clear that dysfunction was weakening the group, as leadership quarrels broke out and a series of bombings failed to produce the desired casualties or failed completely. The anticlimactic end for the remainder of the band came in mid-September after lengthy FBI surveillance of two residences in Daly City. On September 18, FBI agents arrested Bill and Emily Harris as they returned from a jog. Moving quickly to a second known SLA house, two FBI agents and two Los Angeles detectives walked into an upstairs apartment to find Wendy Yoshimura and Patty Hearst sitting at a table; both women were arrested with minimal resistance and arraigned. Steve Soliah was arrested near Hearst's apartment. Kathy Soliah, who changed her name to Sara Jane Olson, remained a fugitive until 1999. James Kilgore was arrested in South Africa in 2002. Mike Bortin quit the SLA in 1975, though, like the others, he did not escape justice.

Patty Hearst's arrest and trial gripped the nation like no media event until the O. J. Simpson trial, and this was before cable television. Defended by famed attorney F. Lee Bailey, Patty spent five months in jail prior to her trial, as her parents refused to pay her bail. On March 20, 1976, Hearst was found guilty of bank robbery and using a firearm in the commission of a felony. President Carter commuted her thirty-five-year sentence to twenty-two months served, and she was released on February 1, 1979. President Clinton granted Hearst a full pardon in early 2001. The remaining SLA members were all eventually apprehended, tried, and served varying prison terms, the last being released in 2009.

The sordid end of the SLA did not end radical violence in the 1970s, though it gradually sputtered out as groups or individuals claiming to be affiliated with the New Word Liberation Front continued to set off bombs well into the latter years of the decade. Efforts to revive the revolutionary fervor of the 1960s had failed disastrously, bringing only chaos and death. Ironically, the violent radical activities of the 1970s had the effect of rejuvenating the image of the FBI, which had been tarnished during the 1960s and early 1970s due to revelations of extralegal activities against protest groups and surveillance of US citizens such as Martin Luther King Jr. The agency ended the decade with a much-enhanced reputation, which would grow in subsequent decades, as both domestic and foreign terrorism threatened American lives.

"THE AMERICAN RIDE IS ENDING"
Energy Crises, Inflation, and the Challenges of a Postindustrial Society

In December 1974, Ed Roberts, owner of Model Instruments and Telemetry Systems (MITS), had just overseen the rollout of the Altair 8080, hailed on the cover of the January issue of *Popular Electronics* as "The World's First Microcomputer Kit to Rival Commercial Models." A machine of laughably modest capabilities by twenty-first-century standards, the Altair was sold as a kit requiring assembly. Fans of the canceled television show *Star Trek* would recognize the name as being that of a fictional planet mentioned in an episode of that program, and the Altair would not have seemed out of place on the bridge of Captain Kirk's *Enterprise*, as it was little more than a small, rectangular black box boasting rows of flashing red lights and toggle switches. The Altair 8080 was bereft of any outward evidence of its function; keyboards and monitor screens were years in the future. Intel, a name to become ubiquitous in the future, had developed the microprocessor for the Altair 8080 in 1974.

Nineteen-year-old Bill Gates, then a student at Harvard University, was in his dormitory room when his friend and fellow computer enthusiast Paul Allen burst into the room holding a copy of the *Popular Electronics* issue that he had spied on a newsstand in Harvard Square and quickly convinced Gates that they could develop software for the Altair that would put them at the forefront of popular computer technology. Only days later, Gates built up the courage to call Ed Roberts and proposed that he be given the opportunity to develop a BASIC (Beginner's All-Purpose Symbolic Instruction Code) for MITS's Altair. Though Roberts agreed, the project was a tremendous gamble on Gates's part. Neither he nor Allen had developed such a code, and it was rather unlikely that they would be able to in the two to three weeks that Gates had promised Roberts. They had neither an Altair nor an Intel 8080 chip. Compelled to improvise, they developed a software code with a PDP-10 minicomputer that seemed capable of mimicking the Intel chip. Working nonstop, the pair completed the promised software in Harvard's Aiken Computation Laboratory and, in late February, Allen flew to Albuquerque to deliver and test the code.

At MITS, Allen loaded the BASIC into an Altair, with which he was completely unfamiliar. To the amazement of Roberts and the relief of Allen, the code worked, and the primitive computer came to life. Satisfied, Roberts agreed to a contract between MITS and the newly named Micro-Soft (the hyphen was later eliminated), to purchase the rights to the Gates-Allen-designed BASIC. The two received $3,000 on signing and a guarantee of royalties up to $180,000 from their software. Unsurprisingly, Gates left Harvard to devote the entirety of his time to the new company that would be a major player in America's high-tech revolution. He, Allen, and their colleagues stepped into a future in which information technology would reshape the nation's economy.

Born into a prominent Seattle family on October 28, 1955, William Henry Gates III, or Trey, was the third child of Bill Gates Sr., an attorney, and Mary Maxwell Gates, a teacher. His parents felt that the active, energetic Trey's precocity would lead to great achievements, and in 1967, he was registered at the Lakeside School, an institution that offered intellectual stimulation. A pivotal event in Bill's life occurred when his math teacher took the class for a visit to the school's computer room, where the teletype machine was connected to a PDP minicomputer in downtown Seattle. Gates was intrigued with the machine and, together with friend Paul Allen, was soon spending much time there. A classic nerd, Gates voraciously read books and pamphlets about computers and began developing his first programs, which included tic-tac-toe, a lunar landing game, and even a computerized version of Monopoly. Gates signed up for advanced math courses at the University of Washington and organized the Lakeside Programmers Group (LPG). A school contract with Seattle's Computer Center Corporation (CCC) afforded Gates and friends more learning opportunities and the chance to aid CCC as troubleshooters and debuggers. In early 1971, Gates, Allen, and Kent Evans signed a contract with Information Sciences to write a payroll program, which mandated that the LPG become a formal partnership. Having done so, the LPG earned $10,000 worth of computer time, which was crucial to their education in computer technology. Soon afterward, Gates and Allen went to work for Traf-O-Data, which analyzed traffic-counter tapes, earning $20,000. As seniors, Gates and Allen were offered employment by TRW, a major defense contractor, to aid in debugging PDP-10 software programs, and the pair moved temporarily to Vancouver.

Returning to Seattle for graduation in June 1973, Gates told a classmate that his future plans included Harvard and making his first million by age twenty-five. Inexplicably enrolling as a prelaw major upon arriving at the Cambridge campus, Gates completed the undergraduate general education requirements but also signed up for upper-division courses in math, physics, and computer science. During the summer of 1974, he and Allen worked for Honeywell, one of the "Seven Giants" that overshadowed IBM. Both men were certain that the computer industry was on the verge of innovations that would inaugurate a new high-tech era. Gates was haphazardly continuing his courses at Harvard when he met Stephen Ballmer, who would also play a major role in Microsoft.

Though few Americans gave thought to owning a home computer in 1975, Gates was convinced that this would change within a short span of time and was determined that Microsoft should retain its position as the leader in software technology to ensure that its products would set the standards for the growing high-tech industries. In the summer of 1975, living in a hotel room in Albuquerque, Gates and Allen began assembling a team of young computer programmers. In their workplace, what they shared in common aside from youth was fanatic dedication, partiality to sloppy attire, unorthodox hairstyles, and loud rock music, all of which drew puzzled looks from passing MITS staffers. Late that year, Gates and Allen collaborated on a floppy disk that MITS was introducing. In the spring of 1976, Gates and Allen assembled a select group of programmers referred to as the "Microkids" in new offices in a bank building. Gates, who had finally dropped out of Harvard, began dedicating his energy to projects that anticipated future markets, such as the development of code for FORTRAN, the second most popular computer language. Later that year, Allen joined Microsoft as a full-time employee, sensing the same future opportunities that Gates foresaw. As the year ended successfully, financially and productively, Gates turned to ensuring that Microsoft became the standard software for newly developed microcomputers. As the Altair 8080 was already dated, the Commodore and Tandy corporations were preparing successors, even as Steve Wozniak and Steve Jobs were on the verge of producing the Apple I, which would have a seminal impact on the industry.

With new opportunities for software sales looming, it was crucial that Gates terminate the agreement with MITS before Microsoft could sell its products elsewhere. But as the MITS agreement included a clause that Microsoft would serve MITS exclusively, a court battle was inevitable, and in April 1976 MITS took the issue to court. Critically for Microsoft, the arbitrator sided with their company. Later that year, Microsoft signed contracts with Tandy and Apple to provide them with BASIC. With that problem resolved, Gates moved the company to Seattle in 1979. Though established on the eighth floor of the staid Old National Bank Building, the two dozen Microsoft employees maintained their unorthodox workplace culture, wearing jeans and often barefoot, working flexible though often long hours. Gates's personal eccentricities contributed significantly to the emerging Microsoft corporate image. Rarely attentive to personal appearance, Gates was easily recognizable by his unruly, rumpled hair and oversized spectacles with hopelessly smeared lenses. Obsessively committed to his company's success and intolerant of the personal inadequacies of others, Gates was capable of cruel sarcasm, and his frequent angry outbursts were legendary. In his drive to make Microsoft successful, he did not spare himself—working long hours, forgoing vacations, and rarely indulging in personal enjoyments. It paid off. Within five years of its founding, Microsoft was generating $7 million in annual sales revenue. Stories spread of Microsoft executives indulging themselves in expensive sports cars and other luxuries.

Microsoft grew rapidly in the late 1970s, cutting a deal with Intel in 1979 to provide BASIC for their new 8086 chip, designed specifically for personal computers (PCs). Moving beyond computer languages, Microsoft established a consumer products division to facilitate a move into application programs, such as spreadsheets, word processing, and games. The company soon moved into hardware with the SoftCard, an expansion card that allowed Apple computers to use Microsoft programs. The company joined the big leagues with an agreement with Xerox to provide BASIC for a PC that company was developing. In July, a much-awaited opportunity arose when an IBM representative contacted Gates about a possible software contract. Big Blue, as IBM was known, wanted to bring Microsoft into its program to develop a PC. It was soon agreed that Microsoft would provide BASIC and a disk operating system (DOS) for IBM's PC, and a contract was soon signed, establishing an often-contentious relationship. Gates had previously arranged for Microsoft to serve as a licensing agent for Seattle Computer Products' DOS, sparing Microsoft the trouble of developing one for IBM's Acorn and making MS-DOS an industry standard.

The next several years established Microsoft as a phenomenal leader in the PC industry. The IBM contract enabled a rapid expansion of Microsoft's workforce, including Steve Ballmer, and enhanced the company's reputation. Microsoft's annual revenues doubled every year after 1975, approaching $16 million by 1981. That same year, as the company moved into larger offices and reorganized, Microsoft became a private corporation with Gates as chair and Allen as director. The company also began offering employees stock options at about one dollar a share. Adroit investment ensured that some would become instant millionaires when the company offered its initial public shares several years later; Gates made $1.6 million from the shares he sold.

As the 1980s dawned, Gates pursued an aggressive corporate strategy based on the slogan "A Computer on Every Desktop Running Microsoft Software." Outselling the Apple II computer, the IBM PC boosted Microsoft along. Gates again got ahead of the curve by examining Xerox's Alto computer, which used an advanced language program called Smalltalk, which allowed on-screen menus and point-and-click technology that obviated that need for keyboarding lengthy and complex commands. The graphic user interface (GUI) technologies he saw there, which would be incorporated in Apple's upcoming Macintosh, pointed Gates in the direction he believed Microsoft had to go. Out of this conclusion grew Microsoft Word, Plan, Chart, and File. The next step was the development of Windows, the first version of which was released in November 1985.

Over the next two decades, as Microsoft's profits ballooned, the relationship with Big Blue soured, and Gates made the most critical error of his business career—he failed to comprehend the significance of the internet. The introduction of Netscape's internet browser in December 1994 finally opened his eyes, leading to the subsequent browser war. With six million computers wired into the internet by 2001, it was crucial that Microsoft enter the market with its Internet Explorer, which was craftily bundled with the popular Windows 95 operating system. The 1990s brought a plethora of federal antitrust investigations, but Microsoft successfully navigated them, as the US government vacated its suit in 2001. At age fifty, in 2005 Bill Gates was the richest man in the world. After 2006, Gates devoted much of his time to the charitable Bill and Melinda Gates Foundation, funded with an initial endowment of $28 billion. The Gates Library Foundation was established to make computers and internet access available in public libraries in low-income communities in the United States and Canada.

As a college student, Bill Gates had a vision of the future that was a critical factor in pulling the American economy out of the postindustrial slump of the 1970s. For the majority of Americans, however, the nation's economic future and their individual financial futures grew more uncertain as the 1970s proceeded. For most, underemployment, lower wages, higher interest rates, climbing energy prices, and financial insecurity were the realities of the decade.

❖

There is a song and a film that speak directly to the economic plight of Americans in the 1970s. "Take This Job and Shove It" was Johnny Paycheck's 1977 number one hit and reflects the anger and frustration of a working man who swears, "I ain't workin' here no more," a sentiment born out of the realization that long hours at a tedious job have not advanced his career or improved his financial situation or marriage. Long before 1977, many workers were experiencing similar situations and resentments as the American economy, flagship of the global economy since the end of World War II, began to take on enough water to capsize it. The 1970s witnessed the severe contraction of the industrial sector even as inflation and catastrophic energy prices slammed Americans, who were quickly being drawn into the uncertainties of a postindustrial economy, which sociologist Daniel Bell defined in *The Coming of Post-Industrial Society* (1973). Bell sought to identify "the way in which the economy is being transformed and the occupational system reworked." The five "components" of a postindustrial society he defined as an economic sector changing "from a goods-producing to a service economy"; occupational distribution featuring the preeminence of "the professional and technical class"; the "centrality of theoretical knowledge as the source of innovation"; a future orientation defined by the "control of technology and technological assessment"; and, finally, the "creation of a new 'intellectual technology.'"

John Updike's *Rabbit Is Rich* (1981) offers a look at what happened to the American economy and society in the 1970s. Updike's central character, Harry "Rabbit" Angstrom, had lost his job as a linotypist ten years earlier and had in *Rabbit Redux* (1971) presciently concluded, "Services and software are where the future is." Now, however, Rabbit is the owner of Springer Motors, a Toyota dealership in Brewer, Pennsylvania. The consequences of the economic changes of the 1970s pervade the novel's first pages. Rabbit enthuses over the Japanese imports that he sells, musing that nothing "on the road gets better mileage than his Toyotas, with lower service costs," a crucial selling point as "the fucking world is running out of gas." He remarks to one of his salesmen that Americans "are running scared out there. . . . They know the American ride is ending." Rabbit's new wealth, gained by marketing imported cars, as well as his perspective on the nation's dilemma, is emblematic of one of the signal changes in the America economy in the 1970s. Noting that one of his salesmen is completing paperwork on a

Figure 5.1. **A flood of imported Volkswagens in a port holding area awaiting delivery to American dealers. The energy crisis of the 1970s led many Americans to opt for more fuel-efficient German and Japanese autos, precipating a decline of the Detroit auto industry.** Source: Library of Congress / Leffler, Warren K.

trade-in 1974 Plymouth Barracuda, even though "nobody wants these old guzzlers," Rabbit touches upon a myriad of interconnected changes that attend the emergence of a postindustrial economy. The US automobile industry, once the global leader, had a significantly reduced position in the 1970s, as fuel-efficient imports began to replace the monstrously large, fuel-hungry vehicles that American manufacturers clung to for too long.

Attendant to the decline in US automobile sales, the steel and components industries that supplied the necessary materials for auto production began to go into decline as foreign competitors in Japan undercut them pricewise while maintaining product quality. As these unionized jobs were among the most prized in the nation, ensuring living wages, benefits, and a path into the middle class, their gradual disappearance left millions of skilled American workers either jobless or relegated to service-sector employment that provided lower wages, little job security, few if any health benefits, and greater financial insecurity. The electronics industry suffered a similar fate, as American brands began to give way to Japanese competitors. Rising inflation, made worse by skyrocketing oil prices and a changing corporate culture, which embraced short-term stock profitability, which produced volatile trading and propelled the move from investment in companies, which demonstrated long-term productivity to complex financial instruments, which promised immediate and massive profits for the few all contributed to economic confusion. Such changes give weight to historian Edward D. Berkowitz's assertion that "even more than Watergate and Vietnam, the economy was the factor that gave the seventies its distinctive character."

The economy of a modern, industrial nation is an extraordinarily complex entity. Its functioning is dependent upon a myriad of variables, some of which are in almost constant flux while others are nearly intangible. Keeping such an economy in balance becomes even more of a challenge in the global age in which the impact of foreign competition is impossible to accurately predict. Labor, productivity, technological innovation, markets, foreign competition, transportation, capital, and available natural resources, especially energy, are but a few of the factors that must be considered. Government policies, including taxation, regulation (or lack thereof), monetary policy, infrastructure funding, continuity, and stability of government (and policies) also play a role, as does perhaps the ficklest component: public opinion. Then there are the changes that the passage of time brings. At the end of World War II, the chief potential challengers to American global economic hegemony were recently defeated enemies Japan and Nazi Germany. Years of warfare had left both nations, and most of the European and Asian continents, industrial wastelands. The Soviet Union, devastated by war and still suffering from decades of inane Stalinist economic policies, was of little concern. Yet within a quarter of a century, Japan and Germany would be in positions to challenge the foundations of American industrial production and wealth. Likewise, the consequences of future foreign wars and unexpected revolutions would pose further problems for America's economic dominance. The 1970s brought a perfect storm of these issues, as confused and worried American people faced the uncertainties and consequences of a new economic world order. Like John Updike's Rabbit Angstrom, many would glumly conclude that "the American ride is over."

As Richard Nixon assumed the presidency in January 1969, the American people were on the verge of a decade that would bring the worst economic shocks since the Great Depression. The economy of the 1970s was shaped by three general developments, which were to varying degrees interconnected, making any solution difficult if not impossible: inflation, an energy crisis, and the decline of American industry and manufacturing. These developments took place in the context of a rapidly changing global economy, which meant that they could not be dealt with in isolation, ensuring that even more variables would be introduced into an already challenging equation. As the first president to confront this ever-growing crisis, Richard Nixon, like his successors, had three chief macroeconomic tools to bring to bear: fiscal policy, meaning the tax rate, the level of federal spending, and the money supply. Political philosophy also played a role, as Republicans and Democrats differed as to the utility of govern-ment invention in the economy, with Republicans historically adhering to the laissez-faire approach of allowing the "free market" to resolve prob-lems. Richard Nixon proved the exception to that traditional approach.

The chief economic issue that Nixon faced upon becoming presi-dent was inflation, which stood at 4.4 percent and was slowly growing due variously to government spending during the Johnson administra-tion, the Federal Reserve Board's decision to expand the money supply when the economy began to stall in 1969, and government borrowing to fund the Vietnam War. Nixon contributed to this by raising social security payments by 10 percent and indexing them to inflation. The congressional Democratic contribution to the fight against inflation was to grant Nixon the authority to implement wage and price controls, convinced that no Republican would take the bait.

Between 1900 and 1970, the average inflation rate was 2.5 percent. The positive side of this, according to what economists call the "Phillips Curve," is that rising or high inflation was understood to correlate with higher employment. There were already signs that this hypothetical might prove inaccurate, but during Nixon's first year in office, the nation's economy took second place in importance to the Vietnam War and the growing opposition to it. There was also serious provocation from North Korea when two of its MIG fighters shot down an unarmed US EC-121 intelligence-gathering aircraft on April 15, but Nixon decided against any precipitate action. Much of his year was taken up with trips abroad and meeting foreign leaders; his first meeting with the Cabinet Committee on Economic Policy occurred in mid-April, when talk of recession clearly bored the president—he hoped to establish his presidential reputation on foreign policy successes. For Nixon, economics was important only as it affected politics—and the next congressional elections were in 1970. The July moon landing by *Apollo 11* astronauts temporarily diverted attention from economic woes. In August, Nixon announced the first indication of a new economic direction: the "New Federalism," by which "revenue sharing" would present the states with monies collected as federal taxes, to be dispensed by state leaders. The nation seemed reasonably quiet—as the conservative *US News & World Report* put it somewhat too complacently, "The war is being phased out; violence in the cities has simmered down; campuses may be quieter; space had brought more respect for the nation; business is good, and most of all, people are living amazingly well." A major element in Nixon's first State of the Union address on January 22, 1970, astonished supporters and opponents alike when he emphasized the need to take initiatives to save the environment.

Events soon directed the nation's and the president's attention elsewhere. By the time of the president's address, inflation had risen to 6.1 percent, the highest in a decade. The previous fall, Nixon had made clear to his economic team and Arthur Burns, his Federal Reserve Board chairman, that recession, not inflation, was what felled administrations. H. R. Haldeman had written in his diary, "P[resident] made a point that he never heard of losing an election because of inflation." By early 1970, there were troubling signs of just that as an illegal mail strike in New York became national by March, due in part to declining wage strength. Wild-cat strikes of longshoremen, taxi drivers, and building service-workers, together with nearly a half million Teamsters, resulted in settlements that brought considerable wage increases. In 1972, a historic wave of strikes, perhaps most notably at the GM plant in Lordstown, Ohio, spoke of further labor troubles.

Though counseled by economist Milton Friedman and Treasury Secretary George Shultz to pursue a policy of gradually "cooling off" the economy by tackling inflation, other voices were sounding the alarm about a new phenomenon that would be widely known by mid-decade as "stagflation"—rising inflation in an economy that was not growing. Burns fretted, "The rules of economics are not working the way they used to." Though he had earlier downplayed the danger of inflation, Nixon was cognizant that the global order established at Bretton Woods in 1944, es-pecially the international monetary system that made the gold-backed US dollar the backstop of international exchange, was now working against the United States, and he expressed his desire to take action against the "gangsters" and "vampires sucking the blood out of every transaction." He feared declining American competitiveness as foreign-made cameras, autos, televisions, shoes, textiles, and other products were threatening the market share of American companies.

After conferring with his economic advisers, Nixon gloated to Haldeman, "This'll put the Democrats in a hell of a place." His April 15 televised speech did much more than that. What grew out of that earlier meeting was a repudiation of conservative orthodoxy and the death of the Bretton Woods system negotiated in 1944. Repudiating the traditional conservative principle of non-interference in the free market, Nixon announced a ninety-day freeze on wages and prices, the first of four phases of freezes tempered by controls, plus a 10 percent tax on imports, various spending cuts, tax cuts, and a border tax. Of much greater con-sequence was his decision to take the dollar off the gold standard and make it free floating. Consisting of four phases that would impose either mandatory or voluntary price controls as economic conditions developed, this was a temporary fix, with no plan as to replacing Bretton Woods or fixing stagflation. In December 1971, an international accord was reached on exchange rates, but it collapsed in 1973, leaving currencies floating.

Whatever its deficiencies, Nixon's economic plan won immediate acclaim. Issues such as the cost of consumables such as food made for a happier public. Inflation was contained at 3 percent and unemployment dropped to 5.5 percent as of election day 1972, an important calculation in Nixon's planning. However, as Nixon biographer John A. Farrell concludes, "The freeze just kicked the can down the road." Free marketeer Milton Friedman warned only weeks later, "Sooner or later . . . it will end as all previous attempts to freeze prices and wages have ended . . . in utter failure and the emergence into the open of the suppressed inflation." As Nixon and Kissinger turned again to the ongoing issue of Vietnam, Friedman was proved correct, in that the system of wage and price controls did not take into account unforeseen events such as those that arose in October 1973 when another Arab-Israeli conflict, the Yom Kippur War, broke out when Egypt and Syria attacked Israel, inaugurating the first of two energy crises that would upend any hopes for slowing inflation. In early October, with Israel's position deteriorating and as the Israeli government pondered using tactical nuclear weapons, Nixon ordered US military aid airlifted to the beleaguered ally on October 12. A hint of what was to come occurred on October 16 when most of the Arab states and Iran announced they were raising oil prices by 17 percent. Nixon's October 19 pledge of $2.2 billion in aid to Israel provoked the oil-producing Arab states to announce an embargo on sales to the United States, as well as production cutbacks. Even as the Arab members of OPEC (Oil Producing and Exporting Countries) extended their embargoes to several western European states, Nixon signed an order authorizing price, production, allocation, and marketing controls. The Yom Kippur War came to an end by October 25, but peace in the Middle East was little consolation, for Americans were facing the greatest economic shock since the Great Depression.

The path to this unenviable position grew out of a long-standing American view of the Middle East as a benighted, distant gas station offering an unlimited product at bargain rates. Western oil companies had long exploited corrupt regional regimes to extract Middle Eastern oil at minimal costs. Periodic threats of nationalization were few, and when they did come, as occurred in Mohammad Mosaddeq's Iran in 1953, covert American and British actions ensured the installation of a more compliant ruler, in this case the Iranian Shah Reza Pahlavi, who became "America's policeman on the Persian Gulf." Middle Eastern oil was of no great concern from

1945 to 1955, as the United States met its own energy needs, and when imports increased in the late 1950s, the oil flowed chiefly from Venezuela and Canada. In the twenty years prior to 1967, the dollar price of a barrel of oil had risen by less than 2 percent per year. From 1959 to 1973, quotas were imposed on foreign oil at the behest of domestic producers, which may have contributed to a relative decline in available crude by the early 1970s even as demand was ratcheting up. Nixon ended the foreign quota system in 1973, as the demand for foreign crude had nearly doubled between 1970 and 1973. Not until the Arab oil embargo would Americans be exposed to a market price of oil that was greater than the posted price, with chaotic results, as American cars averaged thirteen miles per gallon.

Amazingly, as historian Meg Jacobs documents, most Americans were not aware that the nation imported any oil and some three-quarters were convinced that shortages were a hoax produced by "Big Oil." Compelled to address the crisis, Americans responded with often contradictory suggestions, some even asserting that they were under no obligation to accept restrictions on their "rights." Nixon's reaction was to urge greater domestic production and weakening environmental and economic regulations. Predictably, Milton Friedman argued against any government action, which was "the problem, not the cure." California's Governor Reagan insisted that the federal government caused the crisis. Rushing to get ahead of the panic, Nixon took to television on November 7 to acknowledge, "We have an energy crisis," but reassured his listeners that the American people were not headed back to "gas rationing, oil shortages, reduced speed limits . . . a way of life we left behind with Glenn Miller and the war of the forties." With the possible exception of Glenn Miller, almost all of these developments would become features of American life in the next several years. The president later announced the appointment of an "energy czar," William Simon, and Congress followed up with legislation mandating allocation of crude oil and refined products. With the nation now importing one-third of its oil, and New Englanders fretting about winter heating oil, Nixon urged that gas stations close on Sunday; the Emergency Highway Energy Conservation Act reduced maximum highway speed limits to fifty-five miles per hour. The age of conspicuous energy consumption was over as per gallon prices at the pump rose from around thirty-eight cents to more than a half dollar between fall 1973 and summer 1974. Many Americans considered fifty-cent-per-gallon gas as tantamount to a looming apocalypse.

None of these proposals spoke to the dilemma faced by truckers, who saw diesel fuel costs of fifty-four cents per gallon, when they could find fuel, and limitations on purchases that barely permitted them to make it to the next fueling station. In early December, hundreds of independent truckers across five states staged highway stoppages to demonstrate their outrage. That same month, OPEC, led by Iran, raised crude prices from $5.12 per barrel to $11.65, the second doubling of prices in two months. As consumer advocate Ralph Nader railed about "the most phony crisis ever inflicted on modern society," a Senate committee dragged seven oil company executives into a January 1974 hearing in which Henry "Scoop" Jackson denounced their "obscene profits." Late that month, truckers went on the rampage they had threatened unless prices were restored to May 1973 levels, shutting down highway commerce with nails and arson. The violence spread during the next month as eight states called out National Guard troops to stem the anarchy. As consumables disappeared from grocery stores, motorists were affected by the same panic as the truckers, with fights breaking out

Figure 5.2. Frustrated and angry motorists vie for position at gas pumps during the gasoline shortages of the 1970s. Strained tempers led to harsh words, fights, and threats to station operators, even as angry truckers blocked roads and set vehicles afire. Source: Library of Congress / Leffler, Warren K.

in lengthy gas station lines. A Miami Amoco station owner summed up the atmosphere: "If you can't sell them gas, they'll threaten to beat you up, wreck your station, run you over with a car."

Some states implemented "odd-even" rationing, a system in which license plate numbers and calendar days determined who might get gas. The situation was exacerbated by a prolonged stock market crash from January 1973 to December 1974, during which the Dow Jones Industrial Average lost 45 percent of its value.

No consensus solution emerged. Nixon denounced the striking truckers as "desperados" and initiated a voluntary set of price controls, under which inflation rose rapidly. A chorus of voices suggested military action to gain access to the foreign crude. Daylight Saving Time was extended to ten months. NASCAR reduced the Daytona 500 to 450 miles and canceled Sebring. The Arab embargo was lifted in March, but a psychic scar was left on a nation now cognizant that it no longer determined its economic destiny. In the midst of this chaos, Nixon was compelled to resign the presidency in August 1974. Milton Friedman commented that Nixon's energy policy decisions "will prove to have been more harmful to the nation than the misdeeds he has been responsible for in Watergate."

President Gerald Ford, former Michigan congressman, demonstrated his worthiness as a master of understatement in his first address to Congress, in which he observed, "The state of our economy is not so good." One month before, consumer prices were at their highest level since the Korean War, and unemployment stood at 5.4 percent, destined to rise to 7.2 percent by winter. The Gross National Product dropped 7.5 percent by December. In September, Ford, speaking before a World Energy Conference in Detroit, conceded, "It is difficult to discuss the energy problem without lapsing unfortunately into doomsday language." Modestly conceding that he was "a Ford, not a Lincoln," Ford destroyed his initial popular approval by pardoning Nixon. In early October, Ford introduced the "Whip Inflation Now" (WIN) campaign, which was essentially a voluntary program in contrast to the mandatory wage and price freezes that Democrats favored. Symbolized by WIN lapel buttons, the program quickly became the butt of jokes, as Ford proposed that Americans plant WIN gardens, recycle, reduce waste, clean their dinner plates, and even send him lists of ten suggestions as to how inflation might be whipped. By the end of 1974, the inflation rate stood at 13.7 percent.

Ford proposed lowering taxes to stem the recession but was unable to prevent an economic slowdown, heralded by unprecedented work stoppages in both the industrial and public service sectors as wages lagged and unemployment rose. "The disease of the times," a *New York Times* editorial noted, "is no longer simply inflation nor economic stagnation. It is stagflation." Stagflation proved to be a beast that bedeviled Ford, though he was the beneficiary of OPEC price hikes slowing during his tenure, and he was active in suggesting a variety of directions generally involving deregulation of the energy industry, the lessening of auto pollution requirements, and greater use of coal and nuclear energy as well as synthetic fuels. In a televised address in January 1975, Ford laid out the details of what he called the Energy Independence Act. An overwhelmingly Democratic Congress would have to allow controls on crude to expire in August as scheduled; the price of "old oil," about 60 percent of the market, could then rise to the market level of $13 per barrel, which would encourage new exploration and production. Offshore controls on related energy projects would be ended and clean air standards relaxed. The goal was to cut oil imports by 1 million barrels per day by year's end. To achieve energy independence, consumers would be required to bite the bullet. On his own authority, Ford imposed taxes on imported oil.

After months of political acrimony, Congress coughed up the Energy Policy and Conservation Act of 1975, thoroughly revised by myriad special interest lobbyists, authorizing a strategic petroleum reserve, establishing Corporate Average Fuel Economy (CAFE) standards for automobiles, granting the Department of Energy the authority to establish energy conservation standards for appliances, and allowing for coal conversion and the gradual decontrol of crude oil prices over time, which meant rising costs for consumers. The act granted the president the authority to allocate and ration oil if faced with another embargo. An exasperated Ford signed the bill in late December, claiming, "This legislation represents the most constructive bill we are likely to work out at this time." The *Wall Street Journal* derided the act as "the clearest blunder of his administration."

The year 1976 was a presidential election year, and Ford seemed to have little going for him, given the Nixon pardon, the fallout from Watergate, the economic problems, and the simple fact that he was an accidental president with no established political base. His electoral fortunes were not aided by his refusal to agree to a federal bailout of financially crippled

New York City; as the *New York Daily News* famously reported: "Ford to City: Drop Dead." Still, Ford managed to fare reasonably well against Democratic challenger Jimmy Carter, losing the popular vote by only 50.1 percent to 48 percent. In the end, the most conservative president since Herbert Hoover had held his own.

Rarely has an American president entered office with such high expectations and left office so thoroughly repudiated. The former Georgia governor's inabilities to serve effectively as chief executive will be dealt with elsewhere, but his difficulties in dealing with the ongoing energy crisis, inflation, trade imbalance, and unemployment require mention of his fundamental inability to work with a Congress dominated by his own party. Carter has been described as a fiscal conservative, a pragmatist, and a moralist, all of which affected his economic policies. The American people were given fair warning as to Carter's perspective when, in his first presidential address, he told his audience, "We have learned that 'more' is not necessarily 'better,' that even our great nation has its recognized limits, and that we can neither answer all questions nor solve all problems." It was hardly an uplifting message and prefigured Carter's chastising, sermonizing style.

Carter was not the first president to recognize that domestic industry and manufacturing were declining at an alarming rate. If steel may be taken as a model, as early as 1975, US alloy steel was running at less than half of standard capacity after cutting its workforce by 25 percent. Most European steel was government owned and shielded from normal profit requirements; even privately owned steel in Germany and Japan received preferred credit arrangements. When its domestic market contracted, Japan's Ministry of International Trade and Investment compelled domestic price increases and forced exports, diverting more steel to US markets in 1976. From 1964 to 1971, Japanese exports to the United States quadrupled in value. Ironically, both Germany and Japan were embracing something akin to supply-side economics, even as their governments researched new sectors for development. Japanese auto builders proved quite willing to accept lower profits in units sold abroad if this increased market share, and this at a time when US automakers were struggling to develop fuel-efficient autos that might successfully compete with the armada of fuel-saving compacts arriving from Japan. As Japanese exports to the European Economic Community were restricted, the United States became the market of choice, not only for autos, but also for electronics and appliances. Throughout the late 1970s, Carter administration trade negotiators implored Japan to open its market to US manufactured goods, but with little success, other than vague promises to reduce their trade surplus and import more citrus and beef, which would not offset Japanese steel and auto exports. Fuming over the impotence of America's negotiators, a spokesman for a California electronics manufacturer fretted that trends were making the United States "a banana republic." "If we think we are trying to balance our trade imbalance with the Japanese by selling them beef and grapefruit, we'll end up killing our industrial base." That base was, of course, already shrinking rapidly, as industrial production in developing countries such as Brazil, South Korea, Taiwan, and Mexico, which had increased during the 1975 recession, was impacting US markets. There was little domestic investment incentive for US corporations and banks, which began investing abroad. US banks nearly tripled foreign investments during the Carter years, funds that might have been used to modernize and reorient domestic industry. The trade deficit skyrocketed from $5.9 billion in 1976 to $34 billion in 1978. Conservative critics blamed the nation's shrinking industrial base on products that were not competitively priced due to wage inflation, which they blamed on excessive union demands. Union membership was growing to a peak in 1978, but as a proportion of the total labor force, it reached only 22.5 percent that year. The decline in industrial and manufacturing jobs necessarily meant a decline in union wages and benefits, leaving the unemployed to seek other less remunerative jobs and increasing the national slide toward greater inequality in both income and wealth.

These phenomena, as well as a falling dollar, were already underway as Carter assumed the presidency in January 1977. German imports were proving less of a threat than those from Japan, which were beginning to fall that year. Public concern with energy prices and availability had diminished greatly by 1977, and Americans quickly returned to their profligate ways, as the nation imported more than half the oil it used. Detroit had introduced a variety of compacts, many of which did well, but full-size models boasting huge V8 engines remained available. Many of the "muscle cars" born in the 1960s were still available, though pollution controls had emasculated even the mighty Pontiac Trans Am to a measly two hundred horsepower. Americans began to complain of the bite that increased taxes took from the family budget, and in June 1978, Californians voted in favor of Howard

Jarvis's Proposition 13, which slashed property taxes by 57 percent and rolled back tax rates to 1 percent of 1975 assessments. It was a warning of a building tsunami of opposition to taxation.

Carter attempted to awaken the nation to the energy issue with an April 18 address in which he called it the "moral equivalent of war." To emphasize his personal commitment, Carter ordered White House thermostats set to sixty-five degrees, wore sweaters, and had solar panels installed on the roof. The winters of 1976–1977 and 1977–1978 were among the coldest recorded, further driving up energy use. Carter presented Congress with a conservation program that included greater fossil fuel production, greater use of coal, a tax on "gas-guzzlers," as well as increasing the price of domestically produced oil products. Congress, captive to state interests and lobbyists, soon made hash of Carter's proposals, and polls showed that half the public still refused to believe that there was an energy crisis. The bill that emerged from Congress on October 15 bore no resemblance to the administration's initial proposals, containing no provisions that would encourage domestic production or restrain greedy oil companies, but Carter, desperate for anything that he could call a legislative victory, signed it into law in October 1978. Carter did manage to win congressional approval for the creation of a Department of Energy, but any joy was tempered by the loss of three Democratic seats in the Senate and fifteen in the House in the November elections.

The dangers of this insouciant approach to a national security issue became evident when a revolution toppled the Iranian shah in late 1978, and after months of chaos, a virulently anti-American regime led by Islamic cleric Ruhollah Khomeini seized power and stopped oil production. A second energy crisis soon enveloped the nation as crude prices rose 150 percent in the year after December 1978. By spring, gasoline shortages, long lines, and "No Gas" signs began to reappear. Congress refused Carter the authority to ration gasoline and indicated its disapproval when he instituted a gradual phaseout of price controls on domestic crude, which drove prices higher. Congress still refused to impose even a modest windfall profit tax on the prospering oil industry. The Three Mile Island incident that March, which revealed the catastrophic dangers of a potential nuclear meltdown, severely curbed enthusiasm for a nuclear energy alternative. Trucker blockades of interstates recurred, and by June, Carter's approval rate was 28 percent. These events foreshadowed Carter's "malaise" speech, in which after a ten-day retreat, Carter addressed the nation on July 15. Though he never uttered the word "malaise," listeners were left with that feeling, as Carter accurately recounted the trials and tribulations that the nation had been through in recent years, chastised Americans for being too materialistic and lacking in moral fiber, and ultimately confided that he could offer no solution to this "crisis of confidence." Having come across as a presidential Eeyore, Carter did succeed in reducing the number of Americans who still believed the energy crisis was a hoax from 74 to 65 percent but failed to understand that the electorate resented being lectured as if they were misbehaving children.

Through the next year, matters only worsened. Inflation, which was nearing 18 percent, was eating into family budgets for food, housing, energy, and medical costs, which comprised more than 60 percent of the average worker's budget, and Carter's efforts to control energy prices did not dent the bulk of these. December 1979 handed the Carter administration a double whammy with the seizure of the US embassy and its staff in Tehran by radical Islamic extremists, who were encouraged by the regime of Ayatollah Khomeini, and a Soviet invasion of Afghanistan aimed at rescuing a hated Marxist government there. Oil prices jumped to $19 a barrel, while interest rates drove inflation to 14 percent by February 1980. As the nation limped toward the November elections, it seemed unthinkable that Carter would seek reelection, but having staved off a challenge from Senator Ted Kennedy, the Georgian clung to the Democratic standard. The problems that Carter faced may well have been insoluble, at least in the short term. As sociologist Daniel Bell wrote, "I do not think one can yoke a theme that is primarily moral and cultural to a 'cause' or 'crusade' that is so complex as energy."

While energy costs were at the root of the ruinous inflation of the 1970s, even as foreign competition ate away at America's industrial base during this same decade, financiers and bankers began to turn their attention to gradually eroding regulations that they found onerous, and banks began to turn to financing debt, which was more lucrative than investment in infrastructure, laying the foundation for one of the most fundamental structural changes in the economy since the nineteenth century. As economist Jeff Madrick succinctly explains the transformation, "The expansion of debt, facilitated by the commercial banks and then the entire Wall Street community, became the fulcrum on which the economy was levered for the next forty years." Nothing, Madrick writes, "turned out to be as important to economic growth as . . . the expanding capacity to lend and borrow." Not even the new computer technologies rivaled this phenomenon. More and more Americans were funneled into retail and service employment as the industrial and manufacturing base shrank, while inflation and unemployment grew.

These were not issues that could be resolved by a "new spirit of self-lessness" or a "rebirth of the American spirit" that Carter had asked of the American people in his "malaise" speech any more than his grim vision of a future of sacrifice and lessened material circumstances inspire. By 1980, the appeal of Republican presidential candidate Ronald Reagan was evident. With glib optimism, Reagan spoke of unlimited abundance and an American spirit that only awaited to be acknowledged to reignite American supremacy in all areas of endeavor. The future, Reagan insisted, belonged to America. Given the choice between Carter's vision of lessened expectations and Reagan's sunny proclamations of a future that offered untold possibilities, the electorate opted for the latter.

❖

Lee Iacocca joined Ford Motor Company in 1946, moving quickly up the ranks in a family-dominated corporation whose dour, contentious chief, Henry Ford II, was notoriously difficult to get along with. By 1960 Iacocca's meteoric career had made him vice president and general manager of the Ford division. After a slump in automobile sales in the 1950s, the prosperous 1960s compelled auto manufacturers to develop and market vehicles that were competitive in multiple areas, and Lee Iacocca was the moving force behind one of the most successful models in American automotive history. In 1965, Iacocca spoke to the origins of this vehicle. "As early as 1961," he told his audience, "it was becoming apparent that the character of our market was experiencing a major upheaval. The first job was to identify what kind of product the new market was restlessly groping for. . . . From exhaustive market research, the picture of a new car—unlike anything then available—began to take shape." Iacocca was speaking of the first "pony car," the Ford Mustang, which was introduced in April 1964. It could not have appeared at a more propitious time. The nation was moving beyond mourning the recent death of a president, the economy was stable and growing, the new president had a promising vision for the nation, the Beatles had just arrived, and the swamps of Vietnam were not yet in the forefront of public concerns.

The reactions of focus groups were promising, especially when they learned of the price—$2,368 FOB (free on board) from Detroit. The car's name was fixed upon only after Iacocca had an advertising executive develop a list of six thousand possible monikers, including Torino, Cougar, Bronco, Cheetah, and Colt, some of which were appended to later vehicles. As a Ford advertising executive remarked, the name "Mustang" won because "it had the excitement of the wide-open spaces and was American as all hell." The Mustang badge was styled after a famous Frederic Remington sculpture. Iacocca's genius was to ensure that the car was offered with more than eighty options, so that it could be anything from a family fun car to a performance vehicle; a convertible option could be had for a mere $156. Making the car less expensive for Ford to produce, the Mustang incorporated many of the interior, suspension, chassis, and drivetrain components from the already popular Falcon and Fairlane. After the first Mustang went into production on March 16, more than four million people visited Ford showrooms to see the car. The Mustang was featured in both *Newsweek* and *Time*, the latter noting that "Iacocca has produced more than just another new car. With its long hood and short rear deck, its Ferrari flair and openmouthed air scoop, the Mustang resembles the European racing cars that American sports-car buffs find so appealing. . . . The Mustang seems destined to be a sort of Model A of sports cars." By the end of 1964, a quarter of a million Mustangs had been sold.

Lee Iacocca played a role in the development of several other models in the 1960s—the Lincoln Continental Mark III, the Mercury Cougar, the Mercury Marquis, and, later, the Ford Escort, which was marketed in Europe in 1968. The compact, fuel-efficient Escort was a harbinger of the future for the American automobile industry, which had focused on behemoth-sized vehicles since the 1950s and the high-powered "muscle cars" of the mid-1960s. Neither would fare well in the 1970s, as inflation and higher energy prices, as well as increasing numbers of compact, fuel-efficient imports from Germany and Japan, began to eat into US auto sales. Fortunately for Ford, and later for Plymouth, Lee Iacocca would be there to meet the challenge.

Lee Iacocca was born to Italian immigrants Nicola and Antonietta on October 15, 1924, in Allentown, Pennsylvania. The family prospered by operating Yocco's Hot Dogs. Lee graduated from high school in 1942 and obtained an engineering degree from Lehigh University before accepting a fellowship at Princeton, where he studied an odd combination of plastics and politics. Joining Ford as an engineer in 1946, he requested to be transferred to sales and marketing, where his abilities became obvious. He gained favor with the company in 1956 when he conceived the "56 for '56" campaign while working as an assistant sales manager in Philadelphia. The plan was to spur sales by offering loans on 1956 Fords with only $56 a month in payments and 20 percent down. Ford higher-ups were impressed enough with the results that they made the campaign national in scope. That same year, he married Mary McCleary, the first of three marriages (Mary died in 1983). The couple had two children. Iacocca afterward was advanced to the Dearborn headquarters, quickly moving up the managerial ranks until being named president in 1970.

Iacocca was prescient in foreseeing the need for a compact and fuel-efficient vehicle long before the American public was ready to embrace such a vehicle. As historian Douglas Brinkley notes, "To Ford, GM, and Chrysler, the popularity of foreign compacts in the 1950s looked like a fad." This attitude continued well into the 1960s, and Henry Ford II was notoriously resistant to any new model that appeared to be outside the current paradigm. Perhaps still smarting over the egregious failure of the "E" car, the infamous Edsel that was produced for only two years, Ford's son was among those at Ford who were wary of building compacts—if nothing else, the profit margin on those cars was shockingly low. Yet as the 1960s dawned, the Big Three were all designing smaller cars: Chrysler's Valiant was the largest, Chevrolet's Corvair with its rear engine was the most innovative, but it was Ford's Falcon, in production by fall 1959, that was deemed by *Car and Driver* to be the "best looking Ford since the thirties." The chief problem with most early compacts, given their necessarily small engines, was acceleration. The Falcon's zero-to-sixty-miles-per-hour acceleration rate was a dismal twenty-five seconds. Still, *Road and Track* hailed the Falcon, which was eventually available in two- and four-door configurations, a station wagon, and a convertible, as "good, solid, honest transportation."

In 1968, imported cars were showing evidence of threatening US automakers and sales were reaching beyond the one million mark. West Germany's Volkswagen seemed the most troubling, given its growing acceptance by a broad demographic. In 1968, Iacocca first proposed a lightweight, fuel-efficient, low-priced compact based on the European version of the popular Ford Fiesta. John Naughton, the general manager of the Ford division, backed Iacocca, noting that "in 1962, Ford had 36 percent of the small car market. Last year we had only 8 percent." Finally compelled to act, Henry Ford II authorized Iacocca to develop a compact car, to be called the Delta and to be in showrooms by 1969. The vehicle was born as the Maverick in April 1969, using parts from the Mustang, Fairlane, and Falcon. At the behest of Iacocca, in 1971 Ford introduced the Pinto, one day after Chevrolet brought out the Vega. Billed as "the little carefree car," the Pinto, which would later be much maligned and the subject of 117 lawsuits and numerous investigations due to a tendency to explode in some rear-end collisions, initially drew some rave reviews, as *Super Stock Magazine* described the fit and finish as "superior" and *Car and Driver* described the 2.0-liter-equipped Pinto as nimble and powerful. Others were not as laudatory, as *Road and Track* found the suspension lacking and the brakes a "serious deficiency." Nevertheless, more than 350,000 Pintos were sold in 1971 and more than 544,000 left dealer lots in 1978. In 1975, an upgraded version was offered by Mercury as the Bobcat, selling more than 224,000 by 1980, when it was replaced by the Lynx.

By 1978, however, the Pinto's sometimes fatal engineering deficiencies had caught up with it. There were earlier hints of possible future issues. In October 1970, 26,000 Pintos were recalled due to a potential issue with the accelerator sticking. In March 1971, all Pintos manufactured before March 19 of that year were recalled to remedy the possible ignition of fuel vapors in the air cleaner. In 1978, a National Highway Traffic Safety Administration (NHTSA) investigation concluded that 1971 to 1976 Pintos and 1975 to 1976 Bobcats suffered from "fuel tank design and structural characteristics" that made the vehicles vulnerable to "fuel tank damage, fuel leakages, and fire occurrences that have resulted in fatalities and non-fatal burn injuries." The Pinto/Bobcat design defects were responsible for the deaths of between twenty-seven and 180 people, a damning indictment and a public relations disaster. On June 9, 1978, only days before the NHTSA ordered Ford to issue a recall order, the company recalled 1.5 million Pintos and Bobcats, the largest automotive recall at the time. By the time the company technicians had remedied the defects, Ford had lost in *Grimshaw v. Ford Motor Company*, a case in which a Pinto fire had led to a death; the jury awarded nearly $132 million to the plaintiff, which was reduced to $3.5 million by the judge. In August, a grand jury indicted the company in *Indiana v. Ford*, but Ford was found not guilty in 1980.

Before the Pinto/Bobcat debacle, Iacocca seemed to be Ford's savior, having overseen the development of the Falcon, the Mustang, the Maverick, and the Pinto. Named president in 1970, he seemed to be on a glide slope to success and wealth, but as early as 1968, an issue that would bedevil Ford as well as other US automakers was brought up at a stockholders' meeting. Anna Muccioli noted that she had "just one complaint." "When the Thunderbird came out, it was a beautiful sports car," she observed. "Then you blew it up to the point where it lost its identity. The same thing has happened to the Mustang. Why can't you leave a sports car small?" The issue she raised was one of three that would unsettle the industry in the 1970s. First was consumer desire, which was maddeningly ambiguous. Americans demanded more fuel-efficient cars but still bought gas-guzzlers. The other problems were as yet to fully surface: competition from abroad, especially from Japan, and the fallout from the energy crisis, which would bring greater government regulation, dovetailing with demands from environmentalists for cars that polluted less. All three issues seemed to coincide. The Clean Air Act of 1970 compelled the need for engineering costly emissions controls. The best the industry could come away with was the CAFE standard, which allowed for the building of gas-guzzlers as long as their energy use was offset by the selling of fuel-efficient, small cars. The automakers would have to eat the cost of emission controls (or pass them on to consumers) and watch horsepower fall. The Toyota Corona arrived in California in 1966, riding the leading edge of what a *Forbes* writer called "an economic Pearl Harbor." By 1975, 18 percent of all new car sales in the United States were foreign, with a third coming from Europe, while two-thirds were Toyotas, Datsuns, Hondas, Mazdas, and Subarus. Energy crises in 1973 and 1979 made the issue more acute, as Japanese makers captured 20 percent of the market. General Motors tried to straddle consumer desire for "big-little" cars with "X-cars" such as the Pontiac Phoenix and the Chevrolet Citation.

Lee Iacocca maintained that Ford's stumbles in these years were made by Henry II, who nixed front-wheel drive models and a "van-wagon" that was developed in 1977. The minivan of course became a bestseller for many manufacturers in coming years. In late 1975, Iacocca met with Soichiro Honda, presented him with a new Mustang, and asserted that he wanted to build the subcompact Fiesta with a Honda engine and transmission. Soichiro promised that he could produce 300,000 vehicles with low-cost Japanese parts. Henry II rejected the idea, declaring, "No Jap engine is going under the hood of a car with my name on it." He later sourly claimed that "when it finally got down to 1974–75, he [Iacocca] got lost all of a sudden. He got himself into a blue funk over products. I never developed product lines." As publicity about defects in Ford products made headlines in the mid-1970s, sales of some models began to sag. Henry II's disdain for Iacocca manifested itself in a $1.5 million investigation into the company president's life. Though nothing amiss was ever discovered, the writing was on the wall; on July 13, 1978, Iacocca was called before the chairman and fired. Commenting several days later, Iacocca remarked, "Thank God all the bullshit is over."

In August, at the behest of former Florida governor Claude Kirk, Iacocca agreed to a lunch with two member of Chrysler's board. It was not a propitious time to take over the running of any US automaker. In his 1986 *The Reckoning*, historian David Halberstam described the Chrysler corporation as "the embodiment of what had gone wrong with American heavy industry in the last twenty years. . . . It was rotting." Iacocca biographer Peter Wyden concurred. "The Chrysler malaise was so fundamental," he writes in *The Unknown Iacocca: An Unauthorized Biography*, "so downright primitive that its scope is difficult to exaggerate." Just as Iacocca was giving thought to becoming the new Chrysler president, the company sold its European division to Peugeot to raise cash, and recalls of the Dodge Aspen and the Plymouth Volare were driving customers to other makes. Even the compact Dodge Omni and Plymouth Horizon were filling up factory lots. Chrysler's share of the market was a dismal 8 percent. Upon assuming his new post, Iacocca undertook a thorough housecleaning of executives he deemed unproductive and convinced United Auto Workers (UAW) leadership and the rank and file to consider concessions. "We've got lots of jobs at $17 per hour," he declared. "We've got absolutely none at $20 per hour." This would eventually amount to wage reductions of $559,000 annually. Iacocca was also convinced that the company was marketing too many models and trimlines and suggested cutbacks.

Perhaps the most important lifesaver that Iacocca obtained for Chrysler was a $1.5 billion federal loan, which required grueling hearings with skeptical congressmen, assigning other staff to warn state and local officials how a Chrysler collapse would damage their economies, and finally, convincing the House, Senate, and eventually President Jimmy Carter to sign off on the deal in December 1979. The "bailout," as conservative critics denigrated it, came with promises of cost reductions, killing some projects, and major wage concessions by UAW workers. Iacocca had already offered to accept a salary of $1 a year. Whereas Henry Ford II had always ridiculed and resisted the use of foreign parts in his cars, Iacocca's willingness to incorporate foreign parts and engines into Chrysler products significantly cut costs. The front-wheel drive Omni, which was a derivative of Chrysler's European Horizon, was one of the first "World Cars," looking nearly identical to its European counterpart. The minivan that Henry II had rejected was soon put in the hands of Chrysler designers, and in 1983, the Dodge Caravan and Plymouth Voyager did much to get Chrysler back on the road, as did the K-car line featuring the Dodge Aries and Plymouth Reliant.

Iacocca's most far-sighted act may have been the 1987 acquisition of the American Motors Corporation, which brought the Jeep brand into the Chrysler family, and in 1992 the Grand Cherokee was introduced, becoming Chrysler's bestseller in the twenty-first century. Iacocca retired in 1992, though he returned as a television spokesman in 2005. As Chrysler faced yet another financial collapse in the early 2000s, Iacocca told *Newsweek*, "It pains me to see my old company, which has meant so much to America, on the ropes." He urged the Obama administration to act to save Chrysler once more. The ups and downs of that company's fortunes mirrored the rapidly globalizing economy of those years.

Iacocca's noncoporate life involved numerous philanthropic causes as of the early 1980s. Following the death of his first wife, Mary, to type 1 diabetes, he actively supported diabetes research. He also engaged in politics, alternately supporting Democratic and Republican presidential candidates, and authored several books, the last being *Where Have All the Leaders Gone?* in 2007. Though his second marriage ended in divorce, he married for a third time in 1991 to Darrien Earle. His last years were spent in Bel Air, California, where he died of complications from Parkinson's disease in 2019 at the age of ninety-four.

THE "ME DECADE" AND 1970s ACTIVISM

Political commentator David Frum, who described the ethos of the 1970s as "individualism run amok," asserted that "no crank of the 1970s expressed a more extreme version of that individualism than Werner Erhard." The founder of est, or Erhard Seminars Training, Werner Hans Erhard remains one of the most famous proponents of self-improvement, a burgeoning field in the 1970s. Few Americans know that the man who offered the first est seminar in 1971 began his adult career as a car salesman, or that he was born John Paul Rosenberg, taking his new name in 1960 after reading *Esquire* magazine articles about West German economics minister Ludwig Erhard and physicist Werner Heisenberg.

John Paul Rosenberg was born in Philadelphia on September 5, 1935, to Joseph and Dorothy Rosenberg. Joseph, who operated a small restaurant, forsook Judaism for the Baptist Church, later joining Dorothy in the Episcopal Church, as did their son. John graduated from high school in 1953, working with a succession of automobile dealerships. From Ford, where he was mentored by Lee Iacocca, he moved on to Lincoln Mercury and, last, Chevrolet, after which he briefly managed an industrial equipment firm. He married his high school sweetheart, Patricia Fry, in 1953, and the couple had four children. The great shift in his life came in 1960 when he abandoned his family and Philadelphia for Indianapolis and a new life with June Bryde, whom he married after his wife filed for divorce. It was at this point that he changed his name to Werner Erhard.

Under his new name, Erhard found employment as a car salesman in St. Louis. Always in search of new opportunities, he began marketing correspondence courses in the Midwest before moving to Spokane, Washington, where he found work as a training manager for *Encyclopedia Britannica*'s "Great Books" program. His peripatetic existence continued as he took work with the *Parents* magazine Cultural Institute, moving between numerous cities before ending up on the West Coast, where the first seeds of est were planted in the mid-1960s.

The intellectual well from which Erhard drew his "therapy" included Napoleon Hill's *Think and Grow Rich* (1937) and Maxwell Maltz's *Psycho-Cybernetics* (1960), together with the ideas of Carl Rogers and Abraham Maslow, leading figures in the Human Potential Movement. As Erhard's interests migrated to personal fulfillment, he was intrigued by what he heard at seminars by Alan Watts, who emphasized the distinction between mind and self. This led Erhard to journey to Japan to study Zen concepts. Erhard later remarked, "Of all the disciplines that I studied, practiced, learned, Zen was the essential one." Not one to dismiss the works of Dale Carnegie as middle-brow boosterism, Erhard took a Dale Carnegie speaking course in 1967 and was sufficiently impressed to ponder developing a similar course. The later 1960s found Erhard continuing his intellectual journey, exploring Transactional Analysis, Encounter, Enlightenment Intensive, Subud (an Indonesian spiritual movement), and even Scientology. By 1970, Erhard was drawn to Mind Dynamics, a Texas-based seminar company that trained businessmen in personal development techniques. In the meantime, Erhard began offering his own version of Mind Dynamics courses in San Francisco and Los Angeles.

Thus in 1971 was born est, or Erhard Seminars Training. To the uninformed, est would always be perceived as one of a variety of bizarre therapies and cults born in the 1970s, but its objective was far more practical. The personal and professional development workshops, originally termed "est Training," had the objective, according to James Kettle's *The est Experience* (1976), of transforming the manner in which one sees and understands life so that those situations that the individual had been struggling to change or live with simply clear up in the process of living. As Erhard himself stressed, the point was to allow participants to be "free to be" as they increased their effectiveness and the quality of their lives. Erhard led all the early seminars but eventually trained ten others to do so. Werner Erhard &

Associates opened est centers in Los Angeles, Aspen, Honolulu, and New York—among a number of cities—and est drew enthusiastic support from individuals as varied as philosopher Walter Kaufmann and former Yippie Jerry Rubin, along with Yoko Ono and John Denver. Est workshops were offered until 1984, when they were replaced by the Forum, which offered seminars on a variety of topics. As of that time, an estimated 700,000 people had completed training. In 1977, Erhard also established The Hunger Project, a nonprofit nongovernmental organization (NGO) accredited by the United Nations. In 1991, Erhard (who had divorced June Bryde, with whom he fathered three children, in 1983) retired and sold his intellectual property to his employees, who now formed Landmark Education, subsequently renamed Landmark Worldwide.

By 1973, the est Foundation became the Werner Erhard Foundation, which offered financial and organizational support to those engaged in educational or charitable efforts, as well as hosting an annual conference in theoretical physics. Erhard's endeavors drew varied reactions. Historian and philosopher Jonathan D. Moreno grandly described est as "the most important cultural event after the human potential movement itself seemed exhausted." On the other hand, his critics were legion. Psychiatrist Marc Galanter denounced Erhard as having no credentials other than those of "a background in retail sales." Philosophy professor Robert Carroll described est as "a hodge-podge of philosophical bits and pieces culled from the carcasses of existential philosophy, motivational psychology." Social critic John McClearly dismissed Erhard as a "former used car salesman" and est as "just another money-making scheme." New York University professor Paul Vitz went further, claiming that est's "style of operation has been labeled as fascist." James R. Lewis and J. Gordon Melton, in their 1992 book *Perspectives on the New Age*, claimed that est employed "authoritarian trainers who enforce numerous rules," compelled participants to "share" in front of groups, and rejected reason in favor of "feeling and action."

Erhard himself came in for considerable scrutiny, being charged by the IRS in the 1990s with tax fraud, though he won every suit filed against him. There was further controversy when his adult daughter leveled charges of sexual abuse against him, though she subsequently withdrew them. Having followed an unusual path to fame and success, Erhard left a significant legacy, noted in a 2012 *Financial Times* article that acknowledged that his influence "extends far beyond the couple of million people who have done his courses; there is hardly a self-help or management training program that does not borrow some of his principles."

⁘◈⁘

In a controversial article published in *New York* magazine on August 23, 1976, author Tom Wolfe paused at mid-decade to deem the 1970s the "Me Decade." "The new alchemical dream is," he wrote, "changing one's personality—remaking, remodeling, elevating, and polishing one's very *self* . . . and observing, studying and doting on it. (Me!)" Sociologist Christopher Lasch offered a similar observation in the September 30, 1976, issue of the *New York Review of Books*, writing that Americans "have convinced themselves that what matters is psychic self-improvement: getting in touch with their feelings, eating health food, taking lessons in ballet or belly dancing, immersing themselves in the wisdom of the East, jogging, learning how to 'relate,' overcoming the 'fear of pleasure.'" Three years later, as the decade limped to a close, Lasch elaborated on this theme in *The Culture of Narcissism: American Life in an Age of Diminishing Expectations*. "After the political turmoil of the sixties," Lasch wrote, "Americans have retreated to purely personal preoccupations. . . . To live for the moment is the prevailing passion—to live for yourself, not for your predecessors or posterity."

A central historical question confronting those who have examined the America of the 1970s is whether the decade can be dismissed as a ten-year period in which Americans abandoned social commitment and activism in favor of personal pursuits and dubious self-realization programs. Without question, with the end of the war in Vietnam, the implosion of the New Left, the end of mass civil rights demonstrations, and quieter times on campuses and in urban ghettos, a portion of the activist community saw their causes evaporate and the troops disband, leaving them to choose between the alternative of a focus on the self or continuing to pursue collective social action within a transformed paradigm. And equally undeniably, many Americans opted for a focus on the self, be it through new paths to self-discovery, be they fitness regimens, health-food diets, or myriad "therapeutic" programs that promised self-fulfillment.

Examined closely, it becomes evident that the 1970s was a transitional decade, in which many Americans did opt out of collective social and political action, seeing little but ashes as the legacy of the 1960s. Yet it would be a mistake to underestimate the vitality of social, political, and environmental causes in the 1970s. To take but one example, feminist author Ruth Rosen described the decade as "arguably the most intellectually vital and exciting" for women, bringing into being "an amazing array of revelations and changes in social, political, and public thought and policy." The era of mass civil rights marches may have passed, but African Americans engaged in new political arenas, ran for public office, and fought for causes that went far beyond legislated civil rights. Other minority groups, such as Hispanic, Native American, and gay Americans, organized to struggle for justice and equality. The environmental movement gained considerable impetus in the 1970s, as new groups pursuing new tactics and strategies emerged and memberships swelled, even as public opinion was further awakened. It was the simultaneous emergence of the self-obsessed individual and the continued growth of the collective forces of socially committed Americans that defined a decade in which the nation was in transition, still searching for the social consensus that died in the 1960s.

Christopher Lasch recounts a 1976 statement by former Yippie Jerry Rubin which summarized his frenetic search for a new direction in post-1960s America: "In the five years from 1971 to 1975," wrote Rubin, "I directly experienced est, gestalt, bioenergetics, rolfing, massage, jogging, health foods, tai chi, Esalen, hypnotism, modern dance, meditation, Silva mind control, Arica, acupuncture, sex therapy, Reichian therapy, and More House." Having "voraciously" shopped "the spiritual supermarkets of the West Coast," as Lasch characterized this quest, Rubin eventually settled upon a Wall Street career. He died in 1994 after being struck by a car while crossing the street in front of his Westwood, California, penthouse. Writing in 2000, David Frum deemed Rubin "a perfect evocation of the spirit of the time as anybody has put to paper. . . . Seldom did hucksters hunt with greater success than in the 1970s."

Historians denote other eras in which Americans embraced a broad variety of purported methods of improving the physical or spiritual self, most notably during the forty years prior to the Civil War. The 1970s are unique, however, in offering such a broad range of self-improvement/discovery/empowerment methodologies. Traditional religion as a path to spiritual salvation was not abandoned and "born-again" Christians proliferated; even, as Wolfe asserted, the major Protestant sects that had been dominant in the pre–World War II era were "finished, gasping, breathing their last" as evangelical Christianity blossomed. A partial list of popular and often televised evangelical preachers who regularly attracted mass followings includes Pat Robertson, Billy Graham, Jimmy Swaggart, Oral Roberts, Jim and Tammy Bakker, Rex Humbard, and Robert Schuller. Most offered distorted versions of Christianity that would have, in the words of cultural scholar Peter Clecak, "horrified Cotton Mather and Jonathan Edwards." The Jesus People Movement, a charismatic evangelical offshoot, took shape in 1968, its adherents often haunting American street intersections and medians to spread their joy, much to the annoyance of passing motorists.

As historian Leo Ribuffo notes, between 1970 and 1978, the number of Americans who considered religion a prominent part of their lives rose from 14 percent to 44 percent, though concurrently, according to Christopher Hitchens, some 32 million Americans believed in astrology and bookstore shelves groaned with books about the Bermuda Triangle. Many of the new churches of the 1970s emphasized forgiveness over rectitude (just ask Jimmy Swaggart), the emotional over the intellectual, the primacy of the gospel over communion, and an "end times" perspective that made personal salvation all the more urgent. Likewise, as Clecak notes, "as the terms of damnation were relaxed, the widening criteria of salvation came to include various mixes of spiritual enlightenment, psychological gratification, and material security." Prosperity theology awaited just around the corner in the 1980s.

For other Americans, however, especially "Baby Boomers," "New Age" spirituality of the 1970s offered a fresh refuge from the era's uncertainties. The phrase itself denies precise definition, largely because of its eclectic components, which Olav Hammer aptly described as "nineteenth century doctrinal elements such as theosophy and post-theosophical esotericism as well as harmonious or positive thinking . . . now eclectically combined with . . . the religious psychologies: transpersonal psychology, Jungianism and a variety of Eastern teachings." Those seeking a material representation of this bewildering amalgam of beliefs needed only explore the offerings in New Age shops, reeking of incense and aromatic candles, that proliferated. Charles Reich's best-selling *The Greening of America* (1970) promoted the idea that new forms of consciousness emanating from the 1960s would guide the American people in a more positive direction. Others were drawn to astrology as providing life's guideposts, and

Linda Goodman's *Sun Signs* (1968) and *Love Signs* (1978) were bestsellers that bookended the decade.

Also popular were the writings of Carlos Castaneda, who published *The Teachings of Don Juan* in 1968, being a narrative of his tutelage by Mexican Yaqui Indian shaman don Juan Matus, during which he was made aware that he was to be the leader of a party of "seers" into the realm of the "non-ordinary reality." *Teachings* was the first of a dozen books spanning the 1970s that dealt with the shamanistic approach to gaining new knowledge, citing the use of psychoactive drugs such as peyote and jimson-weed in this pursuit. Castaneda was a controversial figure, described in the March 5, 1973, issue of *Time* as "an enigma wrapped in a mystery wrapped in a tortilla." Castaneda's works found an enthusiastic readership among college undergraduates, and *Teachings* was followed by a dozen other works pursuing the theme, which sold more than 28 million copies.

If one saw ultimate knowledge as emanating from the East, the de-cade offered several choices. The Maharishi Mahesh Yogi's *Transcenden-tal Meditation* continued to attract American followers, and in 1974, as his following and bank account grew, Maharishi University was founded in Fairfield, Iowa. As of August 2013, Maharishi International University boasted a student body of some 1,300. An Indian immigrant, A. C. Bhak-tivedanta, founded the International Society for Krishna Consciousness, commonly known as the Hare Krishna movement, in New York City in 1965 and, by 1974, had acquired more than four thousand followers, fifty-four temples, and a chauffeured Mercedes. Hare Krishna was an eclectic meld of Hindu beliefs, Indian folkways, and Aquarian millenarianism that held that an age of peace, love, and unity would soon begin. Critics claimed that "Krishna consciousness" was an exercise in mass hypnosis that led to a rejection of reason, and the group's acolytes soon became the bane of airport travelers, as they hawked their colorful but expensive booklets in terminals.

Claiming to be the incarnation of God, South Korean Sun Myung Moon arrived in the United States in 1974, where he established his Uni-fication Church, which became notorious for its mass weddings, in which bride and groom were selected by Moon. By the end of the decade, Moon had around 10,000 followers and had amassed a fortune with which he pur-chased the *Washington Times* and ended up in federal prison for tax fraud in 1984. Of briefer fame but perhaps drawing more extravagant adulation was

Figure 6.1. The young Maharaji in the 1970s. The Indian holy man was considered "god" by many of his followers, who sought new sources of spirituality. The Maharaji attracted some disaffected 1960s radicals such as Rennie Davis, who declared that he would crawl across the continent on his knees to be at the feet of his new idol. The cult was briefly vibrant, hosting a festival at the Houston Astrodome, but proved ephemeral. Source: Wikimedia Commons / The Prem Rawat Foundation

the eight-year-old guru Maharaji, leader of the "Divine Light Mission" who was held to be "the perfect master," the reincarnation of Christ and Buddha, when he arrived in the United States in the early 1970s.

Some 35,000 followers attended the guru's "Millennium '73" in Houston's Astrodome, where some believed a flying saucer would land. The organization effectively shut down in 1983, the expected UFO having yet to appear.

New Age thought was popularized in David Spangler's *Revelation: The Birth of a New Age* (1976) and Mark Satin's *New Age Politics: Healing and Society* (1976). The emergence of the New Age coincided with the popularity of Erich von Däniken's books *Chariots of the Gods?* (1968) and *Gods from Outer Space* (1971), which offered an alternative to Christian theology, proposing that aliens had first brought civilization to earth. The two books sold more than 6.5 million copies in the United States by

1974. Frum suggests that von Däniken's "science-fiction fantasies satisfied the needs of an age that hungered for mysteries," yet rejected those of traditional religions.

For those desiring a more structured approach to self-empowerment and/or consciousness, the decade offered a plethora of choices. Werner Erhard's est is perhaps one of the most well known. During the same decade, Americans could opt for psychologist Arthur Janov's primal therapy: *The Primal Scream* (1970) sold one million copies. In primal therapy, clients were encouraged to relive and express repressed childhood feelings through screaming out their anguish, if necessary. Janov's method, offered at the Primal Institute in California, was criticized for being little more than a "cash-grab" scheme, as was his claim that his his method could "cure" homosexuality. Drawing the usual celebrity clients, notably John Lennon and Yoko Ono, primal scream therapy remained a phenomenon into the 1980s.

If one was put off by "therapies" that involved screaming, there was the Esalen Institute in California, which was founded by Stanford graduate Michael Murphy and Dick Price in 1962. The intent behind the therapies offered there was to support alternative methods for exploring human consciousness ranging from encounter groups, meditation, massage, Gestalt practice, alternative medicine, yoga, organic food, and Eastern religions and philosophy. Over the years, the Esalen Institute, still in operation, also drew numerous luminaries, including Ansel Adams, Buckminster Fuller, Linus Pauling, Timothy Leary, and Arnold Toynbee. Another attendee was B. F. Skinner, a psychologist whose "behavioral analysis," which he promoted in *Walden Two* (1948), was embraced by some New Agers.

Scientology, founded in 1953, appealed to some New Agers in the 1970s and has been described as a business movement, a cult, and a religious movement, but regardless of its identity, the Church of Scientology has been as controversial as the personal life of its founder, L. Ron Hubbard, born in 1911 in Nebraska. His young years were unremarkable, though he became a prolific science fiction author in the 1930s, which eventually led to the publication of his book *Excaliber* (1938), which laid down some of the cosmology of Scientology. Out of this, Hubbard conceived of the "one command" concept, that being to survive, a theme that was revisited in his later *Dianetics*. Never one for modesty, Hubbard claimed that his book would "revolutionize everything" and that it would have "greater impact on people than the Bible." Hubbard was initially unable to find a publisher for the work, perhaps because, as he claimed, "whoever read it either went insane or committed suicide." During World War II, Hubbard's career as a naval officer brought into question his mental stability after he ordered his ship to depth-charge a nonexistent submarine and later shelled Mexican territory. His military performance was characterized as "substandard."

The 1950s were the foundational years for what would become Scientology, with the publication of Hubbard's *Dianetics: The Modern Science of Mental Health* making the *New York Times* bestseller list for six weeks; it remains, according to religious studies professor Paul Gutjahr, the best-selling non-Christian religious book of the century. Hubbard drew a distinction between Dianetics and Scientology, maintaining that the former was not a religion but a program to improve the individual. A vehement opponent of psychiatry and psychology, Hubbard promoted the idea of reincarnation and past life experiences, which became central to Scientology. Hubbard also invented the "E-meter," an electrodermal activity meter that ostensibly could be used to "audit" or detect changes in a person's mental state. The first of numerous future problems arose in 1951 when the New Jersey Board of Medical Examiners ruled that Hubbard was practicing medicine without a license, bankrupting the Hubbard Dianetic Research Foundation. Hubbard acquired a doctorate from the unaccredited Sequoia University in 1953 and incorporated the Church of Scientology the same year. Hubbard defined Scientology's objectives idealistically as promoting "a civilization without insanity, without criminals and without war; where the able can prosper and honest beings can have rights, and where Man is free to rise to greater heights."

Hubbard retreated to the world's oceans in the 1960s, with a small fleet of ships designated Sea Org, for the purpose of developing the basic cosmology of Scientology and remaining beyond the reach of numerous law and investigative agencies that sought him for a variety of offenses (he went underground briefly in the 1980s). Claiming to have undergone several illuminating journeys through time and space, Hubbard held that the universe was brought into existence by "Thetans" who fell from grace when they lost touch with their original spiritual purity but could, however, be reborn multiple times through a process called "assumption." Without Scientology's training, Hubbard claimed, "the individual's analytical ability remained clouded and hindered from experiencing reality." Scholar David G. Bromley describes Scientology as "part therapy, part religion, part UFO group. It's a mix of things unlike any other religious group out there." Experts suggest that the current number of American Scientologists ranges from 19,000 to 25,000. Today, there are several dozen "Ideal Churches" of Scientology across the United States, all reflecting the wealth of the organization. L. Ron Hubbard, married three times with seven children, died in his Creston, California, home in January 1986.

If the complexities of Scientology seemed too perplexing, there remained other paths to self-discovery and/or empowerment. Though transactional analysis declined in popularity in the 1970s, one could opt for the Silva Method of Mind Control, developed in 1944 by Bolivian electronics repairman José Silva. The Silva Method is a self-help and meditation program that purports to strengthen the individual's abilities through relaxation, higher brain functions, and clairvoyance. One could also opt for orgone therapy, developed by controversial psychoanalyst Wilhelm Reich in the 1930s, which offered the renewal of "life energy" or "orgone," a term derived from orgasm, which he claimed to be a form of biological energy that could be gathered in "orgone accumulators" to defeat neuroses and help bring about a personal sexual revolution. Though he died in 1957, his works, notably *The Function of the Orgasm* (1927), are still found in many New Age bookstores.

Therapies focusing on the body rather than the mind included health food, vegetarianism, veganism, and Rolfing, an alternative medicine developed by Ida Rolf. Typically delivered in a series of ten physical manipulations, Rolfing's objective was to align the body's energy field with the Earth's gravitational field. Less controversial and far more influential was running or jogging, which became a central part of the 1970s fitness revolution. Though many adopted a running/jogging routine of their own volition, the activity became a national phenomenon partly as a result of the publication of Jim Fixx's *The Complete Book of Running*, a 1977 bestseller. Born in New York City in 1932, Fixx demonstrated a high IQ at an early age. In 1967, weighing 214 pounds and smoking two packs of cigarettes a day, Fixx decided to pursue a healthier life and took up running. With his book selling over a million copies, Fixx was a frequent guest on television, hailing the benefits of physical exercise as a means to increasing life expectancy. A 1978 Gallup poll that estimated that some

15 million Americans had taken up jogging. Fixx argued that there was a spiritual aspect to jogging, declaring in his book that a lengthy and strenuous jog could produce "a trance-like state, a mental plateau where they [the joggers] feel miraculously purified and at peace with themselves and the world." It is beyond ironic to note that Fixx died in 1984 at age fifty-two while jogging, though his legacy jogged on into in the twenty-first century.

If one's ambitions tended toward self-advancement, the chief advocate in the 1970s was Robert Ringer. Born in 1938, Ringer was an entrepreneur who saw an opening for a guidebook to personal success, somewhat akin to Dale Carnegie's much earlier works. Ringer's first book, *Winning through Intimidation*, was rejected by twenty-three publishers, so Ringer self-published the book in 1973. It quickly rose to the top spot on the *New York Times* Bestseller List and stayed there for thirty-six weeks. Perhaps his most famous book was *Looking Out for #1* (1977), in which he argued for taking rationally based actions and unashamedly acknowledging the primacy of self-interest. His eight published works, which dot the bestseller lists into the twenty-first century, dealt with a variety of subjects, with *How You Can Find Happiness During the Collapse of Western Civilization* (1983) hinting at Ringer's increasingly right-wing tilt, which is evident on his website. In the 1970s, Ringer was one of the most well-known motivational speakers and writers in a decade that produced more than a few such aspirants, frequently appearing on television.

Obviously, the majority of Americans in the 1970s did not haunt New Age bookstores seeking crystals and astrology books, find refuge in rural communes or salvation in any of the numerous religions and cults, or achieve self-discovery/empowerment through the multitude of therapies that the decade either spawned or rejuvenated. One could reasonably argue that the health food and running regimens probably drew the greater number of adherents and were the most enduring. There was, however, another side to America in the 1970s in which collective action in pursuit of social and racial justice, together with the new environmental activism, prospered and grew, achieving some notable victories even as they altered national attitudes about the challenges that the nation still faced.

By 1970, the era of mass protest demonstrations was coming to an end. It was kept temporarily alive by continued American engagement in Vietnam, especially after the "incursion" into Cambodia in April, which provoked nationwide campus demonstrations, strikes, and shutdowns, as

well as drawing yet another army of protestors to Washington, DC. Subsequent US actions in Vietnam in 1971 to 1973 continued to draw public
protests, but the numbers who could be induced to take to the streets
gradually diminished as American troop withdrawals continued. The
last mass gasp of the counterculture might well be said to have been the
December 1969 Altamont Festival, which drew an audience of 300,000
but was marred by chaos and death. The age of mass civil rights demonstrations trailed off after the passage of civil rights legislation in 1964 and
1965, only to be supplanted by periodic outbursts of rage and violence, as
"ghetto uprisings" marked the late 1960s. Black militance, never a mass
phenomenon, died out with the suppression of the Black Panther Party.
Perhaps the largest mass demonstration by feminists, the Women's Strike
for Equality in New York City, was met with derision by the national
media not to be surpassed until the January 21, 2017, Women's March,
the largest single-day protest in the nation's history. Yet the passing of
the age of mass protest did not signal the end of social and political activism in the 1970s. New and unresolved issues demanded new responses,
which took the movement for racial justice, women's, Native American,
and other minority rights, as well as gay rights and environmentalism, in
new directions, often with surprisingly positive and far-reaching results. It
becomes evident that the 1970s were not years of public somnolence and
apathy but an era in which activism of many types prospered and grew,
laying foundations and expanding boundaries for a new America.

Historian James T. Patterson, in recalling W. E. B. Du Bois's famous
observation that "the problem of the twentieth century is the problem of
the color line," suggests that the African American scholar would "no doubt
have agreed that racial issues stubbornly remained the nation's number one
problem" in the 1970s. Comprising 11.1 percent of the nation's population
in 1970, black Americans had gained much in the course of the 1960s.
Segregation in public educational systems in the South, where it had taken
its most egregious form, often involving shockingly low state funding and
decrepit facilities, was broken down by Supreme Court rulings subsequent
to the 1954 *Brown v. Board of Education* decision, notably *Alexander v.
Holmes County Board of Education* in 1969. As of September 1970, only 14
percent of black children in the South still attended segregated schools.
Significant political barriers were broken down in the 1970s as black candidates won political offices at many levels. While black men had sat in

the House of Representatives since Reconstruction, New Yorker Shirley Chisholm was the first black woman elected to the House in 1968, holding her seat until 1983. In 1973 alone, mayoral victories included Tom Bradley in Los Angeles, Coleman Young in New York, and Maynard Jackson in Atlanta. Between 1970 and 1979, twenty-six black mayors won office across the nation, with Richard Arrington Jr. winning the mayoral election in Birmingham, Alabama, in the latter year. Other political advances included limited home rule for the District of Columbia in 1974 and the appointment of the first black Supreme Court Justice, Thurgood Marshall, who joined the court in 1967.

Yet these advances could not shroud the disheartening inequities that black Americans faced in other areas. Median income for African American households failed to rise in the 1970s, remaining at less than 60 percent of median white incomes. The net worth of black families remained considerably less than that of whites. Between 1970 and 1980, the proportion of black Americans living in poverty decreased only from 34 percent to 33 percent, about three times the rate of whites. As many blacks remained sequestered in the declining and crime-ridden areas of inner cities, social and health conditions remained problematic. Though the rate of black infant mortality declined in the 1970s, it did not match that of whites, and the life expectancy for blacks at decade's end was 68.1 years, compared to 74.4 years for whites.

One of the chief roadblocks to more rapid social and economic advancement for black Americans, as well as integration, was what one historian has termed "suburban victimization." Following World War II, two separate phenomena took place. Middle-class whites, many aided by the low-cost mortgages and loans made available by the Servicemen's Readjustment Act (GI Bill) abandoned crowded, decaying cities for the green spaces of suburbia. Federally subsidized housing developments, new highways, the growth of an automobile culture, the extension of public transportation to suburbs, and the promise of low taxes spurred further suburbanization. The Federal Housing Administration regularly financed middle-class whites, while denying financing to "high-risk" black and minorities. Urban renewal policies and new highway construction obliterated historically black communities even as suburban communities banned multifamily dwellings that low-income minorities could afford. Out of this grew the "bootstrap myth," which held that the urban poor and working class minorities only had themselves to blame for their entrapment in shan-tytowns and urban ghettos. One of the major rights battlegrounds of the 1970s was over minority access to suburban life. Although the Civil Rights Act of 1968 had specifically banned housing discrimination, the legal struggle for minority housing rights continued throughout the decade as white communities fought tooth and nail against grassroots minority challenges to housing restrictions. As indication of the intensity of the fight, the 1983 New Jersey State Supreme Court case known as *Mount Laurel II*, which required "a fair share of low- and moderate-income housing," was denounced by the state's governor as "social engineering on a scale never imagined by Marx or Lenin." America's "crabgrass frontier," a historian has commented, "proved to be an archetypal front porch politics battleground."

The chief glimmer of hope for many black Americans sprang from a marked improvement in educational achievement. By 1980, 51 percent of blacks over age twenty-five had completed four years of high school and 8 percent had four or more years of college behind them, the latter figure being a 100 percent improvement. Yet compared to educational gains made by whites, these were, at best, relative improvements. The struggle for access to higher education had largely been overcome by the 1970s, as students were no longer barred from admittance due to race. More blacks were attending college, even in those states that had maintained segregationist policies in the past. The University of Texas admitted black students in 1956, though their football team remained all-white until 1970. Arch rival University of Oklahoma integrated both the student body and the football team soon after the 1954 *Brown* decision. The University of Alabama, site of then Governor George Wallace's infamous "stand in the schoolhouse door" in 1963, admitted six hundred black students in 1974, fielded an increasingly powerful integrated football team in subsequent years, and crowned a black student as homecoming queen in 1973.

More controversial was the introduction of affirmative action programs in higher education, which generally featured outreach and recruitment efforts. A frequent rationale was that minority students who did not score as well on the oft-used Scholastic Aptitude Test or the American College Test exam did not perform well because the exams were culturally biased. Inevitably, affirmative action and quota or "set-aside" admission processes provoked backlash from white applicants, especially in cases where spots in medical or law schools were limited.

To some whites, this was "reverse discrimination," and the issue came to a head at the University of California's Davis campus when Allan Bakke, a white medical school applicant twice denied admission despite better scores than minority applicants, took the case to the Supreme Court. In *Regents of the University of California v. Bakke*, the court took the case in October 1977 and after eight months arrived at a ruling. In a 5 to 4 ruling, the court held that the medical school's quota system violated the equal protection clause of the Fourteenth Amendment and Title VI of the 1964 Civil Rights Act. "Race," wrote Justice John Paul Stevens, "cannot be the basis of excluding anyone from participation in a federally funded program." The Court's decision nevertheless held that flexible plans that included race or ethnicity among other admissions criteria were acceptable. As Justice Harry Blackman wrote, "In order to get beyond racism, we must first take account of race. . . . In order to treat persons equally, we must treat them differently."

"It has often been said," observes Michael S. Foley, "that whereas the 1960s had the Vietnam War, the 1970s had busing." Indeed, few issues drew such heated responses from white and black Americans as did that of federally mandated busing of students to achieve racial balance. While there were opponents of the court-ordered plans on both sides in the 1970s, it was from whites that sometimes violent opposition sprang. The Fourth Circuit Court of Appeals ruled in May 1970 that "busing is a permissible tool for achieving integration," but white outrage only grew as courts at various levels volleyed the issue to and fro. The most severe battle lines were drawn in Boston, where the Boston School Committee, led by Louise Day Hicks, simply refused to acknowledge that segregation existed. Dubbed "the Bull Connor of Boston" by James Farmer, Hicks had been at the forefront of delaying tactics since the state legislature passed the Racial Imbalance Act of 1965. In South Boston, Restore Our Alienated Rights (ROAR) became the chief antibusing group in 1974, calling for a boycott of city schools. A ROAR-led march to city hall ended with a mob attack on Senator Ted Kennedy when he attempted to address the crowd. The violence ebbed and flowed until busing was ended in 1988. By 2005, 86 percent of Boston public schools were majority black and Latino. The same scenario, usually less dramatic, can be applied to numerous school districts across the nation, as "white flight" to the suburbs bled public school systems of students. The struggle for racial justice and equality would transcend the 1970s.

Black Americans were not alone among those minorities who asserted their rights in the 1970s. Mexican Americans had long known discrimination and even white violence during the Los Angeles Zoot Suit riots in 1943. Even before the 1970s, those who called themselves Chicanos organized along several fronts, creating the Mexican American Legal Defense and Educational Fund in 1968, which established the Chicana Rights Project in 1974. Better known, Cesar Chavez established the United Farm Workers in 1962 and continued the fight for economic justice into the 1970s. The La Raza Unida Party politically represented Chicanos during the same period. Asian Americans, especially in California, organized to fight racism and preserve cultural traditions into the 1970s. Japanese Americans, long represented through the Japanese American Citizens League, won a major victory when, in 1988, a presidential commission agreed to pay reparations for the internment of 120,000 Japanese Americans during World War II.

Though its origins reach back into the 1960s, Native American rights activists gained considerable organizational strength and media attention in the 1970s, largely due to the activities of the American Indian Movement (AIM) and leaders such as Russell Means, Dennis Banks, and Leonard Peltier. Founded in July 1968 in Minneapolis, AIM initially focused on urban issues such as police brutality and poverty. These "urban Indians," comprising almost 70 percent of Native Americans, were largely the product of the 1956 Indian Relocation Act, which sought to encourage them to abandon traditional lands and communal life for greater economic opportunities. That initial focus soon expanded to encompass long-standing grievances over broken treaties and the loss of Indian lands.

Recognizing the value of media attention, AIM inaugurated the decade with the renunciation of the Thanksgiving holiday and the seizure of a *Mayflower* replica in Boston in 1970. The activists also made clear their opposition to the use of images of Native Americans by sports teams. The following year, activists briefly occupied Mount Rushmore, as it was sited on traditionally sacred Lakota Sioux land. AIM members also seized an abandoned Coast Guard station and turned it into a community school. AIM members occupied the Bureau of Indian Affairs in the nation's capital. During the 1972 occupation, Hank Adams composed the group's

Twenty Points, which addressed decades of broken federal promises and demanded remedies.

The most dramatic AIM action was indisputably the Wounded Knee Occupation, which followed close on the heels of protest growing out of the 1972 murder of Raymond Yellow Thunder, an Oglala Sioux from the Pine Ridge, Nebraska, reservation, who was killed by two white men. His assailants were given minimal sentences for manslaughter, despite protests from AIM members, who cited this as a historical pattern of injustice. The 1973 stabbing death of another Lakota, Wesley Bad Heart Bull, in Rapid City, once again by a white assailant, set the stage for a violent confrontation between AIM and local authorities. With characteristic obtuseness, officials decided to hold the trial in Custer, South Dakota. AIM members and other Indians who gathered outside the courthouse in February 1973 were infuriated when the local district attorney appeared to inform them that Bad Heart Bull's murderers would be prosecuted only for second-degree manslaughter. Violence immediately broke out between infuriated Indians, local police, and state highway patrolmen. Sioux men and women joined the fray, as police hurled tear gas and smoke bombs and turned firehoses on the Indians. The protestors succeeded in setting fire to the courthouse and the chamber of commerce building, as well as two police cars. Mary Crow Dog, a Lakota woman who had joined the protestors, recalled how she laughed at a sign reading "WELCOME TO CUSTER—THE TOWN WITH THE GUNSMOKE FLAVOR" as it went up in flames. Crow Dog was among the majority who escaped without being arrested. Bad Heart Bull's killer was acquitted. His mother, Sarah, served time for her part in the protest.

Many of those who participated in the Custer City protest headed for the Pine Ridge Reservation, where discontent with tribal president Richard Wilcox was at fever pitch, due to his misuse of tribal funds, election fraud, reactionary views, and employment of a "goon squad" to enforce his rule. Upon arrival, the dissidents found the town garrisoned by FBI agents backed up by some thirty APCs with mounted machine guns—in addition to the "goon squad" and local white vigilantes. Given the situation, some elder women suggested that a stand be made at Wounded Knee, site of an infamous 1890 massacre. On February 27, 1973, about fifty carloads of Sioux established themselves at the lonely hill; most were not AIM members. The subsequent siege lasted seventy-one days, with the poorly armed Sioux buzzed by F-4 Phantom jets, terrorized by almost incessant gunfire from their besiegers, and harassed by vigilantes who were permitted to penetrate government lines. Periodic meetings with federal officials yielded no results, as the negotiators stated that the US government refused to "negotiate with a gun to its head." Numerous celebrities and Vietnam veterans arrived to offer their support, Indians as far away as New York and the West Coast snuck into the site, and South Dakota's two US Senators met with the beleaguered Indians in hopes of ending the standoff. In March the occupiers declared the Independent Oglala Nation. The siege lasted until May 8; two Indians died from gunshot wounds and a federal marshal was wounded. AIM leaders Russell Means and Dennis Banks were arrested and faced legal troubles for years to come. "What Wounded Knee told the world," Means later wrote, "was that John Wayne hadn't killed us all [the Indians]."

The following year brought internecine trouble as AIM leaders ferreted out suspected FBI informants from their ranks. Suspect Jancita Eagle Deer was killed by a speeding car. Anna Mae Aquash was erroneously identified as a spy and executed at Pine Ridge in late 1975; her killer was never identified. Internal paranoia and numerous prosecutions did not damper AIM's activism, however. In February 1978, activists began the "Longest Walk," starting on Alcatraz Island and ending on July 15 as thousands of supporters arrived in Washington, DC, to bring attention to the continuing erosion of Native American rights. Congress voted against a bill to abrogate treaties with Indian nations and President Carter refused to meet with representatives of the protest. As an indication of enduring Native American activism, AIM led the "Longest Walk 2" in 2008 and continued to call out injustices well into the twenty-first century.

The Gay Activists Alliance and the Gay and Lesbian Activists Alliance joined the Gay Liberation Front in the struggle for gay rights in the 1970s. In 1970 parades marking the Stonewall uprising were held in eight cities. That same year, the Lavender Menace was established by lesbians who felt that men dominated the gay movement. Between 1969 and 1973, six states removed laws that criminalized homosexuality. Numerous cities, including Miami, Florida, passed ordinances granting equal protection to gay Americans. The backlash quickly took shape as religious and conservative activists protested that homosexuality was "anti-family." The most notable of these crusaders was the former Miss Oklahoma Anita Bryant, who was also the advertising face of the Florida orange juice industry. Bryant, who declared homosexuality to be an "insidious attack on God's laws," organized Dade County voters to overturn the recently passed equal protection law. There were setbacks elsewhere, as other cities also rescinded similar antidiscrimination laws. In 1978, after San Francisco mayor George Moscone signed a gay rights ordinance, he was assassinated by Dan White. The 1970s brought giant strides forward for gay Americans, but there remained a sometimes-murderous residue of prejudice.

The forward progress of women's liberation gained momentum in the 1970s, though criticisms voiced by some women and from the New Right would continue (see close-up of Phyllis Schlafly in chapter 9). Considerable support came from publications such as *Redbook, Ladies' Home Journal,* and *Good Housekeeping. Redbook* editorialized that "every human being should have the right and the opportunity to make his or her own choices in every area of life" and asked Gloria Steinem in an interview what "the movement" would tell those women who were happy in the roles of wives and mothers. Steinem made clear that the point of the movement was the right to make that very choice. Steinem's *Ms.* magazine premiered in spring 1972 asserting that "Ms. is . . . a standard form of address by women who want to be recognized as individuals, rather than being identified by their relationship with a man."

The Redstocking collective's 1969 manifesto had its own definition of the objective of the movement, the chief task being "to develop female class consciousness through sharing experience and publicly exposing the sexist foundations of all our institutions." Consciousness raising, which originated among radical feminists, quickly became a central foundation of second-wave feminism and led to the publication of *Our Bodies, Ourselves: A Book by and for Women* (1970), composed by members of the Boston Women's Health Book Collective, spurred in part by the determination to acquaint women with their anatomy, sexuality, health, and reproductive issues and wrest them from a largely male medical profession. The book sold more than four million copies in thirty-three languages and was hailed by the *New York Times* as a "feminist classic" and "America's best-selling book an all aspects of women's health." The book proved an inspiration for reforms in gynecology and obstetrics and preceded an explosion of women's health facilities centers across the nation. By 1975, the new

National Women's Health Network set up more than fifty health centers. The first Rape Crisis Center was established in the District of Columbia in 1972 and within four years more than one hundred such centers had sprung up nationwide. For battered women, Women's Advocates in St. Paul, Minnesota, first took victims into private homes before purchasing the first of four large homes as refuges. In 1978, the National Coalition Against Domestic Violence was formed, and by 1982 three hundred shelters for battered women were established. The ongoing and divisive debate about abortion led to the formation of the National Association for the Repeal of Abortion Laws (NARAL) in 1969 and the Supreme Court settled the issue of the right to choose in 1973 in the *Roe v. Wade* case in a 7 to 2 vote. Much to the dismay of millions, that right was rescinded in 2022 when the court, which had recently been packed with three conservative justices by President Donald Trump, overturned the *Roe* decision in a 6 to 3 vote.

Another area in which new horizons opened for women was in athletics. The Bobby Riggs–Billie Jean King tennis showdown at the Astrodome in the fall of 1973, hyped by the media as the "battle of the sexes," awakened many to the promise of female athletics, as King walloped the mouthy, sexist Riggs in three straight sets for a purse of $100,000. She subsequently established the Women's Tennis Association. The more substantial development was the realization of what Title IX of the Education Amendments of 1972 meant for women's athletics. Growing out of the Elementary and Secondary Education Amendment, Title IX stated that "no person shall, on the basis of sex, be excluded from participation in, denied the benefits of, or be subjected to discrimination under any education program or activity receiving federal finance assistance." While regulations exempted sports that involved bodily contact, Title IX revolutionized women's athletics, especially in higher education, ensuring better funding and instruction. The decade also saw many previously all-male educational institutions opened to women, including all of the service academies in 1975.

The emergence of a new consciousness among the majority of Americans, together with newfound activism, was bound to provoke opposition, much of it founded on the mistaken beliefs that "women's lib" meant that women would be compelled to go to work, be drafted, lose traditional privileges, use unisex restrooms, or "become like men." All of these issues would emerge during the debate over the Equal Rights Amendment (ERA). The women's movement was also challenged by internal disagreements, as younger radical feminists challenged the liberal feminists comprising NOW (National Organization for Women). In 1970, Betty Friedan had warned that the movement needed to "overcome the wallowing, navel-gazing rap sessions, the orgasm talk . . . the rage that will produce a backlash—down with sex, down with love, down with childbearing." While this was an exaggerated characterization of radical feminism, it bore some truth. Friedan healed one of the major rifts in the movement when, in mid-1971, NOW passed a resolution supporting lesbianism "legally and morally." At the 1971 National Women's Conference, Friedan, appalled at antifeminist derogation of lesbianism, won cheers and tears from the delegates when she embraced "our lesbian sisters" from the podium. By mid-decade, scholar Alice Echols argues, the cultural feminism of the NOW mainstream won out over radical feminism because it "promised and end to the gay-straight split." Echols also notes that the marginalization of feminism was "one of the most striking developments in the post-1975 era," largely due to an unwarranted emphasis on the ERA, "which it now seems may have had more symbolic than actual value."

Though conservation and preservation movements had a lengthy history by the 1970s, it could be argued that the first Earth Day in April 1970 signaled a new era of activism and success for environmentalism. During the Nixon years, not only were there major legislative victories with the Clean Air Act (1970) and the Clean Water Act (1972) but also an executive order that established the Environmental Protection Agency (1970). The Sierra Club, the nation's oldest conservation group (est. 1892), continued to enlarge its membership as horrors such as the 1969 Santa Barbara oil spill awakened Americans to the multitude of dangers to the environment. The club employed lobbyists to fight for the preservation of wilderness an end to destructive mining practices, as well as advocating sustainable energy and mitigating climate change. The decade also saw the emergence of more direct-action groups such as Greenpeace, Earth First!, and the Sea Shepherd Conservation Society, all advocating urgent, direct action. Long-established groups such as the Wilderness Society, the Nature Conservancy, the Ocean Alliance, and the Audubon Society likewise grew in the 1970s, broadening public awareness of environmental issues.

Though it often commanded less attention, the disability rights movement made major gains in the 1970s, primarily through the federal courts. In the landmark 1972 Pennsylvania federal district court decisions *Mills v. Board of Education* and *PARC v. Pennsylvania*, the courts ruled that disabled children had a right to a "free and appropriate education." Congress soon took up the issue by passing the Education for All Handicapped Children Act (1975). Having considerably more impact, Section 504 of Title VI of the 1964 Civil Rights Act ensured that handicapped people would by law have access to all hospitals, schools, colleges, urban transportation systems, and other public institutions. The consequence, as a historian wrote, was that "the physical design of America changed in the seventies."

The 1970s, as becomes evident, reflected the duality of the American character. The decade witnessed a new impulse to individualism, either by withdrawing or seeking self-enhancement, as well as toward collective action to confront major social inequities and threats to the environment. How this bifurcation of focus would change in the 1980s remained to be seen.

❖

In 1977, Paul Watson, who had recently left the environmental organization Greenpeace over the latter's rejection of Watson's advocacy of direct, even violent and potentially illegal, actions against despoilers of the environment, had his mind set on the destruction of the *Sierra*, a notorious pirate whaler that prowled the Atlantic, killing whales of every species with no regard for existent laws and regulations. Rumored to have killed more than 25,000 whales, the *Sierra* was a prime target of the global anti-whaling movement. Having failed to purchase an aging vessel from the now uncooperative Greenpeace, Watson found a savior in Cleveland Amory of the Fund for Animals, who provided the funds to purchase a two-hundred-foot trawler, which was rechristened the *Sea Shepherd* in December 1978. A crew was recruited through advertisements in Boston newspapers. The next challenge, following a twelve-day Atlantic crossing, was to locate the *Sierra*. The *Sea Shepherd* was readied for battle, its bow reinforced with one hundred tons of concrete for ramming purposes.

On this maiden voyage, the twenty-eight-year-old skipper of the *Sea Shepherd* learned some important lessons. Following in the wake of the *Sierra*, Watson entered the Portuguese harbor at Portos, where the *Sierra* had anchored. The following day, as the *Sierra* steamed out of port, Watson's departure was blocked by the harbormaster, obviously intent on permitting the pirate whaler to escape. Giving his crew the opportunity to disembark, Watson and two others left Portos aboard *Sea Shepherd* at full speed, soon catching the *Sierra*, which had halted offshore. "In order to get their attention," Watson recalled, he rammed the pirate whaler head-on, hoping to destroy their harpoon mount. Failing that, Watson backed his ship and then rammed the *Sierra* amidships, leaving a six-by-eight-foot-long hole in the whaler's side. The *Sierra* finally limped away, escaping further damage.

Now the *Sea Shepherd* became the hunted, as a Portuguese destroyer forced the ship into Leixões, where the wounded *Sierra* was sheltering. Watson's ship remained impounded for more than four months, after which Portuguese authorities decided that he would have to pay $750,000 in fines, or the *Sea Shepherd* would be forfeited to the owners of the *Sierra*. Inspecting his ship, Watson discovered that it had been largely stripped and decided that his only recourse was to have his chief engineer scuttle the *Sea Shepherd* at its moorings. It was a disheartening lesson in what might be expected from unsympathetic authorities and the vagaries of maritime law, which held the ship, not the captain or crew, responsible. Though the *Sea Shepherd* was lost, justice was not long in coming. In Lisbon's harbor on February 6, 1980, a limpet mine blew a hole in the hull of the newly refitted *Sierra*, which sank in ten minutes. An anonymous call to United Press International affirmed, "We did it for the *Sea Shepherd*." In late April, the Spanish whalers *Isba I* and *Isba II* were also sunk by limpet mines at Vigo, Spain. When Sea Shepherd posted a $25,000 reward for the destruction of the pirate whaler *Astrid*, its owner quickly sold it to a Korean fishing company. "In less than a year," Watson claimed, "we had wiped out the jewels of the North Atlantic pirate whaler fleet." No one was injured in the course of these activities.

Canadian American Paul Watson, founder of the Sea Shepherd Conservation Society, has been lauded as a courageous foe of illegal whaling and fishing as well as the slaughter of baby seals and other marine mammals, even as others labeled him an ecoterrorist, a mutineer, an international criminal, and a violent extremist. Born in Toronto to Anthony Joseph Watson and Annamarie Larsen on December 2, 1950, the future activist grew up in New Brunswick, where he credited his membership in the Kindness Club for his lifelong commitment to "respect and defend animals."

Watson moved to Vancouver in 1967 and afterward served a stint with the Canadian Coast Guard before working as a merchant seaman. Watson's evolution from protest to direct and aggressive activism developed rapidly after he joined a Sierra Club protest of nuclear testing on Amchitka Island in October 1969. A new group, the "Don't Make a Wave Committee," grew out of that action and evolved into Greenpeace, which used dramatic tactics calculated to stop nuclear testing. Watson crewed aboard the *Greenpeace Too!* and later skippered the *Astral* during his time with Greenpeace. Not content with this activity, Watson was also active in the Vancouver Liberation Front and the Vancouver Yippies in the early 1970s. Drawn to the Wounded Knee occupation in 1973, Watson claimed that it was in the course of a sweat lodge experience that he had a vision in which a buffalo told him that he should concentrate on saving marine mammals. This preceded actions in the mid-1970s in which Watson and other activists attempted to interfere with if not stop the slaughter of baby harp seals on the ice floes off Newfoundland. He and his compatriots were the targets of violent attacks by the seal hunters as well as legal prosecutions by Canadian authorities. Both were valuable lessons for the challenges that awaited in the future. Efforts by Greenpeace activists to interfere with whale-harvesting by Soviet ships in 1975 by charging factory ships in Zodiac inflatables proved ineffective and led the captain of the Russian factory ship to make a threatening throat-cutting gesture to the activists. Obviously, some more effective strategy for saving the whales would have to be conceived, though the object of gaining media attention was met.

Watson was ousted from Greenpeace in 1977 as a result of fundamental disagreements over tactics and strategies. "Few changes on this planet," Watson asserts, "have taken place solely because of nonviolent action," to which Greenpeace was committed. Watson soon became an unrelenting critic of Greenpeace, which he claimed had become more of a fundraising organization than one of productive activism, dismissing them as "nothing but the Avon ladies of the environmental movement" and "just an example of eco-corporations, eco-business." Having left Greenpeace, Watson was active throughout the decade with the Defenders of Wildlife, The Fund for Animals, as well as being a cofounder of the Friends of the Wolf and Earthforce Environmental Society.

The latter 1970s were busy years for Watson, having married the first of his four wives in 1979. Having moved his home base to Honolulu, Hawaii, in 1976, he organized Earthforce, which was intended to be international in scope, and in 1978 he journeyed to East Africa to investigate the slaughter of elephants for their ivory. The sea beckoned, however, and in 1977 Watson founded the Sea Shepherd Conservation Society (SSCS) and acquired their first vessel, the *Sea Shepherd*, later scuttled during the controversy over the ramming of the *Sierra*.

Watson's visceral hatred of whaling went back to his Greenpeace days, when he and other activists had tried to stop Russian whalers from killing the giant marine mammals. "There is nothing glamorous about today's whaling ships," he declared. "They stink. They stink so that one is certain to retch when first coming upon them. . . . Blackened with the gore of thousands of deaths . . . they are an insult to the eye." Watson notes that among the members of the International Whaling Commission, Japan and the then Soviet Union are the only ones still maintaining extensive whaling fleets. Japan, he asserts, owned or supported "most of the outlaw ships."

Though SSCS's first direct action in 1979 was aimed at halting Canadian seal hunting, what primarily motivated Watson throughout the

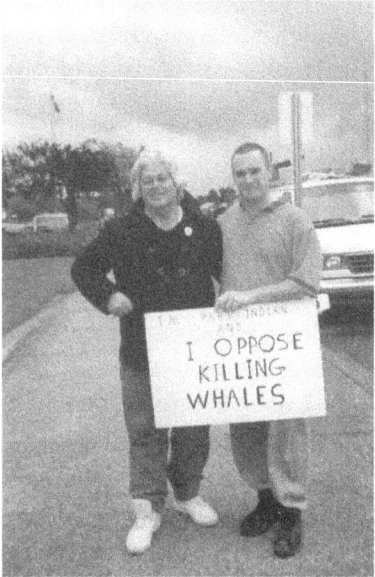

Figure 6.2. Canadian American Paul Watson, cofounder of the Sea Shepherd Conservation Society. Source: Wikimedia Commons / Andrew Parodi

1970s and following decades was the mission of halting illegal whaling, as whaling was not banned by the IWC until 1986. Watson targeted the *Sierra* for two reasons. He saw the pirate whaler as "the most offensive" of the type, as it specialized in hunting "legally protected whales." Second, Watson recognized that the destruction of the *Sierra* would bring about maximum media attention. He was arguably correct about both claims, though the *Sierra* episode marked an increase in the legal troubles that Watson faced in subsequent years. As the decade ended, Watson proclaimed his support of the radical environmental group Earth First!, which resorted to the "monkey-wrenching" tactics celebrated by environmentalist writer and friend Edward Abbey, who advocated sabotaging efforts to alter and deface the environment.

SSCS's activities and renown grew into the twenty-first century, as did the size of its fleet, which numbered twelve vessels in 2021; many of the ships were financed by wealthy celebrities who supported the cause. SSCS, as well as Watson, was featured in the television series *Whale Wars*, which chronicled the group's efforts to halt Japanese whaling in Antarctic seas. Despite favorable rulings by the IWC, SSCS was compelled to abandon its efforts to halt Japanese whaling when Japan militarized its whaling fleet, making interceptions dangerously unfeasible. There remained other crusades, such as stopping shark-finning, halting illegal fishing techniques, and stopping poaching of declining fish stocks by pirate vessels such as the *Thunder*. Two Sea Shepherd vessels undertook a four-month pursuit of the *Thunder* in late 2014, finally cornering the vessel in South Atlantic waters, at which point the captain and crew scuttled the ship rather than face the inevitable fines if the ship was taken into port. Courageous activists who boarded the sinking ship, even as its hold was flooding, discovered tons of illegally harvested fish.

Watson has been condemned as an "ecoterrorist" by the Japanese government for his anti-whaling activities in the South Atlantic. However, in 2000, *Time* magazine named him one of the "Top Twenty Environmental Heroes of the Twentieth Century." In 2002, Watson was inducted into the Animal Rights Hall of Fame, and in October 2012, Watson received the Jules Verne Award, previously awarded only to the late Jacques Cousteau. Watson claims that he and his largely volunteer crews have sunk between six to ten pirate whalers and damaged an additional eight during SSCS's long years of effort to protect marine life and the ocean environment.

His activities also led to arrest warrants and brief imprisonments, and compelled him to avoid several nations out of fear of legal action. His legacy and the Sea Shepherd Conservation Society live on, undertaking numerous campaigns to preserve the earth's oceans and their inhabitants.

"WHAT IS SPECIAL ORDER 937?"
Film, Television, and Theater in the 1970s

The film that made Sam Peckinpah one of the most well-known directors of the 1970s premiered in 1969, presaging a decade in which a new generation of filmmakers would transform American cinema. Largely because of this film, Peckinpah would earn the nickname "Bloody Sam." *The Wild Bunch*, opening on June 18, 1969, was rushed into production partly to counter the wildly popular *Butch Cassidy and the Sundance Kid*. In contrast to the saccharine *Butch Cassidy*, Peckinpah depicted the transitional West as a degraded realm where cruelty was commonplace, violence was the norm, and death indiscriminately visited the innocent as well as the guilty. The film opens in Starbuck, Texas, in 1913, when the last vestiges of the Old West were giving way to a new era and revolution swept Mexico. Riding into the Southern Texas town is the "Bunch," outlaws disguised as US Army troops intent on robbing the railway company office. Then, as Pike Bishop (William Holden) leads his men in the takeover of the railway office, wherein they hold a clerk and several hapless unarmed men and women at gunpoint, he snarls a cold command, "If they move . . . kill 'em!" Little does the Bunch know that they have blundered into an ambush set up by the railroad company, as bounty hunters led by Deke Thornton (Robert Ryan) line building rooftops. With impeccably bad timing, a Salvation Army band begins parading down the main street as the ambushers wildly open fire on the Bunch from above. A lengthy gunfight ensues, replete with blood exploding from panicked townspeople, ambushers, and outlaws. The whirlwind of violence ends with the five survivors fleeing on horseback, the streets littered with the dead and dying, and the gleeful bounty hunters looting the bodies.

The shocking opening scene presages the violent, gruesome episodes that characterize the film. The concluding sequence is a carnival of death, as four members of the Bunch, attempting to rescue one of their own from the clutches of the sadistic Huertista General Mapache, take on the general and two hundred of his soldiers in the courtyard of his headquarters in a ruined hacienda. Rifles, shotguns, handguns, a machine gun, and hand grenades are employed in a lengthy battle that leaves the Bunch, Mapache, and most of his troops dead.

With this film, shot on four locations in northern Mexico, Peckinpah established an unforgettable trademark—films featuring graphic, seemingly endless violence. Prior to filming, Peckinpah promised, "We're going to bury *Bonnie and Clyde*," a 1967 film that shocked audiences as the two leads (Warren Beatty and Faye Dunaway) were riddled with machine gun fire in the final scene. Peckinpah insisted on realistic

Figure 7.1. Director Sam Peckinpah at the Agua Verde location during the filming of *The Wild Bunch*. The extended violent shoot-out betweeen the four survivors of the "Bunch" and the corrupt Mexican General Mapache's soldiers was filmed here. Source: Wikimedia Commons / Sam Peckinpah's *The Wild Bunch*

gunshot wounds re-created by squibs, small packets of red liquid, many supplemented with hamburger meat for added gore, detonated to spray blood from the victims. Some 10,000 squibs were set off during the final sequence alone. More than 90,000 blank rounds were expended by 239 firearms during the film, leaving viewers overwhelmed by the sheer amount of sound, fury, and bloodshed. Peckinpah's West is bereft of heroes—there are only survivors. For the Bunch, the only redemption is in the sacrificial manner of their deaths.

The stellar cast did not temper a barrage of negative audience and critical reactions. At the May premiere in Kansas City, some thirty viewers fled the theater, often vomiting outside. Critics were quick to pounce. William Wolf proclaimed, "There is little justification for discussing this ugly, pointless, disgusting bloody film." Judith Crist warned moviegoers, "If you want to see *The Wild Bunch*, be sure and take along a barf bag," deeming it "undoubtedly the worst movie of 1969." Rex Reed described the film as a "phony, pretentious piece of throat-slashing slobber . . . exploiting and glorifying violence." Film professor Arthur Knight wondered who "could ever come up with a picture as wholly revolting as this film." Others understood what Peckinpah had achieved in *The Wild Bunch*. Pauline Kael belatedly hailed it as "a traumatic poem of violence, with imagery as ambivalent as Goya's." Stanley Kaufmann called it a landmark film, and Vincent Canby concurred that the film was "very beautiful and the first truly interesting American-made Western in years." *Time*'s reviewer proclaimed "its accomplishments are more than sufficient to confirm that Peckinpah, along with Stanley Kubrick and Arthur Penn, belongs with the best of the newer generation of filmmakers." The upcoming generation of filmmakers was also impressed. Quentin Tarantino called the final shoot-out sequence "a masterpiece beyond compare," and George Lucas enthusiastically declared, "This is the best movie ever made!" *The Wild Bunch*, a film historian wrote, "exploded on American screens in 1969 like a shrapnel bomb."

The man both damned and praised for his art was born on February 21, 1925, in Fresno, California, and schooled there. The son of David and Fern Peckinpah spent much of his free time outdoors and at his grandfather's ranch. The West was in Peckinpah's blood from an early age, even as the countryside he loved was gradually being transformed by the encroachment of civilization. Chronic disciplinary problems landed Peckinpah at the San Rafael Military Academy for a year and, in 1943, he joined the Marines and was posted to postwar China, which was rife with violence and inhumanity. Following his discharge, Peckinpah studied history at California State, Fresno, where he married Marie Selland. Gaining two years' experience directing local theater, he found employment as a dialogue coach in *Riot in Cell Block 11* (1954) and later had a minor role in *Invasion of the Body Snatchers* (1956). During this same decade, Peckinpah wrote numerous scripts for television westerns as well as directing several.

By 1960, Peckinpah's alcohol addiction had become evident, perhaps accounting for his divorce from Selland, with whom he had four children. In 1965, he began a tempestuous marriage with Mexican actress Begoña Palacios, which led him to spend much time in Mexico, where he became fascinated with the country's lifestyle and culture; four of his later films were set and filmed there. Peckinpah's directorial career began with the traditional westerns *The Deadly Companions* (1961), *Ride the High Country* (1962), and *Major Dundee* (1965), but his alcoholism began to affect his career and he was fired as director of *The Cincinnati Kid* (1965). Peckinpah's path to redemption came with the offer to direct the television drama *Noon Wine* (1966), scripted from a Katherine Anne Porter short story, after which he began planning for *The Wild Bunch*. Though it received two Academy Award nominations, *The Wild Bunch* won neither, losing out to *Butch Cassidy* for best score. It ranked as only the seventeenth-highest-grossing film of 1969. The film did, however, establish Peckinpah as major director, who went on to direct the western *The Ballad of Cable Hogue* (1970) and *Junior Bonner* (1972), the moving and humorous tale of an aging rodeo performer. *Straw Dogs* (1971) reintroduced Peckinpah's characteristic violence at a horrifically personal level, as a mild-mannered American academic on sabbatical is compelled to fend off murderous locals in the English countryside. *The Getaway* (1972), featuring Steve McQueen as the bank-robbing antihero, brought considerable gunplay to the screen.

By 1973, alcoholism seriously disrupted Peckinpah's life and second marriage, though he pulled things together long enough to direct *Pat Garrett and Billy the Kid*, which was hailed by Martin Scorsese as one of the greatest modern westerns. Peckinpah's reputation went into eclipse with the release of *Bring Me the Head of Alfredo Garcia* (1974) and *The Killer Elite* (1975), both of which were widely panned. Increasingly dependent on alcohol and cocaine, Peckinpah succeeded in putting together one final triumph with *Cross of Iron* (1977), a mildly successful World War II epic. Increasingly desperate for work, Peckinpah agreed to direct *Convoy* (1978), an inane film derived from the hit novelty song by C. W. McCall. Though the film was the highest-grossing film of Peckinpah's career, it was thoroughly derided by critics. In 1982, Peckinpah was reduced to accepting second-unit work on the comedy *Jinxed!* (1982) and the following year directed *The Osterman Weekend* (1983), a poorly received thriller.

Peckinpah's final years were marked by declining health and desperate efforts to find work. His final project, undertaken only two months before his death, was to film two music videos for Julian Lennon. He died on December 28, 1984. Honors and awards for *The Wild Bunch* came belatedly, with the American Film Institute listing it several times among the top one hundred American films. "Bloody Sam's" lasting legacy was to reimagine the western and to pave a path for a new generation of directors who would dominate American cinema in the 1970s.

❖

The most observable impact of the 1960s on the following decade may be seen in the films and television shows of the 1970s. Some of the new directions were presaged by outliers in the 1960s. *Easy Rider* (1969), for example, is now cited by many film historians as prefiguring the New Cinema that dominated the first half of the of the 1970s, driven by a new generation of directors who produced films independent of the major studios, often addressing the grimmer side of American life past and present and providing ambiguous conclusions. Bold, innovative in technique, and often shocking, the New Cinema produced an unsurpassed wealth of critically acclaimed films that have continued to impress film students and lay viewers alike. By mid-decade, however, some in this new generation of directors, along with the major studios, discovered the allure of the blockbuster film, which while less topically challenging, drew huge audiences and predictably lucrative profits, and often laid the path for equally profitable sequels spanning decades.

Film historian Peter Lev notes that "creative moments in film history often take place in periods of social and political conflict," and as the late 1960s bled into the early 1970s, continuing generational and political conflict led some in Hollywood to see the success of *Easy Rider* as evidence that the youth market might continue to prove profitable. However, films such as *The Strawberry Statement*, *Getting Straight*, *Zabriskie Point*, and Dennis Hopper's incoherent *The Last Movie*, all released in 1970–1971, proved dismal box office failures. On the other hand, the traditional syrupy romance *Love Story* (1970) was one of the highest-grossing films of all time. *The Summer of '42* (1971), a coming-of-age film, was likewise a box office success. *The Way We Were*, released in 1973, was another romantic drama set in World War II that garnered numerous Academy Awards. So even as traditional themes remained strong at the box office and a succession of nontraditional films bombed, the question remained as to what direction American cinema might take. Still, 1969's *They Shoot Horses, Don't They?*, directed by Sydney Pollack and starring Jane Fonda, hinted at the darker corners of the American psyche that cinema might explore in the next decade. Set in the 1930s, the film was built around the desperation of marathon dancers, climaxing in a graphic suicide. One critic deemed the film "an epic of exhaustion and futility." The explanation for this cinematic diversity, as William Goldman concluded in 1982, is that the 1970s demonstrated that "nobody knows anything" about Hollywood. Though one can discern a definite fault line in the direction of filmmaking at mid-decade, Lev accurately captures the uniqueness of American cinema in the 1970s with his assertion that "for sheer diversity of aesthetic and ideological approaches, no period of American cinema surpasses the films of the 1970s."

The advent of the New Cinema may be traced to developments reaching back into the previous decade, which saw the major studios, goaded by the success of *The Sound of Music* (1965), indulge in a deluge of costly musicals that did not produce the expected profits. A recession at decade's end and growing indebtedness compelled a drop in production by major studios—the number of films produced by the majors fell 34 percent during 1969–1970. Some of the production gap was filled by new smaller companies such as Avco Embassy, which scored with *The Graduate* (1967), and Allied Artists, which found an audience in *A Man and a Woman* (1966). The distribution of foreign and independent productions gave such start-ups an early boost. The Motion Picture Production Code (MPPC), established in 1934, imposed strict self-censorship on the industry until the Motion Picture Association of America (MPAA) abandoned the code in November 1968 and instituted a rating system denoted by letters (G for general audience, PG for parental guidance, up through R for restricted and X for adult material). The abandonment of the MPC provided an opening for the creative genius of a vast new generation of directors, including Mike Nichols, Francis Ford Coppola, George Lucas, William Friedkin, Robert Altman, Sam Peckinpah, Steven Spielberg, Woody Allen, and Martin Scorsese, among others. These directors brought with them a new generation of actors, many of whom had worked their way up through Broadway, "B" movies, and horror films, as well as television series. Jack Nicholson, Diane Keaton, Clint Eastwood, Roy Scheider, Shelley Duvall, Ellen Burstyn, Robert Duvall, Gene Hackman, Al Pacino, Dustin Hoffman, and Sissy Spacek were among the hundreds of new faces that gained renown in the 1970s.

The New Cinema also incorporated new technologies aimed at making films more captivating and realistic. New lens and camera technology as well as sound reproduction provided the chief instruments of the new cinematography. Film projection had been undergoing constant revision since the introduction of VistaVision (*The Ten Commandments*, 1956), CinemaScope, and Panavision in the blockbusters of the 1950s and 1960s, promoted as means of capturing the full breadth of biblical and historical events. *Lawrence of Arabia* (1962) was filmed in Super Panavision 70, as was Stanley Kubrick's *2001: A Space Odyssey*, which offered a vision of what might be accomplished with the new technologies and an unorthodox screenplay. Projected onto a deeply curved screen in 70mm format with six-track sound, the film produced an unforgettable effect on audiences with its minimalist dialogue, stunning special effects, and controversial conclusion. The *Boston Globe*'s reviewer described it as "the world's most extraordinary film. Nothing like it has ever been shown in Boston before or, for that matter, anywhere." In January 2002, *2001* gained the number one ranking in the "Top 100 Essential Films of All Time" by the National Society of Film Critics.

Rather than immediately turning to the future, some of the new directors turned to the most iconic of American films, the western, which was quickly shorn of the predictability of the past. Films like *Shane* (1953) and *High Noon* (1952), in which the good guys were always discernible, gave way to moral ambiguity in films such as *McCabe and Mrs. Miller* (1971), dubbed an "anti-western" by director Robert Altman. Set in an isolated mountain town in 1902, Altman's West is a wasteland of filth, degradation, mindless violence, drug use, whoring, endless drunkenness, and capitalist enterprises built on murder, where there are no heroes. While films like 1969's *True Grit*, which brought an Oscar for John

Wayne, demonstrated the durability of the traditional western, the "anti-western" gained ground in the 1970s, in large part through the appeal of Clint Eastwood as "the Man with No Name," who had scored with the Italian-produced "spaghetti westerns" of the 1960s, and with Sergio Leone's *The Good, the Bad and the Ugly* (1966), scored by Ennio Morricone, being perhaps the most impressive of the nontraditional westerns of that decade. Don Siegel's 1970 *Two Mules for Sister Sara* had Eastwood reprise his role as a mysterious stranger and mercenary during the Mexican Revolution. In 1973's *High Plains Drifter*, Eastwood, once again the Man with No Name, perhaps even a ghost, rides into the isolated town of Lagos and, in the first several minutes, guns down three men who challenge him before he rapes a woman in a barn. Having cowed the townsfolk, Eastwood instructs them in how to fight off the gunmen who murdered their sheriff, whom they failed to aid as he was whipped to death. Eastwood returns at the film's climax, as the town burns, to kill all the evildoers before literally disappearing as he rides into the distance. John Wayne was so offended by the film that he wrote Eastwood, "That isn't what the West was all about. That isn't the American people who settled the country." Eastwood starred in another anti-western, *The Outlaw Josey Wales*, in 1976, as a farmer pursuing Union troops who had murdered his wife.

Elliot Silverstein's *A Man Called Horse* (1970) depicted the fate of a white man captured by Sioux who gradually comes to appreciate their culture and joins the tribe. That same year, Arthur Penn's *Little Big Man* cast Dustin Hoffman in variety of roles, during which he transitions from settler to gunslinger to drunk to Sioux warrior, managing to be present at most every major western event in the 1870s. Sidney Pollack's 1972 *Jeremiah Johnson* focuses on one trapper's battle with nature's challenges and Indian massacres, but also depicts Native Americans in a positive light and presents the US Cavalry as a callous genocidal force. The year 1972 also saw the premiere of John Huston's *The Life and Times of Judge Roy Bean*, with Paul Newman in the lead role. The drunken outlaw Bean rides into Vinegarroon, Texas, and after suffering a beating by town ruffians, appoints himself judge and the "law west of the Pecos." This is not John Wayne's West—Bean shoots adversaries in the back, robs their bodies, puts a man in a cage with a bear, and sentences prostitutes to remain in town as sex slaves. There are no heroes in white hats here. The real-life Roy Bean died in bed in 1903 in an alcoholic stupor.

Even as the traditional conception of the western was being deconstructed, crime films offered new perspectives on the underworld, as well as images of police who were presented as skirting the law when circumstances required. The era also featured films playing on public fears of crime, which sometimes produced revenge-seeking vigilantes. The year 1968's *Bullitt*, directed by Peter Yates, starred Paul Newman as a San Francisco police officer detailed to protect a mob informant, and prefigured some of the cinematic trends of the 1970s. These themes were given more dramatic treatment in films such as William Friedkin's gripping *The French Connection* (1971), the story of two New York City narcotics officers attempting to track down a massive shipment of heroin imported by Frenchman Alain Charnier. Narcotics officers Buddy Russo (Roy Scheider) and Jimmy "Popeye" Doyle (Gene Hackman) carry out their assignment in a decaying, trash-ridden New York City, employing tactics of dubious legality against suspects (often black). Perhaps most remembered for an unsurpassable heart-stopping car chase as Popeye recklessly races beneath elevated railway tracks to catch the assassin who tried to kill him, the film climaxes on a garbage-strewn Wards Island, where a police contingent confronts the New York gangsters who have purchased Charnier's heroin. In the midst of a shoot-out, Charnier escapes into a decaying factory, where Popeye pursues him, emptying his revolver into a shadowy figure, who is revealed to be a federal agent. As the film ends, viewers learn that Doyle and Russo were transferred out of narcotics and Charnier was never caught, leaving audiences with little but a sense of futility. Framed by a nerve-racking score, the film won Best Picture that year, but the 1975 sequel *French Connection II*, in which Hackman reprised his role, did not fare as well critically.

Two films sought to capitalize on *The French Connection*'s success. *Badge 373* (1973) brought "Eddie Ryan" (Robert Duvall) to the screen as famously tough cop Eddie Egan. Directed by Howard W. Koch, the film recapitulated a grim, filthy New York, where Ryan is compelled to resign after a Puerto Rican suspect "accidentally" falls off of a roof. Ryan spends the remainder of the film searching for the killer of his partner and uncovering a shipment of guns for Puerto Rican nationalists. The film failed at the box office and with critics. *The Seven-Ups* (1973), a reference to a police squad dedicated to solving crimes that carried sentences of seven years and up, brought Roy Scheider back to the screen, again roaming the streets of a grimy, crime-ridden New York in pursuit of a group of murderous gangsters. Too derivative of *The French Connection* (even including a car chase), the film was only a modest success.

Three years later, Martin Scorsese took viewers to the mean streets of New York once again, this time in *Taxi Driver* (1976), featuring Robert De Niro as Vietnam veteran Travis Bickle, a taxi driver disgusted by the human detritus he encounters on a nightly basis. Failing in his efforts to form a relationship with Betsy, an attractive campaign worker (Cybill Shepherd), Bickle purchases an arsenal of handguns, with the evident intent of assassinating the presidential candidate Betsy works for. Foiled at that, Bickle undertakes a personal crusade to save Iris, a twelve-year-old prostitute (Jodie Foster) from a lifetime of degradation, accosting and killing her pimp and several of his associates as he shoots his way to Iris's crib. Despite his murderous rampage, Bickle is played up in the media as a hero, and Iris is returned to her home.

Public anxiety about rising crime likely had much to do with the popularity of the Clint Eastwood vehicle *Dirty Harry* (1971), directed by Don Siegel. Eastwood portrays San Francisco police inspector Harry Callahan, whose reputation for skirting the law, disdain for suspects' rights, and openly expressed racism are the bane of his superiors. Tasked with tracking down the serial killer Scorpio (Andy Robinson), who murders civilians and police alike, Harry's unorthodox methodology is revealed when he responds to a bank robbery. Unlimbering a huge Smith and Wesson .44 Magnum revolver, Eastwood drops one shotgun-wielding robber at the bank's door before killing two others fleeing by car. Confronting the supine wounded robber, Eastwood levels his revolver at the man, who is reaching toward his dropped shotgun, and utters the film's most memorable monologue. "Uh uh," Callahan cautions, "I know what you're thinking. Did he fire six shots or only five? Well, you know, in all the excitement I sort of forgot myself." "But you got to remember," Callahan adds, "this is a .44 Magnum, the most powerful handgun in the world, and it will blow your head clean off. So you have to ask yourself one question . . . do I feel lucky?" Pausing for effect he adds, "Well . . . do ya, punk?" The robber shrinks back from the shotgun as police arrive and as Callahan, in a final taunt, aims the six-and-a-half-inch barrel at the cringing man's head, pulls the trigger on an empty chamber, and walks away smirking. On the trail of Scorpio, who seems to be a psychotic flower child, Callahan first corners him in a nighttime scene in a football stadium, where he drops the killer with a shot to the leg despite Scorpio's effort to surrender, an action that produces enthusiastic audience applause. Freed by "liberal" legalities, Scorpio next abducts a busload of schoolchildren. After a lengthy chase, Callahan runs him to ground and wounds him on a ramshackle pier at a gravel pit pond. Scorpio finds his pistol slightly out of reach, affording Callahan the chance to repeat his "do I feel lucky" taunt once more. Scorpio is not, and a final .44 caliber blast catapults his body into the pond as Callahan tosses away his inspector's badge.

Though *Dirty Harry* was preserved in the National Film Registry in the Library of Congress in 2012 for being "culturally, historically, and aesthetically significant," it drew considerable criticism at the time. Pauline Kael denounced the film's "fascist medievalism" and deemed it a "right-wing fantasy." Roger Ebert claimed, "The film's moral position is fascist." Gene Siskel termed its message "dangerous," and Andrew Sarris called the film "one of the most disturbing manifestations of police paranoia I have seen on the screen in a long time." Nevertheless, its message clearly resonated with a public weary of liberal courts, crime, and criminal rights, while gun dealers reported that they could not keep up with orders for the S&W .44 Magnum. The film was the fourth highest grossing of the year. Sequels *Magnum Force* (1973), *The Enforcer* (1976), and others in the 1980s proved popular and made Harry's later utterance, "Make my day," one of the decade's most memorable lines. In subsequent decades, the film was ranked highly on many lists and is recognized by film historians as one of 1971's best.

The concept of vigilante justice, by cops or citizens, clearly resonated with theatergoers, as the popularity of *Death Wish* (1974) demonstrated. Director Michael Winner's film told the story of Paul Kersey (Charles Bronson), whose wife is murdered and his daughter sexually assaulted by a local gang. Threatened by a mugger, Kersey warns him off with a homemade blackjack, soon graduates to handguns, and prowls the darkened streets of New York City, inviting attacks and killing several thugs. Though drawing negative comments from critics, the film proved popular, as did a sequel in 1982.

The decade also brought two films that sought to present positive views of the police. Richard Fleischer's *The New Centurions* (1972) depicted the daily dangers faced by Los Angeles policemen, receiving only modest reviews. The *New York Time*'s Roger Greenspun, seeming to damn with faint praise, deemed it an "awkwardly modern movie" that offered "pretty traditional" attitudes toward police. Far more controversial was Sidney Lumet's 1973 *Serpico*, featuring Al Pacino as undercover officer Frank Serpico in a semidocumentary examination of the real-life Serpico's eleven-year personal struggle against police corruption in New York, which earned him a bullet in the face when fellow officers refused to back him up in a drug bust. Serpico's heroic testimony before the Knapp Commission was crucial to reducing police corruption in New York. The film won critical acclaim and multiple awards.

The early 1970s fascination with crime produced some notable films about the criminal underworld. The decade produced arguably the most acclaimed American gangster film, Francis Ford Coppola's *The Godfather* (1972), which chronicled the rise of the Corleone crime family in New York City. With starring roles given to Marlon Brando, Al Pacino, Diane Keaton, James Caan, and Robert Duvall, the film was nominated in eleven categories and won three Oscars at the Forty-Fifth Academy Awards and for many years was the highest-grossing film of all time. Critical reception was universally positive. Vincent Canby wrote that Coppola had produced one of the "most brutal and moving chronicles of American life," proclaiming that it "transcends its immediate milieu and genre." Stanley Kubrick wrote unequivocally that *The Godfather* "could be the best movie ever made." Public fascination with the story of the Corleone family fueled two sequels. John Milius's *Dillinger* (1973), starring Warren Oates as the infamous gangster and Ben Johnson as his FBI pursuer Melvin Purvis, drew only modest attention and mixed critical reception. Terrence Malick's directorial debut, the much-underappreciated *Badlands* (1973), brought senseless and unpredictable crime into the heartland. Loosely based on the murder spree of Charles Starkweather, the film starred Martin Sheen as the demented killer Kit Carruthers and Sissy Spacek as his naive girlfriend Holly Sargis, following them through a series of killings that stretch from South Dakota to Montana. Though garnering chiefly negative reviews upon its release, the film won praise from Vincent Canby, who described *Badlands* as "a cool, sometimes brilliant, always ferociously American film," describing Sheen and Spacek as "the self-absorbed, cruel, possibly psychotic children of our time." In 2011, David Thomson wrote that *Badlands* was "by common consent . . . one of the most remarkable first feature films made in America."

Among the most underappreciated films of the era is William Friedkin's inappropriately titled *Sorcerer* (1977). Friedkin conceded that he selected the title in hopes that the public would associate the film with his extraordinarily successful *The Exorcist*, though "Sorcerer" turns out to be only the name painted on a truck in the film.

Friedkin explained that rather than having anything to do with the supernatural, the film was "about revenge, vengeance, betrayal—this is how I feel about life. . . . Fate is waiting around the corner to kick you in the ass." Loosely derived from Georges Arnaud's 1950 novel *The Wages of Fear*, the film follows the fates of four criminals from various countries who seek refuge in Porvenir, a South American hellhole village. The plot follows the desperate lives of the men (one being Roy Scheider as Jackie Scanlon, a hoodlum fleeing a New York mob family) as they seek to earn airfare and out the impoverished dictatorship by hauling two truckloads of volatile, nitroglycerine-covered dynamite over distant mountains to the

Figure 7.2. **An artist's rendition of the ominous and prehistoric looking truck named "Sorcerer," which gave its name to the William Friedkin film of the same title, with which he hoped to capitalize on audience association with his film *The Exorcist*. Rather, this underappreciated film pitted four men running from their pasts and likely fates against a harsh jungle landscape in a race to deliver explosives to a burning oil well in a nameless impoverished South American country.** Source: Wikimedia Commons / Toby Roan

site of an oil well to extinguish the blaze. Having traversed washed-out roads, treacherous bridges, and dense jungles, and killed murderous guerrillas, Scheider, the lone survivor, manages to drive "Sorcerer" back to the village, thus earning a significant cash payment. However, inevitable fate awaits him in the form of two mob hitmen sent to kill him. The film was largely ignored upon release, but decades later critics acknowledged *Sorcerer*'s genius, with Stephen King naming it first on his list of "20 movies that never disappoint" in 2009.

Projecting public fears of youth violence as well as dubious governmental rehabilitation schemes, *A Clockwork Orange* (1971) was Stanley Kubrick's brilliant realization of Anthony Burgess's novel about vicious, drug-fueled delinquents in a dystopian England. The film brought actor Malcolm McDowell growing fame and provoked mixed reactions, with some reviewers denouncing its misogynistic violence while others, like Vincent Canby, perceived conflicting messages, describing the award-winning film as "a brilliant and dangerous work."

Public anxiety over the violence and crime that pervaded much American film in the 1970s may have grown out of a social pathology that led some criminologists to label the decade as the beginning of the "Golden Age of Serial Killers." Indeed, the decade, begun even as the murderous acolytes of Charles Manson were going on trial, produced a number of murderers who kept cities, states, and entire regions in a state of anxiety. Northern California was the home ground of the notorious "Zodiac Killer," who between the late 1960s and early 1970s used both handguns and knives to brutally kill his victims. Zodiac claimed to have murdered thirty-seven individuals and was never apprehended. On the other coast, "Son of Sam" brought terror to New York City for a year beginning in the summer of 1976. Dubbed the ".44 Caliber Killer," Sam murdered mostly female victims, often as they sat in parked cars. In August 1977, New York City police arrested David Berkowitz, who claimed that he was driven to kill the six victims by his neighbor's dog, which Berkowitz insisted was possessed by a demon. He drew six life sentences. The roll call of monsters is too lengthy to fully recount here, but includes Rodney Alcala, the "*Dating Game* Killer"; William Bonin, Southern California's "Freeway Killer"; the infamous Ted Bundy, who killed more than thirty women; a cult responsible for the more than seventy-three "Zebra" murders; Wayne Williams, charged with twenty-three murders in the Atlanta area; Jeffrey

Dahmer, the "Milwaukee Cannibal," who cannibalized seventeen men and boys; and, of course, John Wayne Gacy, the "Killer Clown," who was convicted of thirty-three murders between 1972 and 1978.

Cops and crime did not monopolize the American screen in the early 1970s. Bob Rafelson's 1970 *Five Easy Pieces* brought Jack Nicholson to the screen as Bobby Dupea, a pianist who rejects the elitist pretensions of his artistically inclined family for work as an oilfield roughneck but finds little solace there either. Dupea is a lost soul, finally abandoning his working class girlfriend to hitch a ride on a passing truck. Peter Bogdanovich's *The Last Picture Show* (1971), nominated for eight Academy Awards, was a haunting black-and-white depiction of the emptiness of life in the dying rural Texas town of Anarene (shot in Archer City) where life choices are few and escape seems impossible. Mike Nichols's *Carnal Knowledge* (1971) returned Jack Nicholson to the screen together with Art Garfunkel and Candice Bergen in an examination of modern sexual mores. Though challenged by some groups for its frank discussions of sexual practices, the film was tame compared to 1972's *Last Tango in Paris*, directed by Bernardo Bertolucci and starring Marlon Brando, and *Deep Throat*, whose director chose to be acknowledged by a pseudonym. The latter is said to have fueled "The Golden Age of Porn" from 1969 to 1984. Reviews were understandably mixed, though pornographer Al Goldstein offered the most humorous when he wrote, "I was never so moved by a theatrical performance since stuttering through my own bar mitzvah."

The year 1973 produced several films that abjured crime and sex. George Lucas's *American Graffiti* looked backward to an idyllic past in the coming-of-age film set in 1962. Later in the decade, *Grease* (1978) offered the same appeal. Hal Ashby's underappreciated *The Last Detail* (1973) starred Jack Nicholson as a Navy chief detailed to deliver a less-than-bright sailor to a naval prison, struggling along the way to provide some final pleasures for the hapless convict. Nicholson scored again at mid-decade in Miloš Forman's film adaption of Ken Kesey's *One Flew over the Cuckoo's Nest* (1975). John G. Avildsen's *Save the Tiger* (1973) relates the story of an apparel factory owner (Jack Lemmon) determined to find some meaning in his vacuous life as he is continually haunted by his World War II days. The year's Best Picture Oscar went to *The Sting* (1973), George Hill's tale of an elaborately contrived con game, with its Scott Joplin score also a winner. Martin Scorsese scored an early success with *Alice Doesn't Live Here Anymore* (1974), the moving story of a widow's struggle to build a new life out of the wreckage of a failed first marriage.

The year 1974 brought two compelling mysteries to the screen, with Francis Ford Coppola's *The Conversation* striking a tone of intense paranoia as the Watergate scandal concluded. Featuring Gene Hackman as a lonely surveillance professional who believes he has inadvertently stumbled upon a murder plot, the film concludes with Hackman, fearing for his life, ripping his house apart in search of probably nonexistent listening devices. A standout of the era, and often cited as signaling the end of the old Hollywood system, is Roman Polanski's *Chinatown*, sometimes described as a "neo-noir" mystery, featuring Jack Nicholson as a private detective whose pursuit of a water-diversion scheme in Los Angeles leads him into a web of public corruption, private deceits, incest, and ultimately the triumph of wealth and the power it grants over the public good. The final sequence is guaranteed to leave viewers shocked at life's injustices.

The era did abound with comedies to leaven the more disheartening theater fare, with Woody Allen making multiple contributions with *Bananas* (1971), *Play It Again, Sam* (1972), *Sleeper* (1973), and *Annie Hall* (1977), arguably his masterpiece. Mel Brooks's *Blazing Saddles* (1974) was an absurdist western parody released in the same year as his *Young Frankenstein*. John Landis's *Animal House* (1978), though founded on a minimal plot, was hailed by Roger Ebert for its "manic energy." Ironically, audiences also flocked to disaster films such as *Airport* (1970), *The Towering Inferno* (1974), *Earthquake* (1974), and *The Poseidon Adventure* (1972).

The year 1975 produced a diversity of widely hailed films. Kubrick's epic *Barry Lyndon*, derived from William Thackeray's novel, followed the rise and fall of an aspiring young man whose episodic life in the eighteenth century ends in disability and poverty. Sidney Lumet's *Dog Day Afternoon* starred Al Pacino as one of a hapless pair of bank robbers whose efforts to escape capture end in tragedy. Hal Ashby's *Shampoo* is a satirical examination of the sexual mores of the era. Robert Altman's star-studded *Nashville* is an effort to meld the musical culture of that city with a bizarre third-party presidential candidacy, resulting in a what Pauline Kael termed "the funniest epic vision of America ever to reach the screen," though it climaxes with the pointless assassination of the beloved singer Barbara Jean (Ronee Blakley) at the city's faux Parthenon.

The film that most dramatically captured the growing the public's growing free-floating frustrations, as well as revealed the callous practices behind network television production, was Paddy Chayefsky's *Network* (1976), starring Peter Finch as Howard Beale, a newscaster for the failing United Broadcasting System (UBS) who is driven to increasingly dramatic measures to stay on the air, even threatening suicide on live television. The network's president, desperate for ratings, arranges for a docudrama series, *The Mao Tse-tung Hour*, hosted by the terrorist group Ecumenical Liberation Army (ELA), even as the *Howard Beale Show* scores with Beale's signature rant, "I'm mad as hell and I'm not going to take this anymore!" wins a mass following. As Beale's ratings decline, network executives agree to his televised assassination by the ELA. A concluding voice-over describes Beale's demise as "the first known instance of man who was killed because he had lousy ratings." Critic Roger Ebert praised it as "a supremely well-acted and intelligent film . . . that attacks not only television but also most of the other ills of the seventies."

Rosemary's Baby (1968) prefigured some of the horror films of the 1970s such as *It's Alive* (1974), which featured a murderous mutant infant. *The Omen* (1976) and *Damien: Omen II* (1978) were among a number of films that focused on the demonic, though *The Exorcist* (1973) proved the most convincingly horrific with its compelling presentation of demonic possession. *The Amityville Horror* (1979) closed out the decade, depicting the travails of a New York family driven from their home by evil spirits. Though the film did well financially, Roger Ebert captured the critical response when he described the film as "dreary and terminally depressing"

Though African Americans, such as Sidney Poitier, had starring roles in films in the 1960s, Melvin Van Peebles's *Sweet Sweetback's Badasssss Song* (1971) prefigured the more daring "blaxploitation" films of the 1970s. The most noteworthy was Gordon Parks's *Shaft* (1971), which starred Richard Roundtree as a New York private detective and garnered an Academy Award for Isaac Hayes's masterful score. Sequels *Shaft's Big Score!* (1972) and *Shaft in Africa* (1973) likewise proved popular. Parks's *Super Fly* (1972), directed by Gordon Park's son Gordon Parks Jr., focuses on a New York cocaine dealer who affects gaudy pimp fashions and drives an outlandish pimpmobile, his only redeeming quality being his ability to get over on white gangsters and his expressed desire to get out of the drug trade, which he describes as "a rotten game," but "it's the only one the [white] Man left us to play." Blaxploitation extended into horror with *Blacula* (1972) and crime-fighting with *Foxy Brown* (1974). The decade also brought some serious dramas such as *Claudine* (1974), about a welfare cheat who is valiantly struggling to keep her family together. The low-budget *Killer of Sheep* (1978), directed by Charles Burnett, depicts the crushing, impoverished life of a slaughterhouse worker who fights to keep his family together.

Science fiction and fantasy lagged until the later 1970s, with the exception of Steven Spielberg's *Close Encounters of the Third Kind* (1977), which depicted friendly aliens, drawing large audiences. The following year, Guy Hamilton brought *Superman* to the screen, winning enough devotees to fuel several sequels. With *Star Trek: The Motion Picture* (1979), Robert Wise brought the crew of the *Enterprise* to theaters, leading to numerous sequels.

The truly exceptional science fiction film of the decade, now considered a classic, was Ridley Scott's *Alien* (1979), which Roger Ebert described as "one of the scariest old-fashioned space operas I can remember." The film's eerie soundtrack, masterful pacing, unexpected shocks, and often horrific visual effects provoked audience screams. The plot involves the crew of the deep-space tug *Nostromo* (the name taken from a Joseph Conrad novel) that has been rerouted by a computer command to investigate the source of a signal emanating from a forbidding uncharted planetoid. A scouting team discovers and enters a bizarre derelict alien ship, after which they do everything that the audience is silently pleading with them not to do, resulting in a crewman (John Hurt) having a hideous spidery octopoid creature leap on his helmet's faceplate from a leathery egg, burn through it, and implant an embryo within his body. The horror has only begun, however, as back on the *Nostromo*, the larval form explodes out of its victim's chest and rapidly mutates into a hulking reptilian monstrosity that quickly and horribly reduces the six-person crew to four, including the android science officer. First officer Ripley (Sigourney Weaver), who seeks to learn from the ship's computer how the creature might be killed, discovers an encrypted corporate directive theretofore known only to the ship's science officer. Inquiring "What is Special Order 937?" she finds to her horror that it directed the *Nostromo* to gather a specimen of the unknown organism for the corporation's weapons division regardless of the possible dangers. "ALL OTHER PRIORITIES RESCINDED," the ominous order reads, "CREW EXPENDABLE." In a final nerve-racking sequence, following the destruction of the deceitful android, who had known of the order, and the deaths of her final two crewmates, Ripley arms the ship's self-destruct system and flees down seemingly endless steam-obscured darkened passageways as sirens scream and a voiced countdown blares. Only seconds before the destruction of the *Nostromo*, she escapes in the ship's shuttle, only to find the deadly creature secreted aboard with her. Donning a space suit and decompressing the shuttle, she succeeds in blowing the toothy horror out of a hatch. *Alien* won numerous awards, including a 1980 Academy Award for "Best Visual Effects," wide critical acclaim, and lucrative box office receipts, inspiring three sequels and, decades later, two "prequels."

While films about the Vietnam War lagged, the early years of the 1970s brought two major films about World War II. *Tora! Tora! Tora!* a joint Japanese-American product about the Japanese attack on Pearl Harbor in 1941, drew mixed receptions. Roger Ebert called it "one of the deadest, dullest blockbusters ever made." Nevertheless, it was exceedingly popular and profitable in Japan, and pulled in the ninth-highest gross in North America in 1970. That same year, Americans flocked to theaters to see Franklin Shaffner's bio-epic *Patton*, which starred George C. Scott as the controversial World War II general. The film celebrated Patton's determination in the face of setbacks, his strategic brilliance, and the heroism of US troops in Africa, Italy, and Europe, winning seven Academy Awards as well as critical acclaim.

By decade's end, much had changed as Americans confronted two major traumas. Nixon was gone, driven from office by the Watergate scandal, every shabby detail of which was recounted in Alan J. Pakula's *All the President's Men* (1976), fueling a growing public cynicism about politics. A much deeper psychic scar was left by the Vietnam War, however, which was not seriously addressed until the end of the decade. Not until 1978 did directors begin to seriously wrestle with the nation's most divisive war, as Sidney J. Furie's *The Boys in Company C*, Ted Post's *Go Tell the Spartans*, and Michael Cimino's *The Deer Hunter* compelled theatergoers to begin confronting the harsh realities of that conflict. Cimino's lengthy portrayal of the experiences of three Pennsylvania steelworkers, both at home and in the war, swept up nine Academy Award nominations, won five, and stunned audiences with its often gut-wrenching scenes of war. Leonard Maltin succinctly termed the film as "a sensitive, painful, evocative work." Hal Ashby's 1978 *Coming Home*, which starred Jane Fonda and Jon Voight, dealt with returning veterans disabled physically and emotionally, proved popular approval, and won the Best Actress and Best Actor Academy Awards.

Without question, the Vietnam War film that sparked the greatest controversy in 1979 was Francis Ford Coppola's *Apocalypse Now*, a monumental undertaking that was 238 days in the making. Filmed in the Philippines, the film starred a galaxy of well-known actors, notably Martin Sheen, Robert Duvall, and Marlon Brando. Coppola described the film as a "metaphorical retelling of Joseph Conrad's short classic *Heart of Darkness*, set in Vietnam during war in 1968." The film depicts US Army Captain Benjamin Willard's (Martin Sheen) classified mission up the Nung River into Cambodia, where he is to locate and "terminate with extreme prejudice" rogue Special Forces Colonel Walter Kurtz (Marlon Brando), whose "methods have become unsound." Aboard a river patrol boat, Willard witnesses the myriad insane aspects of the war during the river journey. After locating the ancient temple at which the demented colonel has assembled a private army, Willard hacks him to death, as the dying Kurtz mutters, "The horror! The horror!" The words were borrowed from the ending of *Heart of Darkness*. Back on the river patrol boat, Willard begins the begins the journey downriver, perhaps back to sanity.

Apocalypse Now was released in August 1979 after considerable editing; even then the theatrical version ran 136 minutes. A visual and audio *tour de force* grounded on remarkable cinematography and sound, including a stunning combination of the two as Wagner's "Ride of the Valkyrie" is broadcast by loudspeakers when Colonel Bill Kilgore's (Robert Duvall) helicopter assault armada swoops in on a Vietcong village. Though rock music common to the era is heard throughout the film, it is the Doors' eerie "The End" that accompanies the opening sequence of Willard's mental anguish in a Saigon hotel room and his murder of Kurtz at the film's conclusion. Like other films of the era, *Apocalypse Now* yielded numerous memorable lines, such as Kilgore's "I love the smell of napalm in the morning. . . . It smells like . . . victory," and Chef's prophetic "never get off the boat" after an unexpected jungle encounter with a tiger.

Those critics who lauded the film proved over time to be in the majority. Roger Ebert, who wrote in 1979 that it "achieves greatness not by analyzing our 'experience in Vietnam,' but by recreating, in characters and images, something of the experience," later described *Apocalypse Now* as "one of the greatest of all films, because it pushes beyond the others, into the dark places of the soul." Since its release, the film has sparked discussion about whether it is pro- or antiwar. Coppola insists that more than being antiwar, "it is even more anti-lie." The controversy provoked by the film compelled Americans to begin to sort out their thoughts about a war that they had tried to ignore since 1975.

As early as 1974, critic Stephen Farber perceived Hollywood's turn to "a New Sensationalism" that would produce "gaudier and more lurid" films dedicated to "sensation and visceral shock." The era of the New Cinema (or New Hollywood, as some termed it) came to a slow end at mid-decade as studios discovered the attributes of the "blockbuster," many of which were the creations of the newer generation of directors. Steven Spielberg biographer Molly Haskell affirmed the transition, noting that the "new guys'" fixation with films "seeded with guilt, pessimism, futility" and founded on stories that were "bleak or open-ended" was ending. The celebration of such films, she writes, "will prove to be a media moment rather than a changing of the guard, a rejuvenation rather than a revolution." The so-called "Golden Age" of the "the movie brats" was, she writes, "part mirage, part myth, part fluke and aberration, and was hardly a blueprint for any conceivable golden future." In retrospect, her harsh judgment proved correct. One could argue that the big-budget, broad-distribution blockbuster phenomenon became discernible as early as 1972–1973 with the huge grosses of *The Exorcist* and *The Godfather*, but the truly jaw-dropping receipts become evident after mid-decade, with most film historians crediting Spielberg's *Jaws*. The well-paced tale of a monster great white shark terrorizing a New England beach town sends the shark-fishing boat *Orca*, crewed by its skipper Quint (Robert Shaw), a marine biologist (Richard Dreyfuss), and the town police chief (Roy Scheider) in search of the deadly leviathan. The hunters become the hunted as the shark pursues them until the boat's engines burn out, after which the huge shark pulls a Moby Dick, rams and sinks the stalled *Orca*, and gobbles up the shark-hating Quint. As in *Alien*, allowing the audience to initially view the creature only partially or dimly heightened suspense immensely; in this case, it was due to the serial failures of the three mechanical sharks. *Jaws* opened in 409 theaters and in less than three months outgrossed *The Godfather*. The film won three Academy Awards and mostly positive reviews, Rex Reed being typical in his comments that it offered "nerve frying" action and that it was "a gripping horror film that works beautifully in every department."

Those seeking refuge from horror films could find solace in the feel-good *Rocky* movies of 1976 and 1979 (starring Sylvester Stallone), which generated not only huge profits but also numerous sequels. Additional escapism was to be found in George Lucas's *Star Wars* (1977), which spawned sequels and prequels into the twenty-first century, combining fantasy with science fiction, ultimately becoming the highest grossing of the blockbusters. Its soon-to-be-iconic on-screen introductorion, "A long time ago in a galaxy far, far away," and fanfare offered audiences a desperately sought distancing from contemporary problems.

Those who preferred escapism melded with cartoonlike antics and an absurd screenplay could attend Hal Needhan's 1977 *Smokey and the Bandit*, which successfully showcased several of the most lowbrow characteristics of the decade. Framed around an unlikely plot to bootleg four hundred cases of Coors beer from Arkansas to Georgia, the film introduced audiences to Bo "Bandit" Darville (Burt Reynolds), Cledus "Snowman" Snow (Jerry Reed), and Sheriff Buford T. Justice (Jackie Gleason) as the central cast in a fast-paced cross-country race as "Snowman" drives the beer-laden truck and "Bandit" pilots a 1977 Pontiac Trans Am with the goal of distracting law enforcement, essentially by driving fast and recklessly (ironically, government-mandated emission controls had reduced the once mighty Trans Am to a mere two hundred horsepower V8). Melding fast car chases and numerous wrecks, illegal activity, disregard of the law, CB radios, and Jerry Reed's soon-to-be top hit "East Bound and Down," the film flopped in New York but proved immensely popular in the South (Billy Bob Thornton told Reynolds that Southerners considered the film a documentary) and nearly outgrossed *Star Wars*. The film's regional and elite appeal was evident in Leonard Maltin's sneer that it was "about as subtle as *The Three Stooges*," but the film website Rotten Tomatoes captured the popular response with the comment, "Not much in the head, but plenty beneath the hood . . . infectious fun with lots of car wrecks." The film's impact can be partly measured in subsequent massively increased sales of the Pontiac

Trans Am, two sequels, and the popular 1980s television series "The Dukes of Hazzard."

American films changed much in the 1970s. The New Cinema of the early years of the decade, dominated by directors, gave way to a cinematic culture dominated by executives, agents, and lawyers. It was further eroded by a new emphasis on advertising and marketing. Another change involved the mass release of films into hundreds of theaters rather than attempting to gradually build interest through selective release. By the late 1970s, new technologies such as videocassette players altered the very concept of audience as home viewing became a reality, as did cable television, though only 7.5 percent of US households subscribed as of 1978. As film historian Peter Lev notes, American film in the 1970s "was remarkable for its pluralism, its heterogeneity." This "golden period of American cinema," he asserts, grew out of the "excitement of a dialogue between filmmakers," which led to a "debate on what America is and what America should be."

The case could easily be made that those same creative and inclusive impulses shaped television during the 1970s. On broadcast television, there were hints of the coming inclusion of minorities and controversial issues. *Julia* featured Diahann Carroll as a nurse as early as 1968; private eye *Mannix* had Gail Fisher as an office assistant. One of the most famous episodes of *Star Trek* featured television's first interracial kiss in which the starship *Enterprise's* black communications officer, Lieutenant Uhura, kissed Captain James Kirk (admittedly because of alien mind control). The same show put Japanese American George Takei (who later came out as gay) on the screen as the ship's helmsman. The *Bill Cosby Show* premiered in 1969, a comedy featuring Cosby as a physical education teacher. *The Mary Tyler Moore Show* (1970) foreshadowed the numerous shows that would feature independent, often single women leaving the home to face the larger world's challenges and confront controversial subject matter, notably sex. The shows that had dominated the airwaves since the 1950s, mostly westerns, variety shows, and wholesome family comedies, gave way before the onslaught of more diverse and socially relevant offerings.

Precursors to some of the changes can be found in the late 1960s, but the 1970s saw shows featuring women and minorities blossom. If the Top Ten Nielsen ratings tell us anything about American viewers, they remained attracted to soap operas, family comedies, and dramas (*The Partridge Family*, *The Brady Bunch*, *The Waltons*, and *Dallas*), as well as to westerns such as *Bonanza* and *Gunsmoke* (canceled only in 1975) and *Little House on the Prairie*. Police and private-eye shows, which ran the gamut from the comedic to dramatic, numbered twenty in 1976. Variety shows such as *The Sonny and Cher Comedy Hour*, *Tony Orlando and Dawn*, and *The Dick Cavett Show* retained some popularity, as did medical shows (*Marcus Welby, MD* and *Quincy, ME*). Nostalgia for the 1950s drew viewers to *Happy Days* and spin-offs like *Laverne and Shirley* and, for the desperately nostalgic, *The Waltons*, set in the 1930s.

Perhaps the most noticeable programming change was in shows featuring independent women, a path forged with Marlo Thomas's *That Girl* (1966–1971). In 1970, the truly groundbreaking *Mary Tyler Moore Show* (which spun off *Rhoda*, *Phyllis*, and *Lou Grant*) premiered, featuring a single woman determined to forge her own life path and finding employment as a production assistant at a foundering Minneapolis television station. Consistently in the Nielsen Top Ten and garnering twenty-nine Emmy Awards, the show, which ran until 1977, fearlessly addressed contemporary issues concerning premarital sex, homosexuality, equal pay for women, marital infidelity, divorce, and death (through the unforgettable "Chuckles Bites the Dust" episode). Moore's character remained courageously single throughout the show's run. In 1977, the show won a Peabody Award that lauded it for "a consistent standard of excellence—and for a sympathetic portrayal of a career woman in today's changing society." In 2007, *Time* named the show as one of "17 Shows that Changed TV." Moore's show helped pave the way for *Maude*, in which actress Bea Arthur wrestled with the issue of having an abortion, as well as comedies such as *Alice* and the variety show *The Carol Burnett Show*. Other shows featuring women ran the gamut from the bizarre *Mary Hartman*, to *Wonder Woman*, *The Bionic Woman*, *Charlie's Angel's*, and *Police Woman*.

A major contributor to the change in television was producer Norman Lear, whose *All in the Family*, premiering in 1971, addressed contemporary issues through the bigoted working-class Archie Bunker's clashes with his liberal son-in-law (Rob Reiner), winning Emmys for actors Carroll O'Connor and Jean Stapleton. Spin-off *Maude* outlasted *Archie's Place* and *Gloria*, but the original show was honored by the Television Critics Association with its Heritage Award for its "social and cultural impact on society." Yet another spin-off from *All in the Family* was *The Jeffersons*, which featured Archie's upwardly mobile black neighbor, George Jefferson, which ran from 1975 to 1985, receiving fourteen Emmy Award nominations. *The Jeffersons* was preceded by *The Flip Wilson Show*, a variety program featuring the comedian that ran from 1970 to 1974 and won two Emmy Awards. *Sanford and Son* hit the airwaves in 1972 and ran through 1977, featuring comedian Redd Foxx as a cantankerous junk dealer and named by *Time* in 2007 as among "The 100 Best TV Shows of All Time." *Good Times*, premiering in 1974, was yet another spin-off of *All in the Family* running through 1979, depicting the challenges faced by a black family living in Chicago public housing. Featuring Esther Rolle and John Amos as Florida and James Evans, the series was nominated for numerous awards and won TV Land's Impact Award in 2007.

It was a series about the history and impact of African slavery that drew the largest television audience to date in 1977 when the miniseries *Roots* premiered on ABC. Featuring a stellar cast, the eight-part series followed the travails of Kunta Kinte (LeVar Burton) and his descendants from capture and enslavement, through the horrors of plantation slavery, and finally to the Civil War and Reconstruction. *Roots* received thirty-seven Emmy nominations and won nine. The Nielsen Media Research records that between 130 and 140 million Americans watched the series, the largest viewership ever recorded.

Oddly, *Chico and the Man* was the only television series that featured a Latino, that being the Chicano Freddie Prinze. The show, which ran from 1974 to 1978, grew out of a Cheech and Chong skit and was disrupted by Prinze's suicide in 1977. The producers replaced Prinze with twelve-year-old Gabriel Melgar as Raul, who came under the care of Ed ("the Man"), played by Jack Albertson. Adding Charo to the cast as an aunt from Spain was not adequate to salvage the show.

Reality television made its debut in 1973 with PBS's controversial *An American Family*, which focused on the Loud family of Santa Barbara, California, in a series of twelve episodes that ran between January and March. Intended to chronicle the lives of a typical middle-class family, the series ended up following the outing of their son Lance as gay and the breakup, separation, and eventual divorce of Bill and Pat Loud after twenty-one years of marriage. The show drew more than 10 million viewers and in 2003 was named by *TV Guide* as number 32 in the top 50 television shows.

Musical theater in the 1970s spanned a variety of genres. 1971 suggested a renewed interest in religious-themed musicals, as *Godspell* and *Jesus Christ Superstar* drew large audiences. That same year, *Grease* again spoke to 1950s nostalgia. Tony Award winners in 1970 included *Applause* and *Company*, while 1971 saw the same honor go to *Follies* and *Two Gentlemen from Verona*. Stephen Sondheim's *A Little Night Music* scored a Tony in 1973, as did *A Raisin in the Sun*. That same year brought *The Rocky Horror Picture Show*, the film version of which became a cult classic. *The Wiz* was brought to Broadway in 1975, offering an African American version of the traditional Frank Baum tale. *A Chorus Line* won a Tony the same year, and *The Comedy of Errors* was similarly awarded in 1977. The year 1977's theatrical blockbuster was the award-winning *Annie*, while the following year saw *Ain't Misbehavin'* also win a Tony. The decade's end brought both the uplifting *Songbook* and the more ominous *Sweeney Todd: The Demon Barber of Fleet Street*, reflecting the wide variety of American theatrical musicals.

Far from being a decade of quiescence or stagnation in the visual arts, the 1970s brought a dramatically new look to American film as the New Cinema and the New Hollywood transformed the art, captivating audiences with presentations of a grittier, sometimes more sordid America, as well as providing escapist entertainment. In the aftermath of the turbulent and transformative 1960s, television could no longer offer images of only a white, patriarchal America, but was driven (by ratings and financial reasons, if not by loftier motives) to produce programs featuring minorities and independent women. As had been the case with film, television presented more realistic images of a rapidly changing society.

❖

Steven Spielberg was having a problem with sharks—three of them, to be exact. On location on Martha's Vineyard, Massachusetts, in the shallow coastal waters offshore in May 1974, Spielberg and crew were struggling to complete filming *Jaws* for Universal Studios. With an oft-rewritten screenplay drawn from Peter Benchley's 1974 novel, the twenty-six-year-old director hoped to bring to cinematic life the story of a monstrous great white shark that terrorizes the fictional New England town of Amity Island. An initial plan to use a trained shark never got beyond the talking stage. The backup plan had been to use films of real great white sharks shot off the Australian coast, but that had proved unworkable. A final plan involved three mechanical sharks, all nicknamed Bruce after Spielberg's lawyer, Bruce Ramer. The full-size pneumatically powered sharks included a "sea-sled shark" that could be towed, and two "platform sharks" that could be used for either left-to-right or right-to-left shots, as their opposite sides revealed the complex array of tubing by which they were operated; each required fourteen operators. Problems arose first in July when the platform on which the half-sided sharks could be towed capsized as it was being placed on the seabed. All the sharks proved highly vulnerable to ocean conditions and salt water. Their neoprene skin absorbed salt water, causing them to swell bizarrely, and in almost every scene they could be counted on to malfunction. In large part due to these issues, twelve-hour days often produced only four hours of film.

The unreliability of the mechanical sharks compelled Spielberg to make a decision that made *Jaws* one of the most terrifying movies of all time. The shooting script was revised to leave the shark largely unseen. The creature's first victim, a teenage girl who enters nighttime waters to swim, is abruptly seized by an unknown entity, jerked to and fro, and then disappears, the mutilated remains of her body discovered on the beach the following day. When a young boy floating on a rubber raft off a swimming beach is attacked before a crowd of beachgoers, the audience is shown only the briefest glimpse of the massive shark as it rolls. Another attack in an inlet reveals the huge size of the shark's dorsal fin before its massive jaws are revealed as it engulfs a sailboat occupant who has fallen into the water. The shark's proximity is regularly signaled by a pattern of ominous alternating bass notes, part of a score written by John Williams, who intended the theme to represent the shark's inexorable menace—"instinctual, relentless, unstoppable." Making the shark an unseen or partially seen threat heightened audience anticipation and anxiety. The shark is not seen in its entirety until late in the second half of the film.

The well-known plot revolves around three main characters, Martin Brody, the town's police chief (Roy Scheider), oceanographer Matt Hooper (Richard Dreyfuss), and grizzled shark fisherman Quint (Robert Shaw), who offers to kill the beast for $10,000. Brody, Hooper, and Quint set out to track down their quarry in Quint's well-worn boat *Orca*. Audience anxiety is incrementally increased by the trio's encounters with their intended prey, whose enormous head and mouth emerge from the waters astern of the boat as Brody tosses chum, provoking his memorable line, "You're gonna need a bigger boat." The sea-sled shark makes its first appearance as it swims down the length of the *Orca* and Quint estimates that the beast is "a twenty-five-footer." A lengthy chase and struggle with the harpooned shark conclude as Quint heads the *Orca* into shallower water with the intent of drowning the creature, but the hunters become the prey when Quint burns out the boat's engines. Hooper disappears from the scene when, outfitted in scuba gear, he is lowered into the water in a shark cage, equipped with a poison-tipped spear, only to flee for the safety of the sea floor when the shark smashes the cage. The murderous leviathan next assaults the crippled boat, thrusting its bulk over the smashed transom of the sinking *Orca*, finally revealing its horrific size as Quint futilely struggles to avoid sliding into the monster's toothy maw, which engulfs him in an agonizingly graphic scene. As the *Orca* settles and the shark circles to attack again, Brody takes refuge on the boat's tilting mast, finally dispatching the shark with a rifle shot that detonates a tank of compressed air that had been jammed into its jaws, transforming the beast into massive bloody hunks. Hooper emerges unharmed topside, as the bloody, headless carcass of the monster sinks into the depths.

Originally planned to be completed in fifty-five days, *Jaws* wrapped in October 1974 after 159 days of shooting. Spielberg fretted, "I would never work again because no one had ever taken a film one hundred hours over schedule." He need not have worried. After test screenings, Universal chairman Lew Wasserman commented, "I want this picture to run all summer long." Indeed, some film historians credit *Jaws* with establishing the tradition of the summer blockbuster, with major studios backing directors to whom they gave greater independence than in the past. Given the profits that such films generated, this was a formula that the major studios could eagerly embrace.

Jaws opened across the nation on June 20 and after just seventy-eight days overtook *The Godfather* as the highest-grossing North American film, its initial release bringing in over $123 million. The critical reception was equally encouraging. Pauline Kael described it as "the most cheerfully perverse scary movie ever made." Roger Ebert called it "a sensationally effective action picture, a scary thriller that works all the better because it's populated with characters that have been developed into human beings." Frank Rich of the *New York Times* touched upon the film's success when he wrote, "It speaks well of this director's gifts that some of the most frightening sequences in *Jaws* are those where we don't even see the shark." With his second major film behind him (*The Sugarland Express* was the first) Steven Spielberg was destined for a succession of cinematic successes.

A product of Cincinnati, Ohio, Steven Spielberg was born to Arnold and Leah Spielberg on December 18, 1946. As an Orthodox Jew whose family had lost many members in the Holocaust, Spielberg often struggled to come to grips with his faith, conceding that he was uncomfortable with Orthodox practices. As his family grew with three new sisters and moved to Haddon Township, New Jersey, Steven did poorly in school, distracted by a growing fascination with radio and television. Convinced that he could detect voices through televised static, he also was prone to an overactive imagination, coming to fear a copse of trees outside his bedroom window, which assumed ominous shapes in the dark. These and other childhood fears would later be incorporated in some of his films. The Spielbergs moved to Phoenix, Arizona, in early 1957, where his interest in filmmaking began to take shape. With an 8mm camera gifted by his father, Steven earned a Boy Scout merit badge for photography with a nine-minute western titled *The Last Gunfight*. At age fourteen, Steven produced *Fighter Squad*, a much more complex forty-minute film that won a statewide competition. In 1964, his science fiction film *Firelight* premiered at a local theater and presaged his adult effort *Close Encounters of the Third Kind* (1977). During the summer of 1964, Spielberg did journeyman work as a volunteer assistant in the editorial department of Universal Studios. Shortly afterward, the family moved to Saratoga, California, where he graduated from high school in 1965, a year before his parents separated. Steven moved to Los Angeles with his father, where he was admitted to the Long Beach campus of California State University.

Spielberg's academic career proved short, though he caught George Lucas's student film *THX 1138* (1971) at UCLA, which left a lasting impression. In 1968, Universal Studios signed him to write and direct a short film, which was released as *Amblin'* and deeply impressed the studio's vice president Sidney Sheinberg, who offered Spielberg a seven-year television directing contract. The twenty-one-year-old dropped out of college the following year, just as the first wave of the New Cinema was hitting theaters. But Spielberg already envisioned the sort of film he hoped to direct. "I don't want to make films like Antonioni or Fellini," he confided to a student reporter. "I don't want just the elite. I want everybody to enjoy my films." For the time being, however, Spielberg's directorial talents were focused on television, directing an episode of *Night Gallery* as well as *Owen Marshall, Counselor at Law, Columbo, The Psychiatrist*, and the first episode of *Marcus Welby, MD*. Universal soon signed him to direct four television films, one of which, *Duel*, pitted a hapless Dennis Weaver against an evidently demonic semitruck in a chase across a sparsely settled West, winning high ratings on American television and winning critical and commercial success in Europe as a feature-length film.

Spielberg's *The Sugarland Express* (1974), based on a true incident, starred Goldie Hawn as Lou Jean Poplin, the ditzy wife of minor criminal Clovis, who conspires to spring him from a prison camp and reclaim their infant son Langston from foster care. The path to the fatal, tragic ending begins with the kidnapping of a state trooper and continues as a fleet of police cars pursue the couple across Texas. The pursuit ends at the Rio Grande, where a wounded Clovis, victim of Lou Jean's irrational obsession, dies from a gunshot wound. Opening to largely positive reviews, the film led *The Hollywood Reporter* to announce that "a major new director is in our midst." Pauline Kael described Spielberg as "that rarity among directors—a born entertainer."

Jaws not only took in three Academy Awards for 1975 (though not for direction) but flooded the nation with a single unforgettable image; the movie poster featuring a massive shark with open jaws closing in on an unsuspecting swimmer from below was ubiquitous and soon made its way to T-shirts and other paraphernalia. Despite the film's tremendous success, Spielberg wisely rejected offers to direct sequels, which became successively ridiculous and commercially disastrous. Having driven Americans from the water, Spielberg sought to next turn their gaze skyward as *Close Encounters of the Third Kind* (1977) took shape. These aliens were benevolent, however, and the film's astounding visual effects proved enormously appealing, however absurd the aspects of the plot. The film captured two Academy Awards, though one for directing still proved elusive. Spielberg's friend George Lucas trumped him that year with *Star Wars*.

Not all of Spielberg's films proved as successful as his early efforts. *1941*, a 1979 action-comedy set in a nervous Los Angeles in the days after the Pearl Harbor attack, was described by one wit as "Animal House Goes to War" and was only marginally humorous. The film did reasonably well commercially, but Charles Champlin of the *Los Angeles Times* savaged it as "the most conspicuous waste since the last major oil spill, which it somewhat resembles." If the 1970s ended on something of a sour note for Spielberg, he was on the verge of major directorial fame in the 1980s. He teamed with Lucas to film *Raiders of the Lost Ark* (1981), which led to a series of popular though formulaic sequels. In 1982, Spielberg looked to the sky again for *E.T. the Extra-Terrestrial*, which was ecstatically received at the Cannes Film Festival and won three Academy Awards. Spielberg's filmography during the 1980s and 1990s is immense, including films ranging from the *Indiana Jones* series to those he produced or co-produced through his Amblin Entertainment company, including *The Goonies*, *The Money Pit*, *Back to the Future*, and *Who Framed Roger Rabbit?* There were missteps along the way, such as *Always* (1989), but directorial glory finally came in 1993 with *Schindler's List*, as Spielberg won his long-sought Best Director Academy Award. Marrying actress Kate Capshaw in 1991, Spielberg went on to direct *Jurassic Park* in 1993. He founded the film studio DreamWorks the following year, following up in 1997 with *The Lost World: Jurassic Park* and *Amistad*. His second Academy Award came in 1998 for *Saving Private Ryan*. His lengthy directorial career, which included numerous films not cited here, brought eleven Academy Awards. Spielberg's chief philanthropical contributions have been focused on ensuring that the Holocaust is not lost to historical memory, and he has donated $65 million to the Survivors of the Shoah Visual History Foundation. He was central in establishing the Righteous Persons Foundation, which donated tens of millions to institutions that chronicled the genocide of the Jews, such as the United States Holocaust Memorial Museum, and he remains an active director in the century's third decade.

"BRIDGE OVER TROUBLED WATER"
Popular Music in the 1970s

The year 1970 seemed to mark the beginning of a new musical era as the "supergroups" of the 1960s began to give way to new bands and voices. The Beatles broke up to pursue individual careers, while the Rolling Stones and the Kinks remained intact and doggedly pursued rock 'n' roll. The Doors survived Jim Morrison's death by only two years. Several of the most renowned musical giants of the 1960s fell victim to drugs, as Jimi Hendrix and Janis Joplin died in 1970; Cass Elliot of the Mamas & the Papas followed in 1974, five years after the group had disbanded. Traffic, Steppenwolf, Cream, and Iron Butterfly had all disbanded by 1972, signaling the end of an era dominated by rock 'n' roll and psychedelia. Their passing from the scene did not mean a fallow era in American pop music. Indeed, the 1970s brought new talents to an increasingly diverse musical universe as a new cadre of lyricists, vocalists, and bands quickly filled the void. Female voices that gained fame included some with already lengthy careers such as Judy Collins, Joan Baez, and Laura Nyro, all of whom, together with Bob Dylan, Tom Rush, and Peter, Paul, and Mary had done much to keep folk (or folk-rock) alive. Female musicians who carved out new and enduring niches in folk and later rock 'n' roll included Joni Mitchell, Joan Jett, Pat Benatar, Lita Ford, Suzi Quatro, Chrissie Hynde, and Stevie Nicks. Among the new and innovative male voices to make it to the airwaves and vinyl were Kris Kristofferson, John Prine, Neil Young, David Crosby, Dan Fogelberg, Loudon Wainwright III, Harry Chapin, Michael Bolton, Gilbert O'Sullivan, Don McLean, Michael Murphy, and the duet Loggins & Messina.

Sensing a new direction in pop music, *Time* magazine's October 1966 issue devoted a single page to "The New Troubadours" as a welcome indication of a new literacy and sensitivity in the music world. Among the "troubadours" to emerge in the next few years were James Taylor, Cat Stevens, and Jackson Browne. Taylor's path to success was hindered by drug use and periodic admissions to rehabilitation institutions, though he produced his first eponymous album in 1968. His launching pad to fame was the 1970 release of *Sweet Baby James*, which blended thoughtful, often highly personal lyrics with memorable melodies. Taylor, who married Carly Simon in 1972, found mixed success in a subsequent string of albums, though his performing career, often with Carole King, blossomed. Cat Stevens followed a similar recording path, issuing his first album in 1967 before striking platinum with *Tea for the Tillerman* (1970) and *Teaser and the Firecat* (1971). Though his music remained popular, his recording career came to a halt with his conversion to Islam in 1977. Browne, whose first composition, "These Days," was written the year that the *Time* article appeared, got off to a halting start in the music business during these same years, as he was initially content with composing songs for others to play and record, often playing backup in a variety of venues.

In the of summer of 1969, Jackson Browne came to grips with the dead end that he had blundered into, despite his evident songwriting talents. On the periphery of the popular music scene since graduating high school in 1966, Browne had played with the Nitty Gritty Dirt Band, who recorded several of his songs, before briefly joining Gentle Soul prior to moving to Greenwich Village, where he reported on musical events for Nina Music. For the next two years, he remained in the background, appearing with Tim Buckley and the Velvet Underground's Nico, with whom he had a year-long romantic affair. Nico, as well as the Nitty Gritty Dirt Band, recorded "These Days," which would become one of Browne's signature songs; Nico also predicted that Browne would never record an album. Tom Rush, Steve Noonan, Gregg Allman, Joan Baez, the Eagles, Linda Ronstadt, Ian Matthews, and the Byrds all capitalized on Browne's songwriting genius to record his songs, though Browne, who did not envision himself primarily as a performer, remained reluctant to take the stage. His epiphany came one summer evening in 1969 at the house of music producer Paul Rothchild in Laurel Canyon outside of Los Angeles. The canyon was a mecca for some of the nation's top musicians; anyone of any stature and many current and future greats gravitated there. Laurel Canyon's status was acknowledged in the title of Joni Mitchell's 1970 album *Ladies of the Canyon,* and her home inspired the 1970 Crosby, Stills, and Nash song "Our House." Browne was destined, together with James Taylor and others, to become one of her ephemeral lovers. But all this was yet to come. Browne remembered that what struck him on that fateful night in 1969 was that "I haven't done anything apart from sitting here getting loaded."

It was a harsh assessment of his predicament, as he had kept busy songwriting and performing backup for several years. The path to a breakthrough, as Browne saw it, was on the stage of Los Angeles's famed Troubadour Club, which had provided a venue for many on the way to stardom. Doug Weston, the club's owner, had confronted Browne that same summer and insisted that he consider what might happen if he got that "big break." Weston was a staunch advocate of the Troubadour Club's power to propel striving artists toward greatness. "The people who play our club are sensitive artists who have something to say about our times," he observed. "They are modern-day troubadours." Indeed, the term "troubadours" would soon be affixed to many of the new faces in music who produced tuneful music that carried a story. Journalist Lillian Roxon was already optimistic about Browne's future in her *Rock Encyclopedia*, writing in 1968, "when [Browne] does happen, when he's good and ready, the wait will be worth it."

Jackson Browne was born an army brat in Heidelberg, Germany, to Clyde Jackson and Beatrice Amanda Browne on October 9, 1948, yet another member of the "Baby Boomer" generation. At age three, the Browne family moved to Los Angeles, Jackson having gained three siblings. The boy quickly demonstrated an affinity for singing folk songs and performed at the Ash Grove and the Troubadour Club as he was attending Sunny Hills High School. His songwriting talents became evident at age sixteen, the year he wrote "These Days," a moving and surprisingly mature evocation of heartbreak and lost love. Yet Browne was as yet reluctant to pursue the career of a recording artist or solo performer; he was not yet ready to step up to the mic in a committed fashion. As biographer Dave Thompson writes, "Browne simply didn't play ball." Though Weston was eager to have Browne as a regular at the Troubadour, the quiet, long-haired youngster seemed to lack direction, spending too much time backing up other acts or playing small clubs, or as Thompson notes, Browne did little more than "one-offs and surprises, pickup performances and zero-promotion hoots."

Out of patience, in September 1969 Weston planned a week of performances by Linda Ronstadt with Browne as her supporting act. Having
refused some recording offers, Browne signed a songwriting contract with
Criterion Music. Out of the twenty songs that made it onto acetate between
fall 1969 and spring 1970 were "Doctor My Eyes," "Jamaica Say You Will,"
and "Rock Me on the Water," destined to be hits that would propel his later
recording career.

Having heard a recording of "Jamaica Say You Will," producer David
Geffen perceived a remarkable talent and was willing to become Browne's
manager. Invited to the office of Columbia Records executive Clive Davis
for an audition, both Browne and Geffen were offended when Davis took
a phone call in the midst of Browne's performance of "Doctor My Eyes."
Infuriated, Geffen told Browne to pack up and huffed, "We're leaving."
Columbia Records had, in the words of Browne's biographer, "all but
committed suicide," and Geffen "effectively mothballed his [Browne's]
talents for a year," telling Browne to take some time off and wait for Geffen to contact him. It was fruitful advice—Browne undertook a Jeep tour
through Utah and Arizona that inspired him to write the uplifting and
life-affirming "Take It Easy." Awaiting the appropriate moment to put
Browne's artistry before the public, Geffen was convinced that the early
1970s would be the era of the singer-songwriter. Joni Mitchell and Neil
Young (with the album *Harvest*) affirmed his confidence in 1972. Steve
Goodman's eponymous 1971 album included the engaging "City of New
Orleans," which was subsequently recorded by Arlo Guthrie and Judy
Collins. The Eagles eponymous 1972 album, which included a rendi-
tion of Browne's "Take It Easy," offered further evidence. Yet the more
Geffen was convinced that Browne's time had arrived, the more Browne
seemed uneasy with what fame might bring. His artistry was, he believed,
far more important than transitory fame. Yet Geffen began grooming
Browne to meet his public, providing the musician with money, some of
which Browne grudgingly spent on the clothes that Geffen recommended.

At the close of 1970, Geffen began the process of introducing Browne
to a wider audience, scheduling him to open for Laura Nyro, with whom
Browne had recently begun a relationship, in hope that the pairing would
settle Browne's anxieties. Following a series of concerts in California, it
was clear that the strategy was working. *New York Times* critic Mike Jahn
acknowledged that "Browne has a promising career ahead of him," though

he noted that Browne only played "slow ballads, sticking to a traditional format of songs." Browne was unruffled by such criticism and was quick to own his personal style. As he told *Melody Maker*'s Colin Irwin, "It's therapeutic to be able to tell somebody what you feel." For Browne, lyrics were the essential component of song, and many of his were highly personal, though they often spoke to feelings and experiences that were universal. While critics at home and abroad often gave short shrift to Browne in favor of praising Nyro, Geffen was convinced that Browne belonged in a group of musicians that deserved a home of their own with a new label. Jackson Browne was the first musician to sign with Geffen's new Asylum Records.

Browne's popularity soared after his 1972 debut eponymous album, which included "Doctor My Eyes," "Rock Me on the Water," and "Jamaica Say You Will." As Browne biographer Thompson notes, the album "simply reiterated that kind of set he might have performed at any club over the past few years, alone with a guitar," with the audience respectfully listening to the lyrics. This was the essence of Jackson's art—songs that were often very personal, crafted around heartfelt lyrics accompanied by minimal instrumentation. *Washington Post* critic Alex Ward conceded, "I was convinced that hearing just one more folkie-turned-soft rocker would drive me right around the bend." Having heard *Jackson Browne*, Ward admitted that it was "a downright pleasure to swallow that assumption."

The 1973 follow-up *For Everyman* was completed in nine months as Browne ended his relationship with Joni Mitchell and took up with Phyllis Major, whom he would marry. *For Everyman* was not as commercially successful as his initial album, despite the inclusion of the haunting "Our Lady of the Well," his heartfelt version of "These Days," and his rollicking rendition of "Take It Easy," which he now sought to reclaim. These were productive years for Browne, with 1974's *Late for the Sky* including "Before the Deluge," "For a Dancer," and "Fountain of Sorrow." From 1975 through 1978, Browne toured with the Eagles, Linda Ronstadt, and Toots and the Maytals. Tragedy struck the Browne family when his wife Phyllis committed suicide, leaving Jackson grief-stricken and the single parent of a two-year-old son. *The Pretender* (1976) reflected that grief with "Sleep's Dark and Silent Gate" and "Here Come Those Tears Again." Hardly pausing, Browne released *Running on Empty* (1977), his biggest commercial success, the title song speaking not only to individual exhaustion but clearly reflecting the nation's mood. After mid-decade,

Figure 8.1. Jackson Browne, one of the "troubadors" of the 1970s, in concert. Browne was a brilliant lyricist as well as an engaging performer, scoring early in the decade with hits such as "These Days," "Take It Easy," and "Doctor My Eyes." Subsequent albums assured his enduring popularity.
Source: Wikimedia Commons / Larry Miller

Browne was increasingly willing to move beyond the instrumental minimalism of his early years and expand his backup band.

As the 1970s ended, Browne devoted more of his time to environmentalism, a theme that had run through several of his songs. In June 1978, he performed for opponents of New Hampshire's Seabrook Station Nuclear Power Plant, and after the Three Mile Island accident, Browne and friends Bonnie Raitt and John Hall founded Musicians United for Safe Energy and was later arrested during a protest of the Diablo Canyon Power Plant near San Luis Obispo. Social activism did not preclude artistry and in 1980 Browne released *Hold Out*, which achieved the number one spot on the US pop albums chart. His music became more political with the passage of time, with 1986's *Lives in the Balance* condemning US policy in Central America and benefit concerts for Farm Aid, Amnesty International, and AIDS research. Critically successful albums followed in the 1990s and into the next century with his fifteenth studio album, *Downhill from Everywhere,* appearing in 2021. Inducted into the Rock & Roll Hall of Fame in 2004, Browne's lengthy career continued into the twenty-first century as he participated in numerous charitable causes and benefit concerts. As well as receiving six Grammy nominations in the course of his career, Browne received the Gandhi Peace Award from Promoting Enduring Peace in 2018. As one of the troubadours of the 1970s, Browne played a crucial role in popularizing a musical genre that was a major component of the decade's sound.

Note: Regrettably, the author can claim no relationship to Jackson Browne.

❖

The literature on popular music in the 1970s reflects a veritable contest among cultural historians to identify a specific year that ushered in the new decade's sound. If one forgoes that debate, it becomes evident that, far from being devoid of innovative music, the 1970s produced a superior procession of new voices, bands, and modes as supergroups gave way to superstars in every genre. Musical evolution was continual, though by mid-decade multinational corporations like Gulf & Western and CBS controlled much of the music. As Bruce J. Schulman notes, the success of this approach was evident in the 1976 release of *Frampton Comes Alive!,* a multiplatinum album that featured "a mediocre, undistinguished British rocker" who "offered music with no soul, no message, no recognizable quality," and which, perhaps tellingly, became the best-selling album of all time. A similar phenomenon occurred with the Bay City Rollers, a Scottish quintet hailed as the new Beatles who gained enormous popularity before quickly fading away. It would be unfair to characterize all 1970s music in this way, however. A plethora of new labels appeared to serve a multitude of specific musical genres and tastes. As cultural historian Schulman notes, "The market had fragmented into many niches," and Americans embraced them all.

Many of the most famed musical figures of the 1960s continued their careers into the following decade. While the Rolling Stones adhered to the supergroup model, ambitiously touring and producing albums through the 1970s, the remnants of the Beatles all produced individual albums, with some, such as George Harrison's chart-topping *All Things Must Pass* (1970), receiving wide praise. Paul McCartney scored well with two solo albums before forming Wings, which produced hit albums and toured through 1979. Ringo Starr fared well with 1973's *Ringo*. John Lennon also pursued a solo career, despite wife Yoko Ono's appearance on the John Lennon/Plastic Ono Band album, which had little public appeal. *Imagine* (1971) and *Mind Games* (1973) were received far more positively, though Lennon's separation from Ono and legal troubles led to heavy drinking and a loss of direction. The decade had ended, of course, before Lennon's murder on December 8, 1980.

Following the breakup of Cream, guitarist Eric Clapton enjoyed a brief stint with Ginger Baker and Ric Grech in Blind Faith before recording the remarkable *Layla and Other Assorted Love Songs* (1970), ostensibly by Derek and the Dominos. A double album featuring blues and rock, the standout centerpiece was "Layla," a song of epic length and astounding musicianship that was Clapton's impassioned paean to his secret love, Pattie Boyd, George Harrison's wife. Broadly dismissed at the time, *Layla and Other Assorted Love Songs* was later hailed by critics such as *Rolling Stone*'s Anthony DeCurtis, who termed the album "a masterpiece." Jim DeRogatis of the *Chicago Sun-Times* called it "arguably the greatest blues-rock album ever made." Other 1960s musicians who forged new careers in the 1970s included Traffic's Steve Winwood, Jim Capaldi, Dave Mason, and Chris Wood. The rebuilt group inaugurated the 1970s with *John Barleycorn Must Die*, their highest-charting American album, and went on to produce jazz-rock albums into mid-decade. Pink Floyd, while something of a marginal group in the 1960s, began to make inroads into the American market in the 1970s, and the stunning *Dark Side of the Moon* (1973) assured the group a committed following and hit albums for the remainder of the decade.

Categorizing the new music of the 1970s can be challenging. Various critics and music historians have identified soft rock, Southern rock, country rock, yacht rock, redneck rock, disco, stadium rock, glam rock, and New Wave, among others. A partial review of hit songs and albums beginning in 1970 reflects the mixture of these genres that filled the airwaves, including the Carpenters' syrupy "We've Only Just Begun," which shared the charts with Stevie Wonder ("Signed, Sealed, Delivered"), the Temptations ("Psychedelic Shack"), Simon and Garfunkel ("Bridge Over Troubled Water"), Alice Cooper ("I'm Eighteen"), Black Sabbath ("Paranoid"), and albums by Creedence Clearwater Revival, Santana, and McCartney. The year 1971 brought stardom for David Bowie, Rod Stewart, Pink Floyd, Elton John, Led Zeppelin, Joni Mitchell, Carole King, Carly Simon, and Michael Jackson, among others. 1972 saw Roberta Flack, Helen Reddy, Don McLean, America, Cat Stevens, and Harry Nilsson join these musicians with both hit singles and albums. The following year saw squeaky-clean Tony Orlando and Dawn vie with the distinctly outrageous heavy-metal Kiss for fans. Jim Croce, the Allman Brothers, Billy Preston, Diana Ross, Grand Funk Railroad, and Chicago also produced hits, testifying to the fragmentation of popular tastes, even as Bruce Springsteen joined the fray when *Greetings from Asbury Park, NJ* (1973) and *Born to Run* (1975) put him on the road to becoming one of the industry's best-selling artists. While 1974 brought the annoying hit novelty song "The Streak" by Ray Stevens and Terry Jacks's equally irritating "Seasons in the Sun" (ranked number five in a 2006 CNN poll as "one of the worst songs ever recorded"), the year also saw Eric Clapton, Bob Dylan, Paul McCartney and Wings, Harry Chapin, and the Jackson Five make the charts. Barry Manilow began a lengthy string of hits that extended into the 1980s with "Mandy." Jackson Browne had produced several excellent albums beginning in 1971 with hit tracks such as "These Days," "Rock Me on the Water," "Doctor My Eyes," and "Take It Easy," but hit his stride in 1974 with *Late for the Sky*, followed by *The Pretender* (1976) and the presciently titled *Running on Empty* (1977). The Eagles gained fame in part with Browne's "Take It Easy" but he filled out the decade with a multitude of other hits such as "Hotel California" and "Lyin' Eyes."

Rock 'n' roll in a variety of forms was not absent from the scene during this era, with a myriad of new bands appearing. Badfinger, Journey, Foreigner, Foghat, REO Speedwagon, Van Halen, Boston, Golden Earring, Bachman-Turner Overdrive, Alice Cooper, Tom Petty and the Heartbreakers, and Kiss vied with long established bands like the Rolling Stones. Mid-decade brought the first indications of the coming disco wave with Van McCoy's "The Hustle" and the Bee Gees' "Jive Talkin'." The continued popularity of MOR (middle-of-the-road) pop was reflected in the Captain and Tennille's "Love Will Keep Us Together" and the even smarmier "Muskrat Love," as well as Morris Albert's wooings on "Feelings."

New voices like Freddy Fender vied with Linda Ronstadt, Tanya Tucker, the reconstituted Jefferson Starship, and the long-lived Frankie Valli for audiences and sales. Cultural historian Ronald Brownstein maintains that, as of 1975, "the center of the rock world" shifted away from Los Angeles and toward New York City and London "as darkness encroached on what had been Los Angeles' golden hour" as the New York Dolls, Television, Patti Smith, the Ramones, Blondie, Talking Heads, the Dead Kennedys, the Sex Pistols, and the Clash marked the rapid transition from glitter to punk and New Wave. Guitarist Danny Kortchmar lamented that these new genres that emerged in 1975–1976 "were coming out and giving us all the finger."

What was also evident by mid-decade was the rise of disco, which hit the airwaves with a plethora of hits such as "Play That Funky Music" (Wild Cherry), "A Fifth of Beethoven" (Walter Murphy and the Big Apple Band), "(Shake, Shake, Shake) Shake Your Booty" (KC and the Sunshine Band), and "Disco Lady" (Johnnie Taylor)—all in 1976. The year 1977's *Saturday Night Fever* starring John Travolta not only brought the disco craze to the big screen but vaulted the Bee Gees to musical stardom, as the soundtrack featured six of their falsetto-voiced disco numbers, as well as hits by Tavares, Kool and the Gang, the Trammps, and other disco musicians. The film also introduced Rick Dees's lamentable "Disco Duck."

The year 1977 also saw the founding of perhaps the most colorful and entertaining disco group, the Village People. Consisting of six men outfitted in a variety of outrageous costumes, the group's hits such as "YMCA" and "Macho Man" were obviously aimed at the gay subculture but quickly embraced by the mainstream. As Alice Echols notes in her admirable history of disco, *Hot Stuff: Disco and the Remaking of American Culture*, it was *Saturday Night Fever* that propelled disco into "manic overdrive." Within a year, in the New York metropolitan area alone, one thousand disco clubs were accommodating full dance floors. Echols estimates that by the close of 1978 between 15,000 and 20,000 discos were in business across the nation. The craze even absorbed cinematic soundtracks as Meco recorded a disco version of themes from the film *Star Wars*. Television, never slow to latch on to a fad, likewise responded as *American Bandstand*, *Soul Train*, and even *Don Kirshner's Rock* [!] *Concert* surrendered to the invasive sound. At the February 1979 Grammy Awards ceremony, disco claimed eight of the fourteen awards.

Disco's meteoric rise, however, foreshadowed its rapid collapse. In addition to numerous music critics, an unusual amalgam of forces was organizing in opposition. There had always been the homophobes who saw insidious aspects in disco, but by 1979, the newly powerful evangelical right was taking aim at the dance craze. Singer and Florida orange juice tout Anita Bryant warned her followers that homosexuals were producing disco recordings with the intent of seducing children into that ungodly lifestyle. Evangelist Jerry Falwell listed discos among a catalog of dangers threatening the nation's moral core, together with television comedies, abortion, sex education, and President Carter. The greatest threat to disco, however, was mounted by deejays who worked for classic rock and album-oriented rock radio stations. Dennis Erectus of San Jose's KOME is often credited with organizing the anti-disco movement, which gained momentum through the actions of Chicago deejay Steve Dahl, who was moved to act after he was fired by station WDAI when it embraced a disco format. Hired by Chicago station WLUP, Dahl mocked disco as "homo" music, announced disco titles with a lisp, celebrated the death of Van McCoy, and encouraged one hundred WLUP concert ticket winners to pelt the Village People with marshmallows inscribed with "DISCO SUCKS." (How one wrote on a marshmallow was unclear.) Dahl's anti-disco army grew to an estimated 10,000, many of whom attended Disco Demolition Night on July 12, 1979, at Chicago's Comiskey Park. Dahl promised those who showed up bearing disco records admission for ninety-eight cents, and some 10,000 who did so were among the 50,000 at the game between the White Sox and the Detroit Tigers. By the fifth inning, the field was strewn with records hurled frisbee-style at the players. The main event took place during an intermission when Dahl, wearing military fatigues and a helmet, drove onto the field in a jeep and set off an explosive device inside a crate that supposedly held 50,000 disco records. The detonation signaled 7,000 fans to storm the field, destroying not only the remaining records but also the pitcher's mound and the dugouts. The violence ended only when the Chicago Police Tactical Squad arrived on scene. Not only were there numerous arrests and injuries, but the White Sox had to forfeit the game. Celebrating disco's demise, WLUP played Donna Summer's "Last Dance" for twenty-four hours.

Within a year of disco's domination of *Billboard*'s Top Ten, an official from West End Records conceded that "disco was so officially over." Most major labels dumped their disco divisions, and radio stations that had adopted disco moved back to rock formats. Disco's eulogy might well be said to have occurred in spring 1980, when Gloria Gaynor's prescient "I Will Survive" won the first and last award for 1979's Best Disco Recording. Yet the genre's stubborn endurance, which did take it into the early 1980s, was definitely due to its sheer ubiquity. As Alice Echols argues, disco was "plastic music for plastic people" and that as it was "everyone's music . . . disco had no currency." Yet few phenomena defined the 1970s in the popular mind as did disco and the fashions it inspired.

Variously referred to as rhythm and blues or soul, music by African Americans began to make inroads into the mainstream by the mid-1950s, gaining a separate *Billboard* chart in 1949 and holding a secure niche by the 1960s. Many well-established groups and performers held up well in the 1970s. Aretha Franklin, the "Queen of Soul," produced a lengthy string of number one singles such as "Call Me" (1970), "Bridge Over Troubled Water" (1971), and "Something He Can Feel" (1976), while albums such as *Aretha Live at the Fillmore West* (1971) and *Young, Gifted and Black* (1972) were among her career four platinum albums and twenty number one singles, together with eighteen Grammy Awards. The "Godfather of Soul," James Brown, coasted into the 1970s with a nonstop parade of number one singles such as "Super Bad" (1970), "Hot Pants" (1971), and "Papa Don't Take No Mess" (1974). Brown also released the soundtracks to *Black Caesar* and *Slaughter's Big Rip-Off* in 1973.

Todd Boyd writes, "If there were a Mount Rushmore of the Super-Fly 1970s, the figures represented would be Marvin Gaye, Curtis Mayfield, and Stevie Wonder." All had their beginnings in the 1960s and enhanced their reputations with each passing year. Gaye's album *What's Going On?* contained three number one hits, including the title track "Mercy Mercy Me" and "Inner City Blues." Mayfield gained renown as the composer/performer of the *Super Fly* soundtrack, which made number one on both the rhythm and blues (R&B) and pop charts in 1972. Gaining musical independence in 1971 when he turned twenty-one, Wonder produced a succession of albums between 1972 and 1976 that Boyd describes as "one long, extended musical meditation," from 1972's *Music of My Mind* to the remarkable *Songs in the Key of Life* (1976), which won that year's

Album of the Year Grammy. Scooping up twenty-two Grammys during a career that stretched well beyond the 1970s, Wonder was also one of the first musicians to use electronic sound effects in his recordings. Other significant contributors to R&B came out of Kenneth Gamble's and Leon Huff's Philadelphia International, formed in 1971 as a competitor with Barry Gordy's Motown Records. The label's in-house band MFSB produced the hit 1974 single "TSOP" ("The Sound of Philadelphia") and recorded the O'Jays (best known for "Love Train"), Harold Melvin and the Blue Notes, and Teddy Pendergrass. George Clinton's Parliament-Funkadelic enterprise continued to ride the waves of musical tastes from R&B into the hip-hop era. Other contributors to the R&B hit list of the 1970s were Al Green, the Isley Brothers, Earth, Wind & Fire, and the Ohio Players. No account of 1970s soul would be complete without mention of Barry White, whose Love Unlimited Orchestra scored with "Love's Theme" in 1974 and whose many hit singles featuring White's melodious, seductive baritone voice made both the R&B and pop charts.

One of the most prolific black contributors to jazz and pop music was Quincy "the Dude" Jones, who produced a nonstop succession of albums from 1969 to 1979's *Off the Wall*. Pianist Herbie Hancock drove the transition from jazz to fusion and then funk with albums like *Head Hunters* (1974). Gil Scott-Heron, though often inaccurately characterized as a jazz musician, pushed beyond that genre and toward hip-hop with 1970's *Small Talk at 125th and Lenox*, which featured the brilliant and humorous critique of commercialism and radicalism in "The Revolution Will Not Be Televised." Another piece of social criticism on the album was "Whitey on the Moon," which questioned the expense of the space program when millions of Americans were mired in poverty.

The transitional aspect of the 1970s is evident in the country/western music of the decade, as it evolved into a number of new forms and with both established and new voices. The new polished "cosmopolitan sound" gained popularity through Lynn Anderson, Glen Campbell, Anne Murray, Dottie West, and Tammy Wynette. The "Bakersfield Sound" was well represented by Merle Haggard and Buck Owens, both well-established performers. "Outlaw country" was a new form incorporating honky-tonk, blues, and rock, while often reflecting the resentments of the alienated and was associated with Jerry Jeff Walker, David Allan Coe, Jessi Colter, and, most notably, Willie Nelson and Waylon Jennings, whose 1976

Wanted! The Outlaws went platinum. The decade also witnessed the success of new groups, the most successful during the early 1970s being the Statler Brothers. When the Oak Ridge Boys moved beyond country gospel to embrace country rock, they expanded their fan base. Late in the decade, Alabama won favor with a blend of soft and Southern rock.

Country pop grew in the early 1970s as artists like the Bellamy Brothers, Charlie Rich, John Denver, Olivia Newton-John, B. J. Thomas, and Kenny Rogers gained favor, though there were some, like Charlie Rich, who questioned whether some of these individuals produced anything approaching genuine country. At the 1975 Country Music Association Awards, Rich presented the "Entertainer of the Year" award to "my good friend" the golden-haired John Denver, but only after setting fire to the award envelope with a cigarette lighter. The later 1970s saw Dolly Parton succeed in crossing over to country pop, as did Crystal Gayle, Loretta Lynn, Ronnie Milsap, Eddie Rabbitt, and Linda Ronstadt. Kenny Rogers, whose early success came with the First Edition's psychedelic "Just Dropped In (To See What Condition My Condition Was In)," created a new persona with the hit single "Lucille" (1977) and the wildly popular album *The Gambler* (1978). Country rock expanded its fan base as Bob Dylan, Gram Parsons, and the Byrds devoted albums to the genre, even as Emmylou Harris and the Eagles made significant inroads, with the Eagles' best-selling *Hotel California* (1976) and numerous hit singles establishing that group's enduring fame. Southern rock, which blended country, blues, and rock, grew in popularity propelled by the Ozark Mountain Daredevils, Lynryd Skinner, Charlie Daniels, the Allman Brothers, and the Marshall Tucker Band. Acknowledging the legacy of country/western music's founding giants, Hank Williams Jr. released *Hank Williams Jr. and Friends* in 1975, collaborating with contemporary custodians of that legacy. Perhaps the most annoying country music offshoot was C. W. McCall's CB radio-oriented music, including mid-1970s albums *Wolf Creek Pass/Black Bear Road* (which contained the megahit "Convoy"), *Wilderness*, and the lamentable *Rubber Duck*. Fortunately, the CB radio fad and the insipid music it inspired were ephemeral, though some truly abysmal films grew out of the short-lived phenomenon.

All of these genres were affected by the transitions in the delivery of the medium. Forty-five-rpm records virtually disappeared as long-playing albums (LPs) gained ascendance, in part because the LP afforded musicians the opportunity to pursue a theme in a succession of tracks. Eight-track tape recordings, which afforded only mediocre to poor audio fidelity and had a short life, were gradually succeeded by the cassette tape, which usually offered improved fidelity and greater dependability. Compact disc (CD) players would not be available to consumers until 1982 and then only at tremendous cost. Some sound formats never found a reliable consumer base. Introduced in 1972, CD-4 recordings could be played on standard stereo systems equipped with two left and two right speaker lines, but other quadraphonic recordings (including quadraphonic eight-track tapes!) required specialized playback systems such as SQ and QS, and by the late 1970s, the market dried up. Quadraphonic reel-to-reel tapes were available but generally remained the purvey of only the most devoted audiophiles.

Fears that the demise of the music of the 1960s augured an era bereft of artistic greatness and innovation were fortunately unwarranted. Without question, however, the decade produced some music that could only be charitably deemed puerile. Miami humorist Dave Barry catalogs many of these in *Dave Barry's Book of Bad Songs*, including many truly dreadful "novelty" songs, as well as what he deems "weenie songs," notably Morris Albert's "Feelings," the entire lyrical content of which consists of the word "feelings" and choruses of "wo, wo, wo." Barry's "Bad Song Survey" includes the Captain and Tennille's cringe-worthy "Muskrat Love," described by Barry as "a tender, poetic, squeak-filled ballad about rodents having sex." Numerous 1970s musical luminaries made it onto Barry's list, including Barry Manilow, who actually did not write the lyrics to "I Write the Songs," Olivia Newton-John, deemed a "repeat bad song offender," and the group America, mocked for not naming the horse in "A Horse with No Name." These are outriders, however, in a decade that brought not only new sounds from familiar voices but entirely new directions and genres in popular music, introducing the public to a new generation of brilliant lyricists and talented vocalists as well as bands that quickly filled the void left by the demise of 1960s groups. Popular music took a number of directions during the decade, some drawn from established traditions, some springing from new roots, some ephemeral, and some destined to shape the music of the 1980s, which proved every bit as vibrant as that of the 1970s.

❖

Few record albums have opened with lyrics as provocative as those that led into "Gloria (In Excelsis Deo)," the first track of Patti Smith's 1975 *Horses*. "Jesus died for somebody's sins, but not mine," proclaimed the twenty-nine-year-old poet and singer as she led her band into one of the most unorthodox songs of the decade (the shocking phrase was drawn from her early poem "Oath"). As Smith's spoken-word narration kept pace with a slowly building musical accompaniment, it became clear that this was not just a cover of the song that Van Morrison's Them had recorded years before. As the tempo picked up, matching Smith's increasingly rapid-fire, stream-of-consciousness lyrics, a story begins to emerge that appeared to tell of a party and a (lesbian?) seduction, framed by choruses of the familiar three-chord "Gloria" chant. As the skinny, black-haired singer drives the song to a literal climax, the piece crashes to a finish with Smith's wail that "Jesus died for somebody's sins," a phrase that dies out accompanied by a low feedback drone, before Smith reiterates, "But not mine," before the group joins her shouting out the letters G-L-O-R-I-A to the band's "Gloria" chant in a thunderous rock 'n' roll finish.

Before listeners could fully comprehend what they had just heard, Smith followed with "Redondo Beach," a bouncy, rhythmic number made grimmer by mention of a "pretty girl's" "sweet suicide," then the remarkable "Birdland," a lengthy, lilting spoken-word piece introduced by a quiet piano prelude, with Patti imagining Wilhelm Reich's son's reaction to his father's death. Next, "Free Money" begins with a quiet piano introduction before gradually gaining momentum as a full-out rock 'n' roll number that speaks to Patti's desire to give her mother those things the family could not afford when she was a child. The more poetic "Kimberly" is dedicated to Smith's younger sister, while "Break It Up" grew out of Smith's visit to Jim Morrison's grave in Paris.

"Gloria (In Excelsis Deo)" is *sui generis*, but the nine-minute-long "Land" recapitulates the same innovative combination of a spoken-word story incorporating phrases from Chris Kenner's "Land of 1000 Dances" with an almost hallucinatory tale of a savage locker room knife or sexual attack on "Johnny," during which the victim, a blade at his throat, suddenly imagines "horses comin' in all directions, white shining silver studs with their nose in flames." Into this scenario, Smith suddenly introduces some of the lyrics and melodies from "Land of 1000 Dances," and as the tempo accelerates, shouts "go Rimbaud" and "go Johnny go," mixing her affinity for the

French surrealist with Chuck Berry's "Johnny." A stunning *tour de force* arguably about a homosexual rape and murder, "Land" seemed a fitting place to conclude this remarkable recording, but Smith chose to close with "Elegy," a dreamlike piece devoted to Jimi Hendrix.

Smith had been doing gigs around New York City for several years prior to the release of *Horses,* but it was at the famous CBGB club that producer Clive Davis, who was eager to launch Arista Records with an indisputably innovative group, was first "struck" with Smith, who had been developing a unique stage persona while backed by guitarists Lenny Kaye and Ivan Kral, drummer Jay Dee Daugherty, and pianist Richard Sohl. Smith emerged in the midst of a new generation of bands, including the Talking Heads, Blondie, Television, and the Tuff Darts, who were bringing a new vibrance to the New York City music scene. Davis obviously saw something remarkable in the slim singer/poetess from New Jersey, offering her a $750,000 advance together with a seven-album deal and marketing control; she was the first major signing on the Arista label.

Horses, produced by musician John Cale at Hendrix's Electric Lady Studios, was completed in a month and boasted an award-winning black-and-white cover photo by Robert Mapplethorpe depicting Smith in her iconic outfit of white blouse, black trousers, loosened black tie, and black jacket bearing a horse pin tossed over her shoulder. Arista executives were not pleased with the cover photo; Clive Davis feared that the somber colors and androgynous image of Smith "might confuse the uninitiated." On the other hand, Camille Paglia, in *Sex, Art, and American Culture,* later asserted that Mapplethorpe's photo depicted "one of the greatest pictures of a woman." Upon its release, the album drew nearly unanimous praise from top reviewers. *Rolling Stone*'s John Rockwell deemed Smith a "rock & roll shaman" who "offers visions that embrace a multiplicity of meanings, all of them valid if they touch an emotional chord." Rockwell identified in her music the influence of the Beats and "the Romantic/Surrealist, Blake/Rimbaud sort of visionary mysticism." Discounting Smith's "Martian weirdness," Rockwell attributed her accessibility to the fact that "she anchors her imagination with the sturdy ballast of rock & roll." Describing Smith's singing voice as "more Neil Young than Linda Ronstadt," and her music as "artful rock & roll primitivism," Rockwell concluded that "*Horses* is a great record not only because Patti Smith stands alone, but because her uniqueness is lent resonance by the past." Writing in *Creem,* Lester

Bangs described Smith as "an all-American tough angel . . . combining sulky stalking cat and male aggressor" and credited her with producing "the finest garage band sound yet in the 1970s." "*Horses,* he wrote, "is a commanding record, as opposed to demanding. . . . You don't have to work to 'understand' it or like it, but you can't ignore it either." "Suffice it to say," he concluded, "that Patti has done more here for women as aggressor than all the Liberation tracts published. . . . It's this tough chick who walks like Bo Diddley and yet is all woman that we've been waiting for for so long." Bangs ranked Smith with Miles Davis, Charles Mingus, and Bob Dylan, crediting her with having created "a new Romantism built upon the universal language of rock 'n' roll, an affirmation of life so total that, even in the graphic recognition of death, it sweeps your breath away."

Greil Marcus of the *Village Voice* expressed praise as well as cautions concerning *Horses.* In a November 1975 article titled, somewhat perversely, "Patti Smith Exposes Herself," Marcus termed *Horses* "an authentic record" in which "the music is thin, clean, and brittle: good 1964 rock and roll with a '70s gloss." But he harbored concerns: "if the concepts, sources, and references in her lyrics and in her singing overwhelm the music . . . then, if her record shrinks over the next month or so, it will not

Figure 8.2. Patti Smith performs at the 1976 TMI concert, having recently stunned the music world with her debut album *Horses* and its lead track "Gloria (In Excelsis Deo)," which built a poetic and rock 'n' roll tale of sexual seduction around the framework of the garage band classic "Gloria." Her music was at the vanguard of the punk rock revolution that signaled the end of disco's prominence. Source: Wikimedia Commons / Daigo Oliva

be because the music has diminished in power . . . it will be because her concepts wore out." Singling out "Free Money," a "straightforward rock and roll song," Marcus agreed that "the rest of the album is attractive, but it breaks too easily into its parts under the attention it demands. It seems, in the end, an 'art statement.'" *Melody Maker*'s reviewer was less charitable, declaring that the album was emblematic of everything that "was wrong with rock and roll right now." The "completely contrived and affected 'amateurism'" of the album did not qualify as "good rock and roll." "The old 'it's so bad it's good' aesthetic has been played to death," he wrote. "*Horses* is just bad. Period." The *New Music Review*'s Charles Shaar Murray conceded that *Horses* was among the best of initial albums by any of the great 1960s bands, but was troubled that "it's strange, askew, and flat-out weird. It's neurotic and unhealthy and dank, a message in a bottle sent from some place that you and I have been in the worst moments of self-doubting defeated psychosis." But Sonic Youth's Lee Ranaldo harbored no doubts about *Horses*, declaring, "It's a fucking great rock 'n' roll [that] incorporated all the best elements of a really good garage band . . . and some of the most sophisticated lyrics around." "Within eighteen months," writes Smith biographer Mark Paytress, "*Horses* had incited a huge shift in rock aesthetics, releasing an entire generation from the brush-denim complacency of post-hippie culture." In a decade that had come to be dominated by disco, Southern, and country rock, the advent of punk rock signaled a new energy in popular music.

Though often believed to be a product of New Jersey, Patricia Lee Smith was born on December 30, 1946, to a working-class family in Chicago. One of four children, Patti and family moved from Philadelphia before settling in Deptford Township, New Jersey. A childhood shaped by illness, frequent time for reading and listening to music, and a rejection of her mother's Jehovah's Witness faith contributed to the adult Smith's perspective. In later years, Smith recalled being confused as to her sexuality, as she was thin and developed late. These difficult adolescent years likely contributed to Smith's later adoption of an androgynous image. A growing interest in art and music made her high school years tolerable and she graduated in 1964. Smith's pre–New York years were spent in part as a line worker in a toy factory, which was inspiration for the later "Piss Factory." She discovered Rimbaud during this period as well as jazz and Bob Dylan. A short stint at Glassboro State Teachers College was interrupted by an unwanted pregnancy in 1966, which concluded with Patti giving up the baby girl for adoption. The next phase of her life began as she boarded a train for New York with $16 in savings.

Manhattan was the crucible that shaped the Patti Smith of *Horses*. Finding work at a bookstore, Smith met photographer Robert Mapplethorpe and the two briefly shared an intimate relationship, even as Mapplethorpe wrestled with his sexual orientation. They remained close friends for the rest of his life, and Smith considered him "the artist in my life." Greenwich Village afforded contact with artists, poets, and musicians on the cutting edge of contemporary culture, and a 1969 trip to Paris established Smith's lifelong affinity for French film and literature, especially the poet Rimbaud. Returning to New York that July, Smith joined Mapplethorpe in a room at the Chelsea Hotel, renowned as a haven for unconventional creative spirits: Allen Ginsberg, William S. Burroughs, Gregory Corso, as well as musicians Janis Joplin, Bob Dylan, members of the Jefferson Airplane, and the galaxy of "superstars" that Andy Warhol cultivated. "The Chelsea opened up a whole new thing for me," Smith recalled, "the rock 'n' roll thing." The immediate direction she chose was poetry, having seen in Dylan potential for the fusion of poetry and rock 'n' roll. During the next four years, she was a frequent visitor to Manhattan clubs like Max's Kansas City, where she listened to groups like the New York Dolls and the Velvet Underground. During this same period, as she reset her relationship with Mapplethorpe, she had short-lived affairs with playwright Sam Shepherd, as well as Todd Rundgren and Allen Lanier.

The year 1971 was formative, as Smith gave her first public poetry reading in February at the St. Mark's Church Poetry Project, swaying and gesticulating to the accompaniment of guitarist Lenny Kaye. Among the poems she recited that night was "Oath," which contained the controversial "Jesus died" phrase. Dedicated largely to her poetry was 1972, leading to a London appearance at which she recited the poem that would later be reworked into "Land." In early 1973, she sometimes opened for the New York Dolls at the Mercer Arts Center. A May 1973 performance led a *Village Voice* writer to describe Smith as "a cryptic and androgynous Keith Richard look-alike poetess appliqué." A 1974 appearance at Greenwich Village's cabaret Reno Sweeney provoked *Mademoiselle*'s Amy Gross to describe "this 27-year-old punk who hammered out dirty poetry" as "a little Brando, a little *Blackboard Jungle*. A little Rimbaud, a little rapist, a little off the wall." Enthused by a performance by Television, she and Kaye were joined by pianist Richard Sohl in recording a single of "Hey Joe" and "Pissing in a River," the latter intended as the "B" side. By 1975, the trio, joined by Ivan Kral on guitar and bass, along with drummer Jay Dee Daughtery, drew such an enthusiastic audience response at CBGB that they were booked for a seven-week stand, performing several of the numbers that would make it into *Horses*. Enter Clive Davis.

With *Horses* selling some 80,000 copies in the first five weeks after its release in November 1975 and hitting number 46 on *Billboard*'s Hot 100, Patti Smith was inundated with requests for both televised and print interviews. Some, such as that with ABC's Barbara Walters, revealed Smith's quirky sense of humor. Asked if she ever felt out of control, Smith, fingering her characteristically untamed hair, replied, "I think maybe my hair's out of control." Inevitably, the issue of the opening lyrics of "Gloria" came up. In a 1976 London interview monitored by writer Mick Gold, Smith told an unidentified journalist, "You know, I don't do anything for shock value. . . . I mean, I don't say 'Jesus died for somebody's sins but not mine,' you know, to shock the Catholic Church or the Christian Church. I say something like that because . . . when I do evil . . . I know I'm doing it. *I* do it by my own free will." Twenty years later, in an interview with Mike Goldberg, Smith affirmed that what the lyrics meant was that, "I'd take the blame and I didn't want Jesus to have to worry about me. And I didn't want him to be responsible for my choices." Numerous interviews were accompanied by an April 1976 performance on *Saturday Night Live*, during which Smith performed the controversial song. SNL regular Gilda Radner would later parody Smith on subsequent shows as punk-rocker "Candy Slice."

The band's three-month US tour in 1976 enhanced Smith's fame and influence, as she enthused in an interview in *Back Door Man*, "The possibilities of rock 'n' roll are gonna start being apparent again." Tours in the UK and Europe fueled the band's international popularity, but the group soon faced the dilemma encountered by all newly acclaimed acts—how to follow *Horses* with an equally compelling second album. Now renamed the Patti Smith Group, the band recorded *Radio Ethiopia* in three weeks in the summer of 1976, with Patti clutching the 1957 Fender Duo-Sonic that she refused to learn to play but was content to make noises with. The album was an immense disappointment to Smith fans and fodder for unrestrained critical assaults. The title track, as described by a Smith biographer, was a nine-minute "avant-garde guitar-driven sprawling mess of atonal noise" and with few exceptions the other tracks ("Pissing in a River," "Ask the Angels," "Ain't It Strange," and "Distant Fingers") were instantly forgettable. The critics were merciless. *Melody Maker*'s Marianne Page huffed that "Patti Smith has one hell of a lot to answer for," condemning Smith's "pretentious poetic ramblings" and concluding that "the myth is exposed . . . as cheap thrills." *Rolling Stone*'s Dave Marsh dismissed the Patti Smith Group as "just another loud punk-rock gang of primitives." Charles Shaar Murray of the *NME* could only guess that Smith had "allowed the limitations of the genre to dictate restrictions to her." The *New York Times*' John Rockwell stated what stood out to all: "The level of songs seems lower than on *Horses*." The album failed to climb into the Top 100 in the United States.

A tour to the UK, where the Sex Pistols had just released *Anarchy in the UK* to rave reviews, did nothing to improve Smith's standing in the new genre. Reviewing a Patti Smith Group concert, Maureen Paton was brutal, writing that "Neither Smith nor her band had progressed beyond the totally inept musical standard evident in concert or on *Horses*. The same embarrassing clichés were handed out like food parcels to a largely bemused audience. . . . The guitar that she hadn't even bothered to play properly was toted around the stage as a symbol, nothing more." Matters deteriorated at a press conference when, asked why her shows weren't selling out, Smith shouted "Fuck you!" and hurled a plate of food at the questioner. Back in the United States in early 1977, the Patti Smith Group opened for Bob Seger in Chapel Hill and again at Tampa's Curtis-Hixon Hall. On January 23, the group was six songs into a set featuring titles from both albums when Smith, who was spinning and dancing around the stage, tripped on a monitor and fell fourteen feet off the stage. Taken by ambulance to a Tampa hospital, she was diagnosed with two broken vertebrae in addition to other injuries. Her eyesight was also affected and there was some concern that she might be partially paralyzed. Patti, who had been feeling more and more lost, interpreted the accident as an act of God, which compelled a lengthy recovery and a welcome respite to reassess herself and her music.

While bedridden and undergoing physical therapy, Smith busied herself putting together *Babel*, a collection of her poetry that she conceded was influenced partly by the Percodan she was taking and meanwhile arranging for a gallery show of her drawings. Viewing her recovery as a spiritual and artistic resurrection, she vowed to return to performing by "Easter," the title she gave to one of her new poems. Her resurrection was delayed until May 4, 1977, when she returned to CBGB for a benefit concert, completing a short set including songs from her two albums and some golden oldies, as well as the Velvet Underground's "I'm Waiting for the Man." Time away from the concert circuit gave Smith time to plan a third album to be titled *Easter*, signaling her resurrection.

Recorded in a New York studio, *Easter* was released in March 1978, the cover art and the songs fully reflective of Smith's new direction. The full color cover photo by Lynn Goldsmith was a departure from the past, a waist-up shot of Smith clad in a beige undergarment, sporting feminine jewelry, hands tending long black hair. Clearly, Smith was asserting her womanhood and sexuality, having forsaken the androgynous clothing of the past and unashamedly exposing unshaven armpits. Queried by a reviewer as to whether she feared being seen as "a sex object," Smith replied that she found the prospect "very exciting." The eleven tracks were overwhelmingly rock 'n' roll, punk, and much shorter. Allen Lanier wrote in the *NME*, "*Easter* goes right at you. It has none of the idiosyncrasies which prevented people from deciding whether they really liked her." *Crawdaddy's* Daisann McLain proclaimed, "Musically, this is Smith's best album." Without question, the band was tighter and Smith's voice was greatly improved, showing considerable range in "Till Victory," "High on Rebellion," "25th Floor," "Space Monkey,' "Ghost Dance," "Privilege (Set Me Free)," "We Three," and Smith's only Top -40 hit, "Because the Night," which was built around music by Bruce Springsteen and lyrics by Smith, making it to number 13 on the US charts, while the album reached number 20. The more controversial "Rock 'n' Roll Nigger," was one of two live numbers on the album and caused some consternation in Arista boardrooms and some criticism by reviewers. Nevertheless, the glowing reviews predominated. *Rolling Stone's* Dave Marsh penned a review titled, "Can Patti Smith Walk on Water?" Of a New York concert, Fred Shruers wrote, "Watching the crowd rise out of its seats as Patti walked on stage, you had to clench your fist for her." She was "the Gunga Din of a certain kind of rock magic." Now clearly established as a leading force in popular music, Smith and her band headed for a European tour.

Easter charted well in the UK and British critic Paul Morley described a performance in Germany as "a mesmerizing, sucking hole in time . . . honoring the vibrant spirits, anarchism, and surrealism." Morley praised the Patti Smith Group as "mature" and asserted that "Smith is finding her way back into performing." "They are at a transition period," he prophesized, "one more effort and they are truly great, truly special. Classical." Ironically, even as Smith had become a major force in punk and rock 'n' roll, some observers perceived a weariness in the singer. *Melody Maker*'s Dave Ramsen observed it during a show in London: "She has none of the bounding excess of energy, and sheer childlike exuberance that used to crackle through her performance." Weary or not, Smith and band toured the United States through early summer 1978 before returning to the UK and the continent. In June, the Patti Smith Group opened for the Rolling Stones in Atlanta and ended the year with performances at CBGB. Changes were in the air: in late September, Smith announced her decision to move to Detroit with Fred "Sonic" Smith, formerly of the MC5. As 1979 began, Smith was pushing hard to record a fourth album, though, as Todd Rundgren lamented, "They didn't have material" and were unrehearsed. The consequence was *Wave*, which featured some memorable tracks such as "Frederick" (written for Fred "Sonic" Smith) and "Dancing Barefoot," which proved enduring. A cover version of "So You Want to Be a Rock 'n' Roll Star" seemed to vaguely hint at Smith's simmering cynicism about stardom. Released in May, *Wave* was the group's biggest seller to date but peaked at number 18 in the United States. A *Rolling Stone* reviewer offered damningly faint praise: "Though a long way from being a total disaster, *Wave* is too confused and hermetically smug to be much more than an interesting failure." Fleeing more annoying interviews, Smith and band headed out on a US tour to be followed by European appearances. A biographer succinctly summarized this final foray: "Everything had become stale and Patti was deeply unhappy." Two Italian concerts brought matters to a head. A performance in Bologna deteriorated into chaos when the local Communist Party opened the gates to all comers, and some of the 80,000 fans besieged the stage. An equally chaotic September concert in Florence saw Patti perform "Gloria" for the final time, changing the controversial lyrics to "Jesus died for somebody's sins—why not mine?" Some in the riotous crowd overwhelmed the stage as others trashed the venue. Back at the hotel, Smith told her band that the Patti Smith Group had made its last appearance (the band did make one benefit appearance in 1980). "I was actually at the top of my game," she later told a reporter for the *Philadelphia Enquirer*. "The reason I left was because I had met a man who I deeply loved. Who had been through all of that. Who wanted a quiet life, to raise a family." For Patti Smith, the end of the 1970s meant a lengthy retirement from public life.

Patti Smith's eighteen-year-long hiatus from performing began with her March 1, 1980, marriage to Fred "Sonic" Smith, who taught her how to play the guitar. The couple settled in St. Clair Shores, Michigan, and the births of son Jason Frederick and daughter Jesse confirmed a domestic life that Smith did not disparage. "There's no job harder than being a housewife," Smith told *New York Times* reporter Neil Strauss. "It's a position that should be respected and honored." She instinctively followed the course of popular music in the 1980s, but found no compelling, unitary voice in hip-hop, electric music, stadium rock, hair bands, and dance music, though the decade did produce some new innovative groups. Amid numerous rumors about her disappearance from the music scene, one that she had become a fundamentalist Christian, Smith reemerged in 1988 with *Dream of Life*. She and Fred collaborated on the album's most enduring cut, "People Have the Power," but, as one biographer writes, the album "was a cultural orphan," offering little more to fans than the confirmation that Smith might be on the verge on reentering the arena of popular music, but no clue as to her direction.

Death intruded regularly into Smith's life between 1989 and 1994, as Robert Mapplethorpe died in March 1989, former band member Richard Sohl died in 1990, and within two months in 1994, Fred and her brother Todd both died of heart attacks at age forty-five. A succession of albums that offered both introspection, poetry, and rock 'n' roll took shape in the mid-1990s, with *Gone Again* (1996), *Peace and Noise* (1997), *Gung Ho* (2000), *Trampin'* (2004), and *Banga* (2012), which some critics consider her best recent album. In 2005, Smith gave a live recorded performance of the *Horses* album on its thirtieth anniversary, clearly having lost none of the fire that drove her in 1975, if the audience reaction is any clue. During these same years, as she gathered more honors and awards, Smith published several volumes of poetry, her lyrics often as abstruse as they were personal. In 2010, she won the National Book Award for Nonfiction with her moving autobiographical *Just Kids*, which chronicled her early years in Manhattan with Mapplethorpe and others. *M Train* (2015) and *Year of the Monkey* (2019) were also eagerly grabbed up by her fans. Smith was inducted into the Rock and Roll Hall of Fame in 2007, acted in an episode of *Law and Order*, and began to seriously pursue photography and social activism.

As of the publication of this book, Smith is seventy-six years old and still undertaking a punishing schedule of international appearances, selling out every concert appearance or poetry reading and showing no diminution of the energy that she brought to *Horses*. Joined by both her daughter and son in her band, which still features guitarist Lenny Kaye, Smith continues to inspire tremendous enthusiasm from concert audiences. In 2022, she published *A Book of Days*, a photographic calendar account of a year in her life. Her legacy is not only one of survival over five decades, but also as a major force in redirecting and reinvigorating popular music in the 1970s while paving the way for other women rockers like Joan Jett and Pat Benatar.

"A CRISIS OF CONFIDENCE"
National Politics and Foreign Policy

As Democrats met for their 1972 nominating convention in Miami Beach in mid-July, the specter of the debacle of 1968, which had seen Vice President Hubert Humphrey nominated amid televised images of Chicago police and rioters engaged in bloody street battles, hovered menacingly. The years after Humphrey's defeat were given over to a self-assessment and, specifically, how the nominating process might be reformed. To that end, the Commission on Party Structure and Delegate Selection, chaired by South Dakota Senator George S. McGovern, initiated changes to make the nomination process more open and democratic. The new rules granted greater influence to liberal political activists, women, and minorities, while reducing the influence of traditional party "bosses," such as powerful elected officials, city political machines, and organized labor leaders. The reforms also expanded the field of debate to previously shunned issues such as feminism, abortion, gay rights, desegregation, welfare rights, and an end to the draft. The 1972 platform also proclaimed that Americans "had the right to be different" and "the right to maintain a cultural or ethnic heritage or lifestyle, without being forced into a compelled homogeneity."

Of the thirteen candidates seeking the presidential nomination, only one was black and female. Shirley Chisholm, representative from New York's Twelfth Congressional District, announced her bid for the presidency on January 25, 1972. She was not the first female presidential candidate, as US Senator Margaret Chase Smith had claimed that distinction in 1964. Chisholm was, however, the first African American female candidate. In her January announcement, Chisholm declared, "I am not the candidate of black America, although I am black and proud. I am not the candidate of the women's movement of this country, although I am a woman and equally proud of that. I am the candidate of the people and my presence before you symbolizes a new era in American politics."

Chisholm, born in New York City on November 30, 1924, as Shirley Anita, was a child of immigrants. Her father, Charles Christopher St. Hill, had been born in British Guiana; her mother, Ruby Seales, was a native of Barbados. Her father was a laborer and her mother struggled as a seamstress and domestic worker while raising three girls, who were reluctantly sent to live with a grandmother in Barbados when Shirley was five. She returned to New York in 1934 with a lifelong West Indian accent, attending high school before earning a bachelor's degrees at Brooklyn College in 1946. While a student, she joined the Harriet Tubman Society and advocated the integration of the American military, more courses on

Figure 9.1. Shirley Chisholm, the first black woman presidential candidate, addresses the 1972 Democratic Convention. The speech is famed for her statement that if there was no place provided for one at the table, "bring your own chair." Though she had no expectation of winning, her candidacy signaled the start of an era in which black candidates would regularly win public office. Source: Library of Congress / O'Halloran, Thomas J.

African American history, and more women in government. In 1949, she married Conrad Chisholm, from whom she was divorced in 1977. Neither this nor a second marriage to Arthur Hardwick Jr. produced any children.

Upon graduation, Chisholm worked as teacher's aide at a childcare center, taught in nursery school, and earned a master's degree from the Columbia University Teachers College. During the 1950s, she directed a nursery school and a childcare center while working for the election of a black judge, joining the Brooklyn Democratic Club, the League of Women Voters, and the Unity Democratic Club. Chisholm ran for the New York State Assembly in 1964, easily winning a seat. She served there until 1968, when she sought a seat in the US House of Representatives, running on the slogan "Unbought and Unbossed." Her victory made her the first black woman elected to the US Congress. Working with Robert Dole, she was crucial to the establishment of the Supplemental Nutrition Program for Women, Infants, and Children, also gaining seats on the Veterans Affairs Committee and the Labor and Education Committee. Chisholm was adamant about hiring only women as staff, half of whom were black. Having joined the Congressional Black Caucus in 1971, she worked with fellow New Yorker Bella Abzug to pass a bill for funding for childcare services, which was vetoed by President Nixon as "too expensive."

Though Chisholm drew the support of the National Organization for Women, her 1972 presidential candidacy struggled under several burdens. Many refused to perceive it as serious, viewing it as merely symbolic. Perhaps for that reason, the campaign was grossly underfunded, ultimately collecting and spending only $300,000. Chisholm also felt that she was ignored by the party hierarchy and dismissed by male candidates. "When I ran for president," she noted, "I met more discrimination as a woman than for being black. Men are men." She was especially critical of the attitudes of black men and "the black matriarch thing." "They think I'm trying to take power from them." She agreed that "the black man must step forward," but that did not have to mean that "the black woman must step back." Chisholm was unable to demonstrate strength in any of the primaries that she entered, winning only 3.5 percent of the Florida vote and 4.4 percent of the California vote. Her best showing was in North Carolina, where she pulled in 7.5 percent of the vote. Despite her poor showing in the primaries, Chisholm won twenty-eight delegates and took part in a Democratic presidential debate in June, the first woman to do so.

At the convention, wrangling between McGovern and Humphrey bolstered Chisholm's delegate total when Humphrey released his black delegates to support Chisholm. With defections from other candidates, Chisholm could claim 152 delegates, putting her in fourth place behind McGovern and well ahead of nine well-known white male candidates. McGovern briefly considered Frances "Sissy" Farenthold of Texas for the vice presidency, but instead chose Missouri's Thomas Eagleton. Given the controversy and electoral debacle that ensued in November, Farenthold likely considered herself fortunate not to have been selected.

Chisholm refused to blame her loss on either racism or sexism but, rather, declared that she had sought the presidency "in spite of hopeless odds . . . to demonstrate the sheer will and refusal to accept the status quo." During the campaign she had paid a controversial visit to one of her competitors, Alabaman George Wallace, who had been seriously wounded and crippled by a gunman in May. Several years later Wallace worked with her to pass a bill granting domestic workers the right to a minimum wage. Following her 1972 loss, she continued her work in Congress as an advocate of funding for education, health care, and social services. She was a vocal opponent of the Vietnam War and the draft and supported reduced military spending. She left Congress in 1983 and took up residence in Williamsville, New York, while teaching at Holyoke College in Massachusetts, becoming a cofounder of the National Congress of Black Women the following year. A frequent speaker at college campuses, where she regularly defended tolerance and warned her audiences that their higher education meant nothing "if you don't accept others who are different." She retired to Florida in 1991 and was offered the ambassadorship to Haiti by President Bill Clinton in 1993, but her declining health prevented accepting the post. That same year, she was inducted into the National Women's Hall of Fame. Chisholm died in January 2005, having forged a path for the election of the first African American president in 2008.

❖

As of September 1975, Gerald R. Ford had been president for only little over a year but faced more challenges than many presidents do in a full term. Though supported for acknowledging the end of the Vietnam War,

Ford had been excoriated by liberals for his pardon of Nixon, damned by conservatives for his conditional amnesty for Vietnam-era draft evaders, bedeviled by the crucial issues of inflation and energy, and mocked by much of the public as a clumsy oaf who often fell down stairs and beaned observers with golf balls; there were those who were prone to accept the validity of the late President Johnson's unkind comment, "I think Jerry played football too often without a helmet."

On September 5, Ford arrived in Sacramento, California, to meet Governor Jerry Brown and address the state legislature on the issue of rising crime. As Ford greeted the crowd on the capitol grounds, there was one individual who clearly stood out. Among the well-wishers and only about two feet from the president was a young woman in a bright-red robe and hood—Lynette "Squeaky" Fromme, a follower of condemned cult leader Charles Manson. Strapped to her leg in a holster was a Colt .45 semiautomatic pistol, which she drew and aimed at the president. When she pulled the trigger, a loud click alerted the Secret Service to the threat even as Fromme yelled, "It wouldn't go off!" She was quickly disarmed and pinned to the ground as other agents hustled Ford toward the capitol. Fromme's ignorance of firearms saved the president's life. Unbeknownst to her, the weapon's slide had to be pulled back and released to chamber a bullet, which she had not done. Her rationale for her attack on Ford was that he had failed to protect the environment. Tried in November, Fromme received a life sentence. She was released in 2009 after Ford's death. The president's attraction of would-be assassins was repeated only two weeks later, when he again traveled to California, this time to San Francisco, where he was to tape an interview at the St. Francis Hotel. As Ford strode out of the lobby toward his limousine, the awaiting assassin this time was Sara Jane Moore, a sometime FBI informant who was fascinated by the Patty Hearst kidnapping and enthralled by radical politics. Wielding a .38 caliber revolver, she fired at Ford from across the street but got off only one round before a former Marine knocked the gun down; a ricochet from a second shot wounded one man. Moore was tried and sentenced to life imprisonment but was also released after Ford's death.

Two assassination attempts in less than three weeks were only one of many presidential firsts for Gerald Ford. The first individual to be appointed vice president under the Twenty-Fifth Amendment, former Michigan congressman Ford was never elected to any executive office;

thus, he had no natural national base of supporters when he entered the White House. He succeeded the only US president to resign that office. Arguably the most conservative president since Herbert Hoover, he confronted an overwhelmingly and obstreperous Democratic Congress as the nation came to grips with defeat in war and the new phenomenon of "stagflation," in which an economic slowdown was accompanied by unprecedented inflation. Yet, despite these challenges and others, Ford managed to win his party's presidential nomination in 1976.

Born in Omaha, Nebraska, on July 14, 1913, Leslie Lynch King Jr. was the only child of Dorothy Gardner and Leslie Lynch King Sr. The elder King was given to domestic violence, leading Dorothy to leave him only sixteen days after her son's birth, after which she eventually ended up in her parents' home in Grand Rapids, Michigan. She married Gerald Rudolf Ford in 1917 and the young Leslie, though never adopted, took his stepfather's last name. Gerald Jr.'s adolescence was spent in Grand Rapids where he attended high school and developed a lifelong interest in athletics and football. At the University of Michigan, Ford demonstrated exceptional abilities in football and was named as Most Valuable Player by his teammates. Graduating with a bachelor's degree in economics in 1935, Ford went on to law school at Yale and, in 1941, went into practice shortly before the nation's entry into World War II.

Ford's naval career put him on the aircraft carrier USS *Monterey* as a lieutenant as of May 1943, and he and his shipmates saw much action in the Pacific War. Joining the staff of the Naval Reserve Training Command as a lieutenant commander, Ford was discharged in February 1946 and immediately gravitated to a career in politics. There he defeated an incumbent Republican congressman in Michigan's Fifth District, where he served from 1948 to 1973. During a long era of near-total Democratic congressional dominance, Ford never authored a piece of major legislation. He described himself as "a moderate in domestic affairs, an internationalist in foreign affairs and a conservative in fiscal policy." Appointed to the Warren Commission in 1963, Ford also supported the crucial civil rights legislation of the Johnson years. However, his views on the Vietnam War bordered on political expedience. A strong advocate of containment, Ford criticized Johnson's conduct of the war, though his private doubts about American success grew along with public disaffection with the war. Still, when Nixon won the presidency in 1968, congressman Ford dutifully fell in line with Nixon's shifting policies. Perhaps most importantly, during his long tenure in Congress, Ford gained a reputation for personal modesty, honesty, fairness, and general likability.

The national mood was confused during the hot August days of 1974. A discernible feeling of relief that that system had worked and a criminal and arguably unbalanced president had been driven from office collided with the less-optimistic perception that the constitutional and legal guardrails had only barely held. Had it not been for a free and relentlessly investigative media, a Democratic-controlled Judiciary Committee, the courts, and the ironclad ethics of a few important individuals both in and out of Congress, the outcome could have been far different. The undeniable reality was that the United States was not the exceptional nation that it was believed to be—both its president and vice president had proved to be criminals, aided and abetted by a coterie of lawbreakers and moral cowards, dozens of whom went to prison.

In the earliest days of his presidency, Gerald Ford benefited immensely from the nation's willingness to place its trust in a man who had, as he took the oath of office, promised honesty and transparency. "I assume the presidency under extraordinary circumstances," Ford acknowledged. "I am acutely aware that you have not elected me as your president by your ballots and so I ask you to confirm me with your prayers." Promising a brighter future, the former vice president declared, "My fellow Americans, our long national nightmare is over." The nation's media was immediately charmed by the new president, who opened his Alexandria, Virginia, home to journalists. The sinister bunker mentality that had characterized the Nixon presidency evaporated in the light of this new antiseptic brightness. Only hours after his swearing in, Ford was in the press room promising reporters that "we will have an open . . . and candid administration." The change in governments was evident on the first morning of Ford's presidency, as he walked out onto his driveway in pajamas to retrieve the morning paper while photographers jostled for position. This new, open style was vastly reassuring to Americans, who had grown restive at Nixon's paranoid reclusiveness. Apprised of Nixon's "Enemies List," Ford scoffed that "a person who can't keep his enemies in his head has got too many enemies."

More than a change in style, however, it was necessary for Ford to establish his own White House; he needed to assemble a loyal and competent cabinet and staff. Some Nixon holdovers were adamant about their indispensability. Chief of Staff Alexander Haig self-servingly insisted that he had personally held the government together during the final eight to ten months of Nixon's presidency. The ever-dissembling Henry Kissinger retained his position by disingenuously warning Ford that his removal as Secretary of State would result in dire consequences around the world. Haig was soon replaced by Donald Rumsfeld, with Dick Cheney as his deputy. William Simon replaced the disgraced John Mitchell as attorney general and James Schlesinger remained as secretary of defense until succeeded by Rumsfeld in 1975. David Broder praised Ford's choices as "one of the most competent staffs I've seen." The only misstep was the selection of Secretary of Agriculture Earl Butz, who was compelled to resign in 1976 after he regaled listeners with a series of obscene and racist remarks.

Determined to establish his authority and independence, Ford nominated the moderately liberal New York governor Nelson A. Rockefeller as his vice president. As a Ford biographer noted, "the American people accorded Ford a honeymoon for simply *not being* Richard Nixon." A late August Gallup poll gave Ford a 71 percent approval rating. Reaching out to previously shunned groups, Ford invited the Congressional Black Caucus and AFL-CIO president George Meany to the White House. In hopes of erasing some of the wounds of Vietnam, on August 19, Ford courageously announced before the national convention of the Veterans of Foreign Wars a policy granting conditional amnesty to Vietnam-era draft evaders and deserters. The policy was generally well received, leading presidential historian Richard Reeves to later observe that the speech "was the most striking example to date that Richard Nixon was gone." In September, however, Ford took an action that instantly ended the public honeymoon.

On September 8, Ford appeared on nationwide television to announce that he was granting "a full, free, and absolute pardon" to Nixon "for all offenses against the United States" that the former president "may have committed." A majority of Americans reacted with shock and anger upon learning that Nixon would never be held responsible for his misdeeds, even as many of his underlings were going to prison. Jerald terHorst, Ford's press secretary, resigned that same morning. A sample of press opinion makes clear the consensus opinion—the *New York Times* declared that Ford's "blundering intervention" badly eroded the president's "credibility, as a man of judgment, candor, and competence," a *Boston*

Globe editorial fumed that the pardon was "a gross misuse, if not abuse, of presidential power," while the *Washington Post* worried that the pardon was a "continuation of the cover-up." A *Time* staff writer opined that "the unreal glow is gone, and it will probably never return." A Gallup poll found 59 percent of respondents disapproving of the pardon, and Ford's approval rating subsequently fell from 71 percent to 50 percent. Ford was stunned by the negative outcry. Believing that the humiliation of forced resignation was adequate punishment for Nixon, Ford had told terHorst, "I know there will be controversy over this, but it's the right thing to do and that's why I decided to do it now." Nothing Ford did could shake the rumor of a secret bargain with Nixon, even an unprecedented appearance before the House Judiciary's Subcommittee on Criminal Justice, during which he pounded the table and asserted, "There was no deal, period, under any circumstances." Ford biographer Yanek Mieczkowski termed the Nixon pardon "the defining event of the Ford presidency" and concluded that "it may also have cost him the election in 1976."

Despite his congeniality, Ford remained the target of mean-spirited mockery that centered on his ostensible clumsiness and marginal intelligence. He had the great misfortune to be president when *Saturday Night Live* premiered in 1975 with Chevy Chase's slapstick impressions of Ford's supposed klutziness, some of which was inspired by events such as Ford's fall down an aircraft's stairway in Salzburg, Austria, a tumble while skiing in Vail, swimming into the wall of the White House pool while doing laps, and tripping while entering the presidential helicopter. A joke circulated about a "Jerry Ford doll" that when wound up, would run into whatever was nearby. The reality was that Ford was no lamebrain—he held a bachelor's degree and a law degree from Yale, and his athletic prowess and physical poise had been demonstrated while at Michigan State.

The next two years were no kinder to Ford, as he faced a succession of crises not of his making. When Ford took office, the nation's economy was suffering from the unprecedented phenomenon of stagflation, which wedded a slowing economy to growing inflation; the traditional remedies for both were contradictory. The president's initial thinking was that inflation and recession were the greater threats and placed his confidence in the public's willingness to reduce spending. Thus was born the ill-fated WIN (Whip Inflation Now) campaign in October 1974 and a ten-point economic plan that included a higher tax on corporations and high earners. Americans proved loath to reduce personal spending. In November, Ford reversed course, withdrew the tax increase, and two months later proposed a tax reduction, which became law in December 1975 with the Revenue Adjustment Act, which included spending cuts.

The energy issue was inextricably related to inflation and the threat of recession, which most Americans had ignored after the worst impact of the 1973 oil embargo passed. Few positive options existed, though Ford preferred the decontrol of oil, which would let the price of "old" oil rise to market level. In his 1975 State of the Union Address, Ford urged reducing oil imports, stockpiling domestic oil, exploring alternative energy sources, and congressional action to impose an excise tax and import fees on oil and an excise tax on natural gas. Ford also threatened the use of presidential authority to achieve these ends if Congress stalled; when he did so in February, Congress suspended this authority for ninety days. As expected, public and corporate responses to his program were generally negative and surveys revealed that one in three Americans believed the energy crisis was a hoax. The reality was that there were powerful corporate and regional political forces arrayed against any solution Ford proposed. While Congress debated the concept of "right turn on red" to save gas, the House Ways and Means Committee, at the behest of Detroit, eliminated a proposed "gas-guzzler" tax. Ford glumly complained that there were "535 energy programs up on Capitol Hill," all driven by parochial and regional political considerations.

In November, the Energy Policy and Conservation Act (ECPA) emerged from the congressional chaos, rolling back oil prices prior to phased decontrol. The act also required states to submit energy consumption reduction plans in order to qualify for federal grants, while establishing a strategic petroleum reserve and setting fuel economy standards for new cars and trucks after 1977. While development of nuclear power languished, Ford urged the doubling of coal production by 1985 and vetoed a bill banning strip-mining, but signed the EPCA in December. As it kept domestic oil prices artificially low (gas averaged less than $0.40 per gallon in 1976) any resolution of the energy crisis was delayed.

Recession, which had taken second place to the energy crisis until 1976, again emerged as an issue during the presidential election year. Rather than do nothing, Ford agreed to a tax cut with vague promises from a Democratic Congress that it would consider economies at a later point. The president recaptured some ground in late October when he promised to veto any bill aimed at bailing out a nearly bankrupt New York City. The city's *Daily News* responded with the memorable headline: "Ford to City: Drop Dead." Ford's rejection of an outright bailout won over some conservatives, and he gained congressional support for a succession of federal loans to the city in return for efforts to reduce expenditures. However, Ford's later decision to drop Vice President Rockefeller from the Republican ticket in favor of the more conservative Kansas Senator Bob Dole did much to alienate New Yorkers.

Domestic concerns were not Ford's only challenges. He had the misfortune to be in office when the Saigon regime finally collapsed in the spring of 1975. A Democratic congress steadfastly refused to appropriate an additional $722 million in military aid that Ford requested. Throwing in the towel, on April 23, Ford told an audience of Tulane University students, "Today America can regain a sense of pride that existed before Vietnam. But it cannot be achieved by refighting a war that is finished as far as America is concerned." Loud cheers and lengthy applause greeted his comments. On April 30, US Marines evacuated the remaining US citizens from the Saigon embassy, producing the iconic photos of helicopters lifting the last personnel off the embassy roof as North Vietnamese units rolled into the city. America had officially washed its hands of Vietnam, though Ford humanely agreed to admit 125,000 refugees. What remained was for Americans to come to grips with the reality that their nation had lost a war at the cost of more than 58,000 dead.

Americans hardly had time to ponder the consequences of the defeat in Vietnam before the possibility of conflict with another Southeast Asian nation. The radical Khmer Rouge were establishing a murderous communist regime in Cambodia, and on May 12, a Cambodian gunboat seized the American merchant ship *Mayaguez*. Inaccurate intelligence led the administration to send a marine detachment to Koh Tang Island, where it was believed the ship and crew were being held. Even as the Marines engaged a Cambodian force on the island, the Cambodian government was releasing the crew and ship. Some forty-one servicemen died in the fighting, but the public response generally supported Ford's decision. Nevertheless, it remains a controversial decision to this day.

Ford's conduct of foreign policy was influenced by the enlarged congressional role in international affairs signaled by the 1973 War Powers

Act and congressional concern over intelligence agency misconduct at home and abroad. Ford created the Rockefeller Commission to investigate evidence that the Central Intelligence Agency (CIA) had carried out domestic covert operations that violated its charter, and Senate committees overseen by Senators Sam Ervin and Frank Church likewise investigated possible intelligence agency illegalities and misconduct. The Church Committee, established in January 1975, documented assassination plots against foreign leaders, a devastating account of covert CIA activity in Chile, and a National Security Agency (NSA) "Watch List" that included thousands of Americans. The committee's investigations exposed the threat posed to open democratic government by the absence of congressional oversight of the nation's intelligence agencies. Ford's chief response in February 1976 was to issue Executive Order 11905 banning political assassinations, but the damage to the credibility of America's intelligence apparatus was done. Both houses of Congress established intelligence oversight select committees.

During his short presidency, Ford was confronted with numerous crises: a three-way dispute between Cyprus, Greece, and Turkey; a civil war in Angola, which drew in Soviet and Cuban support for one faction; and Indonesia's invasion of East Timor. Irritated at Israeli stalling over a Middle East peace treaty, Ford threatened cutting off US aid for military arms. The Soviet-sponsored Conference on Security and Cooperation in Helsinki, Finland, had been underway for two years when, in July 1975, Ford determined that the United States should take part, hoping that the conference would work to improve détente. The Helsinki Accords focused on a treaty that covered three areas of concern: respecting national borders and sovereignty; lowering barriers to economic, scientific, and cultural exchanges; and, perhaps most importantly, recognizing human rights. A Ford biographer deemed it "one of the finer legacies of his presidency," establishing human rights as a major international issue.

The year 1976 was not only that of a presidential election but also a year marking two hundred years of American independence. Bicentennial celebrations were somewhat muted given recent national shocks, and there was even less enthusiasm over the presidential election. While Ford fought off a strong challenge from Ronald Reagan, the Democrats nominated former Georgia governor James Earl "Jimmy" Carter, hailed as a representative of the New South, freed from the segregationist bigotry of the past. Ford's greatest weakness was the economy; as of September, unemployment had risen for the previous three months, GNP (gross national product) growth had faltered, and inflation seemed to defy any solution. In September, Ford hurriedly initiated a national vaccination campaign against a swine flu epidemic that never materialized. The presidential debates were not only boring but went largely in Carter's favor. The third debate blew up in Ford's face when he remarked that the nations of the Soviet Bloc "did not consider themselves dominated by the Soviet Union." Ford meant to assert that those nations did not consider Soviet domination legitimate—but the damage was done. Ford's running mate, Bob Dole, did the president no favors when he referred to both world wars and the Korean War as "Democrat wars." The chief threat to Carter's election came from his own missteps, as when he admitted to a *Playboy* reporter that he had "lusted after women in his heart." The public accepted Carter's explanation that his faith had aided him in overcoming these common male sins.

Carter won a close election, garnering 297 electoral votes and 40.8 million popular votes, making this the tightest presidential race since 1916. Carter gained his meager edge in large part because he was a new face in national politics, entering the race with only 2 percent name recognition. Upon telling his mother he planned to run for president, she had responded, "Of what?" In December 1973, he had stumped the panel on the television game show "What's My Line?" when no one could identify him. Herein lay his strength: Carter ran as an outsider, someone untouched by Washington's corrupting miasma, someone who could bring new solutions to the nation's problems. Many voters were won over by his simple declaration that he would never lie.

James Earl Carter Jr. was born into the Baptist household of the senior James and Lillian G. Carter on October 1, 1924, in Plains, Georgia. The town never recovered from the Great Depression, and the young James Jr. grew up among poverty, befriended black field hands, and was given his own acre of farmland, on which he grew peanuts, which were to become a mainstay of his adult income. Graduating high school in 1941, Carter studied engineering at Georgia Southwestern College before transferring to Atlanta's Georgia Institute of Technology. Admitted to the Naval Academy in 1943, when he met his wife, Rosalynn, he graduated with a bachelor of science degree in 1946. Between 1946 and 1953, he served in both the Atlantic and Pacific fleets before being attached to the

Navy's nuclear submarine program in 1952, where he was mentored by Captain Hyman Rickover. Gaining a hardship discharge upon his father's death, Carter returned to Plains and oversaw the family's peanut business.

Carter won election to the Georgia state senate in 1963, careful not to tread on the feet of segregationist colleagues, though he denounced literacy tests and stressed expanding education. In 1966, he ran for governor, improbably describing himself as "conservative, moderate, liberal, and middle-of-the-road." This effort to cover all bases failed, and Georgians ultimately elected the racist, segregationist Lester Maddox as governor. Shortly after his defeat, Carter declared himself a born-again Christian as his fourth child, Amy, was born. Running again in 1970 as a conservative populist, Carter courted the segregationist vote by praising George Wallace and promising to "return control of our schools to local people." However, Carter rejected racist politics after winning, asserting in his 1971 inaugural address, "the time of racial discrimination is over," dismaying many of his white supporters. As governor, he reorganized state government, merging three hundred state agencies into twenty-two, reduced spending to avoid a deficit, and aggressively fought for educational improvements. He brought many blacks into state agencies and, as a champion of free-flowing waterways, vetoed a dam on the Flint River. In 1971, a *Time* cover featured Carter as "the face of the New South."

Pursuing a presidential bid in 1976, Carter defeated sixteen other candidates for his party's nomination before selecting Minnesota's Senator Walter F. Mondale as his running mate. In addition to running as a Washington outsider, Carter benefited, according to Lawrence Shoup, from "the acceptance and support of elite sectors of the mass communications media." Carter came into the presidency in January 1977 with broad public support and genuine hopes for his success, though the danger lay in disappointed hopes that could quickly turn into resentment and rejection. Carter clearly deserves credit for abandoning the imperial presidency, with all its secrecy and connivances. During his inauguration, he and the new First Lady walked more than a mile down Pennsylvania Avenue, waving to cheering, hopeful crowds. Carter strove to project the image of a man of the people, often wearing casual clothes, traveling in standard government vehicles, and requesting that "Hail to the Chief" be played only on special occasions. He sought to set an example by turning down White House thermostats and donning sweaters to save energy, as well as installing solar panels on the executive mansion's roof. Attempting to reach the public directly through televised "fireside chats," Carter hoped to bring to Washington the populist aura that he had brought to Georgia.

These laudable symbolic acts could not insulate the Carter presidency from the complicated problems that the nation faced, nor could they ensure a symbiotic relationship between the Democratic Congress and a president who showed little interest in working with powerful Democrats such as Speaker of the House Tip O'Neill. This proved disastrous for Carter's initiatives; these powerful congressmen were offended at Carter's snubs and "I'll go to the people" threat when faced with congressional opposition. The absence of any definable presidential ideology was also worrisome. Carter's obsession with "comprehensive' solutions made for questionable legislative success—his national energy program consisted of 113 proposals, while his welfare reform plan ran sixty-two pages, out-done by a 178-page urban policy memorandum. Still, with high approval ratings, Carter began his presidency with an act of clemency, granting a limited pardon to Vietnam draft resisters and next set to work reducing government regulations and deregulating business. Deregulation of the airline industry was authorized in 1978. In 1979, Carter deregulated the beer industry, legalizing the sale of the necessary ingredients for beer brewing to home brewers with astounding results—by 2017, a microbrew culture had brought about the establishment of more than six thousand microbreweries and brewpubs.

Issues involving energy, the economy, and the environment remained to be addressed, however, and public patience was short. The resolution of any one of these issues was made more complicated by the inextricable con-nections between them and the reality that powerful lobbies and regional interests would also be players. Carter attacked the energy issue during the televised "cardigan speech" in which the sweater-clad president promised "comprehensive long-range energy policy by April"; in August, Carter signed a bill creating a Department of Energy. Taking to television, he deemed the fight for a national energy policy "the moral equivalent of war." Though there was broad public support for such a program, the adminis-tration's proposal, which included a "gas-guzzler" tax, taxes on domestic oil production, gas consumption, and autos with low fuel efficiency, as well as tax credits for energy conservation, was immediately dissected and killed by Congress. Not until October 1978 did a congressional bill emerge deregulating the sale of natural gas, ending pricing disparity between inter- and intra-state gas, and providing tax credits to encourage energy conservation and alternative energy sources. Carter later complained that enacting an energy policy was like "chewing on a rock that lasted the whole four years."

Carter's advocacy of environmentalism compelled him to acknowledge the power of the special interests represented in Congress. Hoping to reform national water resources policy, only weeks after taking office, Carter targeted twenty-two projects such as dams, locks, and canals as "prime candidates for extermination." As these projects involved jobs in the affected states, their representatives drove the projects through, against the president's express wishes. On a more positive note, the Carter administration acted quickly in 1978 when toxic wastes required the evacuation of eight hundred families from the Love Canal area in Niagara Falls, New York, signing the Superfund law that was intended to provide funding for containing and remediating the toxic waste matter.

Even as a solution to economic issues had eluded Ford, they likewise baffled Carter. The Carter presidency saw three years of solid, rapid economic growth and unemployment abated marginally. This growing economy, however, was the parent of increasingly hair-raising inflation and a falling dollar, even as the likelihood of a recession loomed in the future. Upon entering office, Carter had advocated a small tax reduction, public works and public service programs, and a one-time taxpayer rebate of $50. Alert to overspending, Carter withdrew the measly tax rebate in April 1977. He recouped his losses with a minimum wage bill and data showing some 625,000 new jobs in public works and services, but none of these measures ameliorated out-of-control inflation. Treading the same path that Ford had pursued, Carter pushed a program of voluntary wage and price restraints in 1978, which had little impact. The inflation rate, which stood at 6.5 percent in 1977, was headed for a devastating 15 percent in 1980, crushing consumer spending, especially on big-ticket items such as houses and autos. Carter's approval rate inversely mirrored the inflation rate, falling to 33 percent in June 1979. His hopes for a national health care plan foundered in 1978, though he did succeed in creating a Department of Education.

Events came to a head in 1979 when OPEC nations began increasing the price of oil in the aftermath of the Islamic Revolution in Iran, which caused a cessation of Iranian oil production. The doubling of the price of a barrel of oil over twelve months to a historical high produced chaos in the United States, with angry fuel-seeking motorists fuming in long lines at gas stations. Enraged truckers blockaded highways and set vehicles aflame. Some state governors suggested odd-even gas sales days, determined by license plate number. The national speed limit had already been reduced to fifty-five miles per hour in 1974, so that option was already in effect. On March 1, 1979, Congress asked Carter for a standby rationing plan but later denied him the authority. Weeks later, a serious accident at the Three Mile Island nuclear plant in Pennsylvania brought into question the adoption of nuclear energy as an alternative fuel. Following a succession of public assertions of the urgency of energy conservation, Carter canceled yet another such address and retreated to Camp David.

What grew out of Carter's withdrawal to Camp David, during which he met with political, economic, business, and religious leaders as well as intellectuals, became known somewhat inappropriately as the "Malaise Speech," though the president never used that word. On April 15, Carter took to national television to speak of a "crisis of confidence" growing out of a lengthy succession of national tragedies and disappointments. At the heart of the president's analysis of the nation's loss of meaning lay an interpretation that sprang from his spiritual convictions as well as from sociological analyses. "In a nation that was proud of hard work, strong families, close-knit communities, and our faith in God, too many of us now tend to worship self-indulgence and consumption. Human identity," he asserted, "is no longer defined by what one does, but by what one owns. But we've discovered that owning things and consuming things does not satisfy our longing for meaning. We've learned that piling up material goods cannot fill the emptiness of lives which have no confidence or purpose." This striking paragraph spoke to a truth that many in the president's audience did not want to acknowledge.

Carter noted "a growing disrespect" for government, churches, schools, and the news media and declared that this "is the truth and it is a warning." Future events would bear him out. However, Carter could offer no solution other than "we simply must have faith in each other, faith in our ability to govern ourselves." A lengthy account of his planned energy program preceded his affirmation that "working together with our common faith, we cannot fail." In many ways, the "Malaise Speech" was a brilliant summation of the roots of American discontent, but many were offended by its preachy tone and lack of solutions. FDR's "Fireside Chats" succeeded because he not only honestly apprised Americans of the dire challenges that they faced, but always concluded with an uplifting assurance that all would come right. Carter's speech was at heart a Puritan jeremiad warning his flock to repent from their materialistic ways or face divine retribution. Americans do not like being told that they are responsible for the problems that they face, be it true or otherwise.

The remainder of the year was not kind to President Carter. Scandal stained his administration as Office of Management and Budget director Bert Lance resigned in 1977 over allegations of misconduct as board chairman of a Georgia bank. Further embarrassment in 1978–1979 grew out of "Billygate," which involved the president's brother Billy's registration as a foreign agent for the Libyan government. This followed Billy's embarrassing marketing of "Billy Beer" in 1977. By 1979, the press seemed almost eager to depict Carter's misfortunes and capitalized on the "Killer Rabbit" episode. The incident grew out of Carter fishing in a Georgia pond when a rabbit jumped into the water and swam toward his boat, where Carter used a paddle to deflect the creature. The story hit the front page of the *Washington Post* on August 30 under the headline "Bunny Goes Bugs: Rabbit Attacks President." Press Secretary Jody Powell claimed in a 1986 book that the offending creature was dangerous, "a swamp rabbit . . . perhaps berserk . . . making strange hissing noises and gnashing its teeth" with the obvious intent of "climbing into the presidential boat." Carter critics howled with laughter. Much worse was yet to come.

Carter hoped that his conduct of foreign policy would serve to usher in an era of international peace, and his stress on the primacy of respect for human rights in American relations with the world bore the stamp of this spiritual convictions. His greatest achievement was the Camp David Accords. Determined to defuse Middle East tensions, Carter brought Israeli Prime Minister Menachem Begin and Egyptian President Anwar Sadat to Camp David in September 1978 and essentially compelled them to remain until an agreement was reached. The resulting Camp David Accords laid the grounds for a peace treaty between Egypt and Israel in 1979 and the transition to elected governments in the West Bank and Gaza. Begin and Sadat shared the Nobel

Figure 9.2. Egyptian President Anwar Sadat, President Carter, and Israeli Prime Minister Menachem Begin at the signing of the Israeli-Eyptian peace treaty in 1979. *Source:* Library of Congress / Leffler, Warren K.

Peace Prize in 1978. In 1981, the treaty cost Sadat his life at the hands of radicals in his own army.

In October 1977, Carter addressed African delegates at the UN, stressing his hope for a "free and prosperous Africa" and a resolution to the issue of minority white rule and apartheid in South Africa. In May 1979, the Senate lifted economic sanctions on Rhodesia, greatly dampening Carter's hopes. Completing Nixon's opening to the People's Republic of China, Carter granted formal diplomatic recognition to that nation in 1979. In Central America, the Carter administration withdrew US support of the corrupt and brutal Somoza government, which was overthrown by the popular Sandinista Revolution that year. The eventual emergence of a Marxist regime under Daniel Ortega would leave Carter open to allegations that he had enabled the establishment of communism in Central America.

The same year saw American relations with the Soviet Union deteriorate rapidly as the latter invaded Afghanistan in late December 1979 to bolster a faltering Marxist regime. In summer 1978, Carter had sought to engage the Russians in a second round of nuclear weapons limitation talks

(SALT II), but the president's insistence on including discussions of human rights only brought a Soviet crackdown on dissidents such as Andrei Sakharov; the Soviet invasion of Afghanistan effectively killed *détente*. Carter also imposed a grain embargo on the USSR, promised renewed aid to Pakistan, halted participation in the SALT II talks, and called for a boycott of the 1980 Moscow Olympics. In addition, he authorized a program to provide arms for the *mujahideen*, Afghan guerrillas who fought the Soviets. Decades later, the blowback from this policy would prove catastrophic. The 1980 Carter Doctrine asserted American willingness to resort to military force to protect its national interests in the Middle East. As often happened when national security was threatened, the public rallied to Carter, his approval rating soaring from a dismal 32 percent to 61 percent in one month.

Carter had the great misfortune to be president when one of history's greatest examples of "blowback" (unexpected consequences) took place. America's decades-long support for the cruel dictatorship of Iranian Shah Reza Pahlavi, who seized power following a 1953 CIA-backed coup that overthrew Mohammad Mosaddeq maintaining control through SAVAK (meaning, in English, Intelligence and Security Organization of the

Figure 9. 3. President Carter congratulates Ruth Bader Ginsburg on her appointment to the federal court of appeals.
Source: Wikimedia Commons / Jimmy Carter's Presidential Photographs, 1/20/1977–1/20/1981

Country) a brutal secret police force, and American arms blew up in the Carter administration's face in the late 1970s. Despite national security adviser Zbigniew Brzezinski's warning about rising anti-Shah sentiment, Carter visited Tehran in 1978 and proclaimed the Shah's Iran "an island of stability in a turbulent corner of the world." One of those who took note was the aged Shia cleric Ayatollah Ruhollah Khomeini, around whom anti-Shah resistance was coalescing. Khomeini advocated a strict Islamic regime and the end of "corrupting Westernization." Exiled first to Iraq and then Paris, Khomeini spread his message of Iranian renewal through the Islamic Revolution as popular demonstrations erupted across Iran. As almost every element of Iranian society joined the opposition, the Iranian army turned on the Shah. On January 16, 1979, the Shah fled Iran; on February 1, Khomeini arrived in Tehran to head the new government, which by was dominated by Islamists and radical students who embraced Khomeini's "government of God." Khomeini's denunciation of the United States as the "Great Satan" attained greater force once Carter made the disastrous, if humane, decision to admit the Shah to the United States for cancer treatment in October. Two failed attempts to invade the US embassy in Tehran were followed by a third successful effort on November 4. Thousands of chanting Iranians surrounded the complex as a group of armed radicals disarmed the marine contingent and seized sixty-six embassy personnel. The 444-day-long Iranian hostage crisis that largely defined the final year of the Carter presidency had begun.

Though fourteen hostages, mostly women, were released, the nation and its president became fixated on the remaining fifty-two. Hosted by ABC's Ted Koppel, *America Held Hostage*, a specialized news program, effectively captured the national mood with its title. Out of this grew *Nightline*, a late-night news show that offered daily updates. Carter became the chief hostage to the crisis, remaining in the White House for more than one hundred days during a presidential campaign year, pledging not to authorize any military action that "would cause bloodshed or arouse the unstable captors of our hostages to attack them or punish them."

Planning for such a mission had already begun on November 6, 1979. Having announced economic sanctions against Iran on April 7, about two weeks later Carter gave the go-ahead for Operation Eagle Claw, a mission to free the hostages, the success of which seemed highly improbable to any objective evaluator. The complexity of the planned operation was staggering, involving all three military branches. On April 24, eight Sea Stallion helicopters would launch from an aircraft carrier in the Persian Gulf to meet up with three C-130 transports flying from an island off Oman to rendezvous at an Iranian salt flat called Desert One, some two hundred miles southeast of Tehran. From there, the helicopters would airlift an assault team to Desert Two, closer to Tehran. All US forces would remain in place overnight. The following morning, trucks secured by in-country CIA agents would drive the rescue team into Tehran, where its members would secure the embassy and the Iranian Foreign Affairs building, where two hostages were being held, before loading the hostages into the trucks, which would head for Amjadieh Stadium, where all would be picked up by the Desert Two helicopters. The helicopters would then fly the hostages to a nearby abandoned airbase, where they would board C-141s for a flight to Egypt. All the helicopters would be abandoned and destroyed.

To the great misfortune of all involved, these events did not occur as planned. The fate of the mission was sealed when three of the eight helicopters were delayed or disabled by a sandstorm, which fouled air intakes and wreaked havoc on electrical systems, while one suffered a cracked rotor blade. As the mission's success required a minimum of six helicopters, Carter aborted the mission after consulting with the military commanders. The real horrors began as the units at Desert One prepared to depart. As one of the helicopters attempted to move another that needed refueling by a process called "hover taxi," the pilot of the airborne helicopter, blinded by sand, crashed into a nearby C-130, setting off an explosion and fire that killed eight. In the chaos of the firelit scene, it was decided to abandon the remaining helicopters, which could not be destroyed as they were filled with fuel and ammunition that would endanger the C-130s. The remaining personnel at Desert One lifted off in the C-130s, leaving behind the dead, intact helicopters, and a scorched landscape.

The following day, Carter made what must have been the most heart-wrenching announcement of his presidency. Having hoped to announce the freeing of the hostages, Carter instead went before the television cameras at 7:00 a.m. to announce the dreadful news that the effort had failed catastrophically. Iranian television gleefully ran film of the carnage at Desert One; one segment showed a cleric spitting on burned American bodies. The hostages were subsequently moved to diverse locations to discourage another such attempt. Carter's advisers had been divided over the use of force or a military rescue. National Security Adviser Brzezinski had advocated that the United States "bomb the hell out Tehran and risk having the hostages killed," as it would rally the public to a decisive president. Secretary of State Cyrus Vance warned that he would resign if Carter agreed to the raid and made good on his word. For the rest of his term, the hostage crisis followed Carter like a dark cloud, as the Iranians made clear that the hostages would never be released during his presidency. Every evening, network news anchors ticked off the number of days that the crisis endured. Democratic leadership seemed to have failed at home and abroad.

During these same years of apparent American impotence, a powerful and diverse conservative movement coalesced in opposition to most everything that Democratic liberalism stood for. The genesis of the New Right goes back to the 1950s, when moderate liberalism still held sway. Conservative economic theories were largely discredited during the Hoover presidency and in the 1950s conservatism was often identified with isolationism, segregation, red-baiting, racism, and extremism. The John Birch Society, the Ku Klux Klan, the American Nazi Party, and Southern racists, though on the fringes of conservatism, did much to discredit the ideology. One of the first steps toward redefining conservatism came in 1955 with the founding of William F. Buckley Jr.'s *National Review*, which aimed to marginalize the kooks and bring together libertarian, religious, and anti-communist conservatives under the banner of a coherent and respectable ideology. The first indication that the new conservatism had found a home in the Republican Party came in 1964 when Arizona Senator Barry Goldwater, who had voted against the 1964 Civil Rights Act, won the Republican presidential nomination denouncing federal overreach, social security, and spending on social programs while demanding an aggressively anti-communist foreign policy that did not exclude the use of nuclear weapons. His philosophy was accurately summed up in an oft-repeated statement in his acceptance speech: "Extremism in the defense of liberty is no vice. Moderation in the pursuit of justice is no virtue." Though Goldwater went down in ignominious defeat, losing the election by the widest margin in history to President Johnson (52 to 486 electoral votes), few could have guessed that most of his ideas would be embraced by a majority of the electorate only sixteen years later. Actor Ronald Reagan, who endorsed Goldwater in an October speech, claimed the California governorship in 1966 as a stepping stone to the White House. In his presidential campaign of 1968, former Alabama governor George Wallace espoused a populist message that spoke to the "angry white man," who believed that liberal politicians coddled hippies, criminals, student protestors, and black radicals. The Republican Party and the New Right both absorbed these messages.

The New Right movement of the 1970s was a truly grassroots phenomenon, as millions of Americans, alarmed by what they saw as the excesses of 1960s liberalism and the threat posed by counterculture values, took action locally and at the ballot box. The New Right was given national coherence by several individuals, most notably Richard Viguerie, who perfected direct mail as the most efficacious communication method among the New Rightists, maintaining that it was one of the "Four Keys to Our Success." The identification and mobilization of single-issue groups such as the National Rifle Association (NRA), STOP ERA (Equal Rights Amendment), and antiabortion groups was equally important. Additionally, new organizations such as the American Conservative Union and the National Political Action Committee were crucial to establishing agendas, organizing pressure groups, fundraising, and grassroots activities.

Out of these groups came new leaders such as Paul Weyrich, Terry Dolan, and newly elected Georgia representative Newt Gingrich, who voiced these issues in Congress. These activists helped create a New Right network to bring together a politically potent coalition that focused on national defense, anti-elitism, challenging the liberal establishment, and promoting "family values." The latter came to include antifeminism, opposition to LGBTQ+ rights, and protests against "biased" school textbooks and sex education in schools.

This "pro-family" coalition was a key component of the emerging Christian Right, the growth of which was fueled by the Supreme Court's ban on school prayer in 1962 and court-ordered integration and efforts by the Carter administration to tax private Christian academies. These issues found organizational voice in the 1979 founding of the Moral Majority by Baptist minister Jerry Falwell, whose Liberty College (later Liberty University) in Lynchburg, Virginia, became a crucial linchpin in the Christian Right movement, which soon drew in other evangelical ministers and churches, many of whom could propagate their beliefs through radio and television. As James Dobson's "Family Forum" flourished on radio, "televangelists," including Falwell, Pat Robertson, Jim and Tammy Bakker, Oral Roberts, and James Robison, among others, all charged liberalism with causing America's decline.

The New Right also boasted its own intellectual cadre, including Norman Podhoretz of *Commentary*, Irving Kristol at the *Public Interest*, and of course William Buckley Jr., many of whom were regular commentators on television. The new ideology of neoconservatism rested chiefly on opposition to liberal big government and adherence to free market capitalism, but not to the extent of opposing all regulation. In foreign policy, the "neocons" supported aggressive opposition to communist expansion and a robust defense policy, which meant opposition to the 1977 Panama Canal Treaty and support for expanding the military. Many neoconservatives were former liberals who had become disenchanted with that ideology. Irving Kristol famously described neoconservatives as "liberals who have been mugged by reality." Through their writings in newspapers and a growing profusion of periodicals, such as *Human Events, Conservative Digest, Washington Weekly*, and *American Spectator*, and in television appearances, the neoconservatives gave conservatism the intellectual foundation that it had lacked in previous years.

According to historian Bruce J. Schulman, the issue that was embraced by all elements of the New Right was the tax revolt of the late 1970s. Lowering taxes was an innately popular position and those on the New Right could easily make the case that stagflation, rising property assessments, and wasteful federal spending on costly and abused social welfare programs promoted by liberals were the causes of outrageous taxation. Claims that taxpayer money was used to fund abortion and sex education enraged many in the movement. One of candidate Ronald Reagan's favorite anecdotes involved a fictional "welfare queen" living in public housing and growing wealthy on fraudulently acquired taxpayer money through the use of multiple aliases and nonexistent dependents. The unspoken implication was that this individual was black, which corresponded with the widespread falsehood that most "welfare" funds went to blacks. In 1978, Howard Jarvis led the first major tax revolt in California with the passage of Proposition 13, which limited property tax increases to 2 percent annually. The emergence, convergence, and dynamic growth of the populist, religious, and intellectual strands of the New Right during the 1970s went largely unnoticed or were dismissed by the liberal establishment until it was too late to effectively refute them. In

1980, these pigeons came home to roost, with disastrous consequences for Democratic politicians.

Carter was determined to win reelection in 1980, attacking his Republican opponent as too old, too radical, uninformed, and prone to inexplicable gaffes, once claiming that trees were a primary producer of carbon dioxide. Ted Kennedy again challenged Carter but made little headway. A debate schedule became problematic when Carter refused to participate in the first debate if a third-party candidate, moderate Republican John Anderson, was present. In the second presidential debate between Reagan and Carter, the president hoped to put Reagan away. But the smiling, relaxed Republican brushed aside Carter's attacks with the line, "There you go again," suggesting that the president routinely mischaracterized Reagan's policies. Reagan's positive can-do attitude, together with his assurance that Americans would not have to settle for the diminished future that Carter seemed to represent, meshed well with a public desire to embrace his conservative vision of American renewal. In November, Reagan won in a landslide of 489 electoral votes. Several long-serving liberal Democratic senators likewise suffered defeat as the Republicans took control of the Senate for the first time since the 1950s, signaling a lengthy national turn toward conservatism.

Only hours after Reagan's inauguration in January 1981, the American hostages in Iran were released. Carter's presidency had begun with tremendous (perhaps exaggerated) hopes, but events, coupled with Carter's unfamiliarity with Washington and his unwillingness to accord congressional Democrats the respect they demanded, undercut his presidency from the beginning. As early as late 1977, commentators noted growing public disenchantment with the "man from Plains." Carter bore no responsibility for the foreign or domestic crises that beset his presidency, but his inability to effectively deal with them contributed to an image of weakness and/or ineptitude that his successor promised to remedy. In his postpresidential years, Carter continued to play a role in international diplomacy, often to the chagrin of more than one sitting president. In his later years, Carter devoted much of his time to humanitarian organizations and activities, notably Habitat for Humanity. Though often ranked by historians as one of the less successful presidents, many commentators have praised Carter as the nation's "best ex-president." A devout Baptist who has endured and conquered numerous illnesses in old age, Carter's most enduring triumph may be that he faithfully lived the life of the Christian creed he embraced.

❖❖❖

In the late 1970s, the new feminism appeared to have unstoppable momentum. Growing out of the National Organization for Women, founded in 1966 by Betty Friedan and two other feminist activists, modern feminism had greatly advanced the national debate over women's roles in society, politics, employment, sports, and many other areas of public endeavor. This was not without often snide derision. When Friedan led the Women's Strike March in New York City in 1970, media figures and politicians derided the marchers; a West Virginia senator referred to the protesters as "braless bubbleheads." Even CBS's respected anchorman Walter Cronkite described the participants as "a militant minority." Yet within a few years, substantial progress was undeniable. The Equal Rights Amendment (ERA), drawn up in 1923 but shuffled aside in a conservative decade, was revived in 1971 and was overwhelmingly supported by both the House and Senate prior to its ratification by thirty-five of the required majority of thirty-eight states. By 1977, ERA seemed on its way to assuring equal legal rights for American women as the 1977 National Women's Conference met in late November in Houston, where a wide range of issues were addressed by the conferees. They could never have imagined how profound an impact on the ERA that gathering across town would have.

Meeting in Houston's Astro Arena, an overflow crowd of 15,000 flocked to a "Pro-Life, Pro-Family" rally organized by lawyer and right-wing activist Phyllis Schlafly, where the attendees heard speakers denounce the ERA, liberalism, feminism, lesbianism, and abortion as threats to the American family while praising "traditional family values." Though Schlafly's rally drew little media attention and was viewed as inconsequential, within a shockingly short span of time it became evident that Schlafly and the sentiments expressed at the Houston rally presented a potentially fatal threat to passage of the ERA and represented a significant backlash against modern feminism. Within a few years, many feminist spokeswomen grudgingly conceded that Schlafly, who was to become the *bête noire* of modern feminism, was a "maddeningly" difficult debate opponent, an articulate spokeswoman for the "family values" that were the cornerstone of New Right politics and a brilliantly effective organizer of opposition to the ERA. As law professor Joan C. Williams explains, "ERA was defeated when Schlafly turned it into a war among women over gender roles." Political scientist Jan J. Mansbridge affirms Schlafly's crucial role, noting that the ERA would

Figure 9.4. Phyllis Schlafly, organizer of the STOP-ERA movement and the Eagle Forum, whose activities did much to prevent the ratification of the Equal Rights Amendment. Source: Library of Congress / Leffler, Warren K.

have been ratified "had it not been for Phyllis Schlafly's early and effective effort to organize potential opponents."

Phyllis Schlafly's attraction to and involvement in right-wing politics long predated the ERA battle of the 1970s. As early as 1946, Schlafly was employed by the American Enterprise Institute as a researcher, and she subsequently worked for Republican congressional candidates and sought congressional office herself several times in the 1940s and 1960s. She first gained national attention in 1964 when, hoping to nudge the GOP away from a moderate presidential candidate, Schlafly wrote and self-published *A Choice Not an Echo* with the intent of bolstering the candidacy of Arizona Senator Barry Goldwater. It was a formidable task in a nation that had long embraced the moderate center of national politics. Goldwater was an outspoken conservative who opposed Social Security and the Civil Rights Act, and was seen by many as uncomfortably willing to consider the use of nuclear weapons. Schlafly's chief fight was within her own party, which she believed had, for too long, allowed Northeastern "kingmakers" to nominate moderate conservatives like Thomas E. Dewey or even former Democrats like Wendell Willkie as presidential candidates. Schlafly identified with the

Western and Midwestern wings of the party, which were traditionally isolationist and anti–New Deal, favoring candidates like Ohio's Robert A. Taft.

Schlafly believed 1964 was the crucial year for conservative Republicans to ensure that their party was not bulldozed into nominating the liberal New Yorker Nelson A. Rockefeller, Michigan's George Romney, or Pennsylvania's William A. Scranton. Distributing her book in mass quantities, including to the Republican National Committee (RNC), she intended to distribute a half million copies of *A Choice Not an Echo* in California, where a primary victory would be critical to a Goldwater nomination. The John Birch Society helped by handing out 300,000 copies of the book. Actor Ronald Reagan aided considerably with his nomination speech "A Time for Choosing." Schlafly and party conservatives were rewarded when Goldwater wrested the nomination away from the Northeastern liberals in July 1964. Gardiner Johnson, California RNC member, attributed Goldwater's nomination in large part to Schlafly's book. The triumph proved temporary—Goldwater lost the general election in a Democratic landslide. No one could have guessed that the monumental defeat signaled the future electoral dominance of the Republican Party.

Born in St. Louis, Missouri, on August 15, 1924, to John B. and Odie Stewart, Phyllis S. Stewart's youth in a Catholic household was shaped partly by the Depression, when her machinist father was briefly unemployed. As a teenager she worked as a model before graduating high school and from St. Louis's Washington University, where she earned a bachelor's degree in 1944, later earning a master's degree in government at Radcliffe. After doing defense work during World War II, she returned to Washington University for a law degree and earned her degree in 1978. In 1946, she worked at the American Enterprise Institute and on the congressional campaign of Claude Bakewell. Taking time out to marry Fred Schlafly in 1949, she briefly settled into the role of housewife, and the couple eventually had six children. Unsuccessfully seeking congressional seats in Illinois in 1952 and 1960, her rightward direction continued as she and her husband authored the American Bar Association's "Report on Communist Tactics, Strategy, and Objectives." In 1960, she raised her profile in Republican national politics as leader of a revolt of "moral conservatives" who opposed Richard Nixon's stands against racial segregation and discrimination. After the Goldwater debacle, Schlafly ran unsuccessfully for the presidency of the National Federation of

Republican Women. Still on a losing streak, she was defeated in a 1970 Illinois contest for a seat in the House of Representatives.

Fame was not long in coming, however, and even before the 1977 Houston rally she quickly rose to lead the "Stop Taking Our Privileges" movement, better known as STOP ERA. The name itself spoke directly to Schlafly's conception of the dangers presented by second-wave feminism—it was at base an effort to deprive women of their traditionally privileged position in society. Those privileges, according to Schlafly, included the "dependent wife" benefits provided by Social Security, alimony, child custody, separate restrooms for men and women, and exclusion from the military draft. Beginning her campaign against the ERA in 1972, Schlafly was a frequent radio commentator in Chicago from 1973 to 1975 and on the *CBS Morning News* from 1974 to 1975. She adamantly opposed the Supreme Court's 1973 *Roe v. Wade* decision, denouncing it as the "worst decision" in the court's history, "responsible for the killing of millions of unborn babies."

The wording of the ERA seemed to offer little reason for controversy. The heart of the amendment is in the first of three articles, reading, "Equality of rights under the law shall not be abridged by the United States or any State on account of sex." The other articles gave Congress the power to legislatively enforce the amendment and stated that it would go into effect two years after ratification. Initially, Schlafly and those who shared her views seemed to be struggling against strong headwinds. The Democratic and Republican parties had included support for the ERA in their platforms since the 1940s. Until the late 1960s, the ERA was strongly supported by Republican women and prominent Republicans, including Presidents Eisenhower and Nixon. The amendment was sent out to the states in 1972 and twenty-two state legislatures rapidly approved, with eight more signing on in 1973. That same year, Ruth Bader Ginsburg, writing in the *American Bar Association Journal*, supported ratification, asserting that the ERA "looks toward a legal system in which each person will be judged on the basis of individual merit and not on the basis of an unalterable trait of birth that bears no necessary relationship to need or ability." ERA advocates began to fret, however, when only five additional states ratified the amendment between 1974 and 1975, and the 1979 deadline for final approval was approaching.

These were the same years in which Schlafly's STOP ERA group, renamed the Eagle Forum in 1975, began to demonstrate its strength in opposing the ERA. In a decade that brought a significant backlash to the liberalization of American society, Schlafly's Eagle Forum condemned. the ERA as a product of radical feminism and an instrument that threatened traditional gender roles. Feminists, she claimed, were acting out of self-hatred. "The women's liberationist," she declared, "is imprisoned by her own negative view of herself," making it necessary "for women to agitate and demonstrate and hurl demands on society in order to wrest from an oppressive male-dominated social structure the status that has been wrongfully denied to women." The ERA, she claimed, was designed to benefit young career women and threaten the security of middle-aged housewives who lacked job skills. Schlafly's opposition to gay rights likewise played a role in her opposition to the ERA. In 1977, she declared, "Another silliness of the women's liberationists is their frenetic desire to force all women to accept the title Ms in place of *Miss* or *Mrs*. If Gloria Steinem and Betty Friedan want to call themselves *Ms* . . . their wishes should be respected. . . . Most married women . . . worked hard for the 'r' in their names, and they don't care to be gratuitously deprived of it." According to Schlafly, an accomplished lawyer, women also lacked basic intellectual capabilities. In a 1977 comment on the nature of women, Schlafly glibly remarked, "Men are philosophers, women are practical, and 'twas ever thus. . . . Women don't take naturally to a search for the intangible and the abstract."

Little wonder that feminists fumed at Schlafly's faux sociology, denigration of female intellectual capabilities, and regular belittling of legitimate feminist objectives. What made the situation worse was that Schlafly, perhaps because of her legal education, was a formidable debate opponent, capable of provoking feminist opponents to furious rebuttals, while remaining calm and responding with a condescending smile. Any feminist who debated Schlafly undoubtedly sympathized with Betty Friedan, who after just such an encounter in 1973 exploded in frustration, telling the anti-ERA activist, "I would like to burn you at the stake. . . . I consider you a traitor to your sex, an Aunt Tom." Of course, that was exactly the response that Schlafly sought, to prove that feminists were all nothing more than "angry women."

Salting the national debate with a continuing series of anti-ERA and antifeminist comments, Schlafly and her Eagle Forum played a major role in the slow death of the ERA by a thousand cuts. Between 1973 and 1979, Nebraska, Tennessee, Idaho, Kentucky, and South Dakota rescinded their ratifications of the ERA. In five states, only one legislative house approved ratification. By the late 1970s, as efforts to extend the ratification deadline wound their way through several state legislatures and numerous lawsuits were filed, passage appeared far from certain. The 1980 Republican Party platform fudged the issue by claiming that it was now up to state legislatures and the courts. The US Supreme Court finally ruled in October 1982 that the ERA's ratification effort had expired in 1979 and that the state recissions stood. The ERA died three state votes short of the required thirty-eight for ratification.

The consequences were significant. As historian Judith Glazer-Raymo notes, "The ERA's defeat seriously damaged the women's movement, destroying its momentum and its potential to foment social change." The political consequences, however, were equally important. "Eventually," Glazer-Raymo notes, "this resulted in feminist dissatisfaction with the Republican Party, giving the Democrats a new source of strength." That trend continued as Schlafly became a powerful voice within conservative circles for more than four decades, denouncing the concept of marital rape, gay rights and gay marriage, immigration reforms, women in combat, and sex education. As to the latter, Schlafly claimed that "sex education classes are like in-home sales parties for abortions." Higher education also posed a threat, as "radical feminists . . . staff women's studies departments at most colleges." In the workplace, she claimed, "sexual harassment . . . is not a problem for virtuous women." Schlafly was an ardent supporter of all Republican presidents and accused President Obama of compiling "a record of hostility to religion that is unmatched by any other president." She found no irony in supporting the adulterous Donald Trump for the presidency in 2016, despite multiple allegations of sexual assault, his vulgar comments recorded on the *Access Hollywood* tape, or a $130,000 payment to a porn star for her silence. An ambitious author of right-wing books, pamphlets, and articles in her later years, Schlafly died in September 2016. Her role in the battle for the ERA is recounted in the controversial FX miniseries *Mrs. America*, in which Cate Blanchett played the role of the conservative provocateur.

"ARE YOU BETTER OFF NOW. . . ?"
The End of the 1970s

T he general election of 1980 inaugurated a lengthy era of conservatism, overseen by the septuagenarian Republican president
Ronald Reagan, who advocated economic policies that were born
in the 1920s, social policies that negatively impacted the least wealthy
and underprivileged Americans, fiscal policies that rewarded the wealthy,
and a foreign policy that seemed drawn from the most contentious and
dangerous years of the Cold War in the 1950s. The nation embarked on
a course characterized as "neoconservatism" or the New Conservatism,
hawking conservative policies that had been relegated to the margins of
politics for forty years. The altruistic activism of previous decades seemed
to recede in the face of a new ethos that celebrated wealth and material
acquisition. Hippies gave way to yuppies (young upwardly mobile professionals) and the new creed was, as proclaimed by the fictitious broker and
corporate raider Gordon Gekko (Michael Douglas), portrayed in 1987's
Wall Street, "greed, for lack of a better word, is good."

An aggressively anti-communist foreign policy brought renewed fear of
nuclear war of an intensity that Americans had not experienced since the
1950s and early 1960s. Those same policies led to US interventions in the
Caribbean and Central America, as Marxism was deemed a major threat in
those regions, resulting in a US invasion of the tiny island of Grenada and
open and surreptitious aid to right-wing regimes and guerrillas in Central
America. Instability in the Middle East and North Africa drew the United
States into a costly intervention in Lebanon, where 241 Marines died

in a terrorist bombing in 1983, and several military confrontations with Muammar al-Qadhafi radical regime occurred in 1986, during which US aircraft bombed several Libyan cities.

Ronald Reagan won reelection in a landslide in 1984, defeating hapless Democrat Walter Mondale. Reagan's campaign proclaimed, "It's morning in America," crediting the president's policies with restoring national pride (to which there is some truth) as well as the nation's international standing, bringing inflation under control as employment statistics rose, and offering a much-sought new direction. Perhaps most surprising, by mid-decade, Reagan's earlier visceral anti-communism gave way to the president's desire to avoid nuclear war and willingness to meet with Mikhail Gorbachev, the new Soviet general secretary. Nuclear anxieties abated as the two met on multiple occasions and got along well. Efforts to defuse Soviet-American tensions continued under the presidency of George H. W. Bush, elected in 1988, leading to nuclear arms reduction treaties and the dissolution of the Soviet Union in 1991.

The more "radical" aspects of the Reagan Revolution gave way to a "kinder, gentler America" during the presidency of George Herbert Walker Bush, even as the consequences of a decade of unrestrained corporate and financial greed and misdoings were uncovered in a savings and loan scandal and revelations about the damage done by "junk bonds" and other dubious financial instruments pushed by Ivan Boesky and Carl Icahn. As a recession set in, the glory years of the Reagan recovery faded in the face of growing industrial unemployment and the realization that worker wages and benefits had been greatly eroded in an age of corporate greed. Ideological conservatives turned their ire on the moderate Bush, who was damned for requesting a tax increase to help pay off a burgeoning national deficit and for abandoning Reagan's more radical policies. As the conservative revolution was undone by infighting and public perceptions that some aspects of the Reagan Revolution had been carried to injurious extremes, the door was opening for alternative approaches to government, proffered during the 1992 general election by Democrat Bill Clinton and Reform Party candidate H. Ross Perot.

Many aspects of 1960s and 1970s activism survived the 1980s intact and, in numerous cases, strengthened. Racial justice, minority rights, women's rights, and environmentalism all demonstrated new energy as the nation moved into the 1990s. American national politics have demonstrated a historical tendency to swing between liberal and conservative tendencies. Columnist Russell Baker wrote in the mid-1970s that, given the tumult of the 1960s, "Americans hungered for boredom. A sleepy government, some peace in the streets. . . . It seemed an unattainable dream of paradise. Now we may have it and may even by enjoying it." Careful readers of this book will perceive the flaws in this interpretation. American life was anything but boring in the 1970s, and far from being a decade in which "nothing happened," the 1970s were in fact a crucial transitional era between the liberal, even radical 1960s and the conservative decade of the 1980s. It was an era in which Americans confronted a series of life-altering crises that defied solution, and struggled to identify the path forward through a fog of uncertainty. Two chief developments help explain why the 1970s seemed so trying to many Americans. Though the 1970s have a dreary reputation in public memory and among many intellectuals, the nation had survived much worse, including a civil war, two world wars, and an interceding depression, wars in Korea and Vietnam, and the threat of nuclear Armageddon for several decades. What made the shortages and uncertainties of the 1970s seem so unbearable was that they followed more than two decades of economic progress in which the majority of Americans could see the material consequences of postwar prosperity in the homes, cars, and possessions that they acquired. That uplifting reality faded quickly as the 1970s began.

The second major development that ensured that the 1970s would seem so grim was the fact that the social consensus that had bound Americans together during and since World War II eroded quickly after 1965. The war had compelled a sense of collective sacrifice toward a laudable goal—the survival of "the American way of life" and world democracy. Americans could take pride in knowing that their collective sacrifice had played a major role in defeating the worst tyranny of the twentieth century. The advent of the Cold War did much to preserve this sense of national unity in the face of communist aggression. That crucial social consensus began to shred rapidly by the mid-1960s, torn apart by deepening fissures over the war in Vietnam, racial polarization, campus unrest, urban violence, and rising crime. By 1970 much of the promise of the 1960s had proved elusory. Barely able to process the significance of the tumultuous and alarming events of the late 1960s, Americans entered the next decade only to be confronted with a sequence of equally disturbing and often incomprehensible developments. Dazed by the events that preceded the 1970s, and confused by what followed, the American people confronted the decade divided, uncertain, and anxious about what awaited them.

BIBLIOGRAPHIC ESSAY

Chapter One "I'm Wasted, and I Can't Find My Way Home": The End of the 1960s

While there are shelves of histories of the 1960s, a recent new study of that decade may be found in Robert C. Cottrell's *The Activist Sixties: Striving for Political and Social Empowerment in America* (Jefferson, NC: McFarland, 2023). Though there are numerous books about 1968, there are fewer that deal fully or partially with 1969. Rob Kirkpatrick's *1969: The Year Everything Changed* (New York: Skyhorse, 2009) challenges 1968's preeminence as the most turbulent year. Philip Jenkins's *Decade of Nightmares: The End of the Sixties and the Making of Eighties America* (New York: Oxford University Press, 2006) argues that some social movements that gained impetus in the 1960s took root and had a notable impact in subsequent decades, provoking a conservative reaction. Bryan Burrough's *Days of Rage: America's Radical Underground, the FBI, and the Forgotten Age of Revolutionary Violence* (New York: Penguin, 2015) follows the radical movements of the 1960s through the 1970s. Kirkpatrick Sale's *SDS* (New York: Vintage, 1974) is the standard work on that organization up through 1972. *The R. Crumb Handbook* (London: MQ Publications, 2005) by R. Crumb and Peter Poplaski offers a fascinating look into the life, mind, and artwork of the best-known underground cartoonist of the later 1960s. *Miracle Year 1969: Amazing Mets and Super Jets* (New York: Sports Publishing, 2016) covers two major sports of that year.

Chapter Two "A Decent Interval": America's Exit from Vietnam, 1969–1973

Among the numerous books about the American war in Vietnam, the best brief summary is George C. Herring's *America's Longest War: The United States and Vietnam, 1950–1975,* 5th edition (New York: McGraw-Hill Education, 2015). Stanley Karnow's *Vietnam: A History* (New York: Penguin, 1997) has been the standard comprehensive account of the conflict for decades. Newer entries are Max Hastings's *Vietnam: An Epic Tragedy, 1945–1975* (New York: HarperCollins, 2018) and Robert Mann's *A Grand Delusion: America's Descent into Vietnam* (New York: Basic Books, 2001). Brian VanDeMark's *Road to Disaster: A New History of America's Descent into Vietnam* (New York: HarperCollins, 2018) examines the war up through 1969. Neil Sheehan's *A Bright Shining Lie: John Paul Vann and America in Vietnam* (New York: Vintage, 1989) stands out as an excellent recounting of an American army officer's efforts to formulate a strategy for victory. Max Boot's excellent *The Road Not Taken: Edward Lansdale and the American Tragedy in Vietnam* (New York: W. W. Norton, 2018) examines the impact of CIA operative Edward Lansdale on American policy in Vietnam. Henry Kissinger's role in war strategy and diplomacy are examined in Robert K. Brigham's *Reckless: Henry Kissinger and the Tragedy of Vietnam* (New York: PublicAffairs, 2018); Greg Grandin's *Kissinger's Shadow: The Long Reach of America's Most Controversial Statesman* (New York: Henry Holt and Company, 2015); and Jussi Hanhimäki's *The Flawed Architect: Henry Kissinger and American Foreign Policy* (New York: Oxford University Press, 2004). Christopher Hitchens's *The Trial of Henry Kissinger* (New York: Verso, 2008) argues that Kissinger's Vietnam policy, as well as that regarding Chile, constituted war crimes. Two books that focus on how the ground war was waged are *Tiger Force: A True Story of Men and War* (New York: Little, Brown and Company, 2006), which details the atrocities of a unit that was ultimately disbanded after it got out of control, and Nick Turse's *Kill Anything That Moves: The Real American War in Vietnam* (New York: Henry Holt and Company, 2013), which posits that American atrocities were far from being exceptional. Some of the best fictional accounts and oral histories of the war are Graham Greene's *The Quiet American* (New York: Penguin, 1955) and *The Things They Carried* (New York: Houghton Mifflin Harcourt, 1990) by Tim O'Brien. See also

Everything We Had: An Oral History of the Vietnam War (New York: Random House, 1981) by Nick Santoli.

Chapter Three "Should Have Destroyed the Tapes": The Collapse of the Nixon Presidency

The literature on Nixon's life and presidency is voluminous. Stephen Ambrose provided one of the most ambitious analyses with his three-volume work, *Nixon, Volume I: The Education of a Politician, 1913–1962*; *Nixon, Volume II: The Triumph of a Politician, 1962–1972*; and *Nixon, Volume III: Ruin and Recovery, 1973–1990* (New York: Simon & Schuster, 1988, 1989, and 1991, respectively). Evan Thomas's *Being Nixon: A Man Divided* (New York: Random House, 2015) attempts to explain the contradictions inherent in the man. John A. Farrell's *Richard Nixon: The Life* (New York: Doubleday, 2017) offers a portrait of "our darkest president." Richard Rovere's *President Nixon: Alone in the White House* (New York: Simon & Schuster, 2001) and Tim Weiner's *One Man Against the World: The Tragedy of Richard Nixon* (New York: Henry Holt & Company, 2015) both depict an isolated, vindictive, and unstable president. Rick Perlstein's *Nixonland: The Rise of a President and the Fracturing of America* (New York: Scribner, 2008) and *The Invisible Bridge: The Fall of Nixon and the Rise of Reagan* (New York: Simon & Schuster, 2014) are complementary volumes that chronicle the rise of conservativism. Jefferson Cowie's *Stayin' Alive: The 1970s and the Last Days of the Working Class* (New York: New Press, 2010) has some enlightening observations on Nixon's efforts to forge a "New Majority" with working-class whites and labor. David Paul Kuhn's *The Hardhat Riot: Nixon, New York City and the Dawn of the Working-Class Revolution* (New York: Oxford University Press, 2020) offers an in-depth examination of working-class resentment of elites. Daniel Frick's *Reinventing Richard Nixon: A Cultural History of an American Obsession* (Lawrence: University Press of Kansas, 2008) examines the "reinvention" of Nixon that accompanied changing American attitudes. Perhaps most damaging to Nixon's reputation are the transcripts of a selection of the "White House Tapes" from June 1971 to August 1974 published in *Abuse of Power: The New Nixon Tapes* (New York: Free Press, 1997). Anthony Summers's *The Arrogance of Power: The Secret World of Richard Nixon* (New York: Viking, 2000) is an encyclopedic chronicle of Nixon's crimes and misdeeds, which, according to this account, define his presidency.

Revisionist works on Nixon include Kasey S. Pipes's *After the Fall: The Remarkable Comeback of Richard Nixon* (Washington, DC: Regnery, 2019), which struggles to depict Nixon as a redeemed senior statesman, and Conrad Black's lengthy *Richard Nixon: A Life in Full* (New York: PublicAffairs, 2007), which a reviewer for the *New Yorker* described as "providing an exculpatory gloss for seemingly every grimy facet of Nixon's career." Perhaps one of the more balanced is Joan Hoff's *Nixon Reconsidered* (New York: Basic Books, 1994), which argues that Nixon had many positive accomplishments.

Nixon was the author of nine books about his life and political career, the earliest being *Six Crises* (New York: Doubleday, 1962). Postpresidential works include *RN: The Memoirs of Richard Nixon* (New York: Grosset & Dunlap, 1978); *The Real War* (New York: Sidgwick & Jackson, 1980); *Leaders* (New York: Sidgwick & Jackson, 1982); *Real Peace* (New York: Simon & Schuster, 1984); *No More Vietnams* (New York: Arbor House Publishing, 1985); *1999: Victory Without War* (New York: Simon & Schuster, 1988); *In the Arena: A Memoir of Victory, Defeat, and Renewal* (New York: Simon & Schuster, 1990); *Seize the Moment: America's Challenge in a One-Superpower World* (New York: Simon & Schuster, 1992); and *Beyond Peace* (New York: Random House, 1994), published in the year of his death.

Chapter Four Bringing the War Home: Last Spasms of the Radical Left

Perhaps the most comprehensive examination of the radical left after 1969 is Bryan Burrough's *Days of Rage: America's Radical Underground, the FBI and the Forgotten Age of Revolutionary Violence* (New York: Penguin, 2015). Burrough does an exemplary job of following the various mutations of Students for a Democratic Society (SDS) after the disintegration of the organization and the decision to go "underground," as well as examining a number of lesser-known radical groups. The standard history of SDS up to 1972 is Kirkpatrick Sale's *SDS* (New York: Vintage, 1974). Among the more recent studies of SDS's later permutations are Ron Jacobs's *The Way the Wind Blew: A History of the Weather Underground* (New York: Verso, 1997); Dan Berger's *Outlaws of America: The Weather Underground and the Politics of Solidarity* (Oakland, CA: AK Press, 2006); and Arthur M.

Eckstein's *Bad Moon Rising: How the Weather Underground Beat the FBI and Lost the Revolution* (New Haven, CT: Yale University Press, 2016). A study of radical women is Mona Rocha's *The Weatherwomen: Militant Feminists of the Weather Underground* (Jefferson, NC: McFarland & Company, 2020). A work that puts the Weather Underground into the broader context of global radical leftism is Jeremy Varon's *Bringing the War Home: The Weather Underground, the Red Army Faction and Revolutionary Violence in the Sixties and Seventies* (Berkeley: University of California Press, 2004). There are numerous memoirs dealing with the lives of specific Weather Underground radicals, including *Underground: My Life with SDS and the Weathermen* (New York: HarperCollins, 2009) by Mark Rudd; Susan Stern's *With the Weathermen: The Personal Journal of a Revolutionary Woman* (New Brunswick, NJ: Rutgers University Press, 2007); Cathy Wilkerson's *Flying Close to the Sun: My Life and Times as a Weatherman* (New York: Seven Stories Press, 2007); and Bill Ayers's *Fugitive Days: Memoirs of an Antiwar Activist* (Boston: Beacon Press, 2001). Bernardine Dohrn, arguably the most prominent figure of the late SDS, has edited, along with Bill Ayers and Jeff Jones, *Sing a Battle Song: The Revolutionary Poetry, Statements and Communiqués of the Weather Underground* (New York: Seven Stories Press, 2006). Harvey Pekar has edited *SDS: Students for a Democratic Society: A Graphic History* (New York: Farrar, Straus and Giroux, 2009). The title declares the subject of *Tonight We Bombed the US Capitol: The Explosive Story of M19, America's First Female Terrorist Group* (New York: Atria, 2020) by William Rosenau. Books dealing with the Symbionese Liberation Army and the Patty Hearst kidnapping are Vin McLellan and Paul Avery's *The Voices of Guns: The Definitive and Dramatic Twenty-Two-Month Career of the Symbionese Liberation Army* (New York: Putnam, 1977); Jeffrey Toobin's *American Heiress: The Wild Saga of the Kidnapping, Crimes and Trial of Patty Hearst* (New York: Anchor, 2016); William Graebner's *Patty's Got a Gun: Patricia Hearst in 1970s America* (Chicago: University of Chicago Press, 2008); and Gregory Cumming and Stephen Sayles's *The Symbionese Liberation Army and Patricia Hearst: Queen of the Revolution* (Pechanga, CA: Great Oak Press, 2019). Editor Dan Berger has produced a fascinating study of lesser-known radical entities in *The Hidden Seventies: Histories of Radicalism* (New Brunswick, NJ: Rutgers University Press, 2010). Robert Cottrell and Blaine Browne's *1968: The Rise and Fall of the New American Revolution* (Lanham, MD:

Rowman & Littlefield, 2018) contains a concluding chapter that speaks to the direction of left radicalism after 1968. Robert C. Cottrell's *All-American Rebels* (Lanham, MD: Rowman & Littlefield, 2020) examines the direction of left radicalism in the 1970s.

Chapter Five "The American Ride Is Ending": Energy Crises, Inflation, and the Challenges of a Postindustrial Society

David Halberstam's *The Reckoning* (New York: William Morrow and Company, 1986) offers a comprehensive analysis of the decline of American auto manufacturing in the 1970s. *Cars of the Sensational '70s: A Decade of Changing Tastes and New Directions* (Lincolnwood, IL: Publications International, 2000) by James M. Flammang et al. offers a magnificent pictorial review of the decade's autos as well as yearly capsule updates about the auto industry. Any of the presidential histories mentioned in this book offer insight into economic policies and the course of the US economy in the 1970s. Jefferson Cowie's admirable *Stayin' Alive: The 1970s and the Last Days of the American Working Class* (New York: The New Press, 2010) presents one of the most comprehensive examinations of the economic, social, and cultural impacts of America's transition to a postindustrial society. Cowie's essay "'Vigorously Left, Right, and Center': The Crosscurrents of Working-Class America in the 1970s" in Beth Bailey and David Farber's *America in the '70s* (Lawrence: University Press of Kansas, 2004) offers further elaboration. Lane Windham's *Knocking on Labor's Door: Organizing in the 1970s and the Roots of a New Economic Divide* (Chapel Hill, NC: University of North Carolina Press, 2017) speaks to the challenges facing organized labor. Michael Stewart Foley's *Front Porch Politics: The Forgotten Heyday of American Activism in the 1970s and 1980s* (New York: Hill & Wang, 2013) offers several chapters about the response of average Americans to the economic tumult of the decade. A superior examination of the transition to a postindustrial economy can be found in Judith Stein's *Pivotal Decade: How the United States Traded Factories for Finance in the Seventies* (New Haven, CT: Yale University Press, 2010). Jeff Madrick's *Age of Greed: The Triumph of Finance and the Decline of America, 1970 to the Present* (New York: Alfred A. Knopf, 2011) offers further insight into the topic. Indispensable to a comprehension of the energy crisis is Meg Jacob's *Panic at the Pump: The Energy Crisis and the Transformation of American Politics in the 1970s* (New York: Farrar, Straus and Giroux, 2016).

Chapter Six The "Me Decade" and 1970s Activism

On Erhard, consult Pat R. Marks's *est, Werner Erhard: The Movement and the Man* (Los Angeles, CA: Playboy Press, 1976) and William Warren Bartley III's *Werner Erhard: The Transformation of a Man, the Founding of est* (New York: Clarkson N. Potter, Inc., 1978). Other personal growth programs are examined in Marc Galanter, *Cults: Faith, Healing, and Coercion* (New York: Oxford University Press, 1989); John McCleary, *The Hippie Dictionary: A Cultural Encyclopedia of the 1960s and 1970s* (New York: Ten Speed Press, 2004); and Paul Vitz, *Psychology as a Religion: The Cult of Self-Worship* (Grand Rapids, MI: William B. Eerdman's Publishing Company, 1979). Thomas A. Harris's *I'm Okay, You're Okay: A Practical Guide to Transactional Analysis* (New York: Harper & Row, 1969) was ubiquitous on bookstore shelves well into the 1970s despite the lessening influence of that therapeutical approach. On the jogging craze, see Jim Fixx, *The Complete Book of Running* (New York: Random House, 1977). On Wilhelm Reich, see *The Function of the Orgasm*, 2nd edition (New York: Farrar, Straus and Giroux, 1973). Though there is no biography of Robert Ringer, his website (http://www.robertringer.com) offers an enlightening glimpse into a reactionary mind. Two general histories of the 1970s that examine a wide range of social and cultural phenomena are *The Times of the Seventies: The Culture, Politics, and Personalities That Shaped the Decade* (New York: Black Dog & Leventhal Publishers, 2013), edited by Clyde Haberman, and Thomas Hine's *The Great Funk: Styles of the Shaggy, Sexy, Shameless 1970s* (New York: Farrar, Straus and Giroux, 2009).

The breadth of social activism in the 1970s is the topic of a number of studies. Second-wave feminism receives a thorough examination in Alice Echols, *Daring to Be Bad: Radical Feminism in America, 1967–1975* (Minneapolis: University of Minnesota Press, 1989). Michael Stewart's *Front Porch Politics: The Forgotten Heyday of American Activism in the 1970s and 1980s* (New York: Hill & Wang, 2013) includes several valuable chapters on the subject, as does Barbara Epstein's *Political Protest and Cultural Revolution: Nonviolent Direct Action in the 1970s and 1980s* (Berkeley: University of California Press, 1993). The emergence and activities of the American Indian Movement are well represented in Dennis Banks's *Ojibwa Warrior: Dennis Banks and the Rise of the American Indian Movement* (Norman, OK: University of Oklahoma Press, 2004); *Lakota Woman* by Mary Crow Dog (New York: HarperPerennial, 1991); and *Where White Men Fear to Tread* by Russell Means (New York: St. Martin's Press, 1995). The birth of modern environmentalism is recounted in Tom Turner's *David Brower: The Making of the Environmental Movement* (Oakland: University of California Press, 2015). For the "new environmentalism," Rik Scarce's *Eco-Warriors: Understanding the Radical Environmental Movement* (Walnut Creek, CA: Left Coast Press, 2006) is indispensable. The philosophy and activities of Greenpeace may be found in Rex Weyler's *Greenpeace: How a Group of Ecologists, Journalists, and Visionaries Changed the World* (Vancouver, BC: Rodale Books, 2004). The struggle to preserve the West and Southwest is powerfully presented in Edward Abbey's *The Journey Home: Some Words in Defense of the American West* (New York: E. P. Dutton, 1977), one of numerous books he wrote on the subject. Abbey's heartfelt *Desert Solitaire: A Season the Wilderness* (New York: Random House, 1968) was instrumental in igniting the new environmentalism and has been described by writer Russell Martin as "a kind of *Catcher in the Rye* for the coming-of-age of the environmental movement." For a close look at Sea Shepherd founder Paul Watson, see his own *Sea Shepherd: My Fight for Whales and Seals* (New York: W. W. Norton & Company, 1982); Lamya Essemlali's *Captain Paul Watson: Interview with a Pirate* (Buffalo, NY: Firefly Books, 2013); and David B. Morris's *Earth Warrior: Overboard with Paul Watson and the Sea Shepherd Conservation Society* (Golden, CO: Fulcrum Publishing, 1995).

Chapter Seven "What Is Special Order 937?": Film, Television, and Theater in the 1970s

For Sam Peckinpah, the best biography is David Weddle's *"If They Move . . . Kill 'Em": The Life and Times of Sam Peckinpah* (New York: Grove Press, 1994). W. K. Stratton's *The Wild Bunch: Sam Peckinpah, a Revolution in Hollywood and the Making of the Legendary Film* (New York: Bloomsbury, 2019) is especially illuminating regarding both the film and the changes it wrought in American cinema. Biographies of Steven Spielberg include Molly Haskell's *Steven Spielberg: A Life in Films* (New Haven, CT: Yale University Press, 2017) and Kathi Jackson's *Steven Spielberg: A Biography* (Westport, CT: Greenwood Press, 2007). Andrew Gordon's *Empire of Dreams: The Science Fiction and Fantasy Films of Steven Spielberg* (Lanham, MD: Rowman & Littlefield, 2008) offers an analytical examination of some of Spielberg's films. There are numerous excellent works on the New Cinema of the 1970s, including Sam Wasson's *The Big Goodbye: "Chinatown" and the Last Years of Hollywood* (New York: Flatiron Books, 2020). The most encyclopedic account may be found in David A. Cook's *Lost Illusions: American Cinema in the Shadow of Watergate and Vietnam, 1970–1979* (Berkeley: University of California Press, 2000). Barbara Jane Brickman focuses on youth in 1970s films in *New American Teenagers: The Lost Generation of Youth in 1970s Film* (New York: Bloomsbury, 2012). Francis Ford Coppola's *Apocalypse Now* gets an in-depth examination in Peter Cowie's *The Apocalypse Now Book* (New York: Faber & Faber, 2000). Those interested in the making of *Apocalypse Now* should view the DVD documentary *Hearts of Darkness: A Filmmaker's Apocalypse* (Hollywood, CA: Paramount, 1991). Books offering a broader look at 1970s film are Robin Wood's *Hollywood: From Vietnam to Reagan . . . and Beyond* (New York: Columbia University Press, 2003); Peter Lev's *American Films of the 1970s: Conflicting Visions* (Austin: University of Texas Press, 2000); Leonard Quart and Albert Auster's *American Film and Society since 1945* (Westport, CT: Praeger, 2002); Jonathan Kirshner's *Hollywood's Last Golden Age: Politics, Society, and the Seventies Film in America* (Ithaca, NY: Cornell University Press, 2012); Ryan Gilbey's *It Don't Worry Me: The Revolutionary American Films of the Seventies* (New York: Faber & Faber, 2004); and Peter Riskind's *Easy Riders, Raging Bulls: How the Sex-Drugs-and-Rock 'n' Roll Generation Saved Hollywood* (New York: Simon & Schuster, 1999). Michael Benson offers an in-depth examination of the making of Stanley Kubrick's *2001: A Space Odyssey* in *Space Odyssey: Stanley Kubrick, Arthur C. Clarke, and the Making of a Masterpiece* (New York: Simon & Schuster, 2018). Ronald Brownstein's *Rock Me on the Water: 1974, the Year Los Angeles Transformed Movies, Music, Television, and Politics* (New York: HarperCollins, 2021) covers film as well as other media. Sam Wasson's *The Big Goodbye: Chinatown and the Last Years of Hollywood* (New York: Flatiron Books, 2020) focuses on the impact of that film. *Those Girls: Single Women in Sixties and*

Seventies Popular Culture (Lawrence: University Press of Kansas, 2011) by Katherine J. Lehman offers some trenchant observations on that aspect of 1970s film as well as other media. Blaxploitation films, black films in general, soul music, and black celebrities are covered in an entertaining manner in *The Notorious PhD's Guide to the Super Fly '70s* by Todd Boyd (New York: Broadway Books, 2007). American theater is comprehensively covered in the James Fisher's *Historical Dictionary of Contemporary American Theater: 1930–2010*, 2 vols. (Lanham, MD: Scarecrow Press, 2011)

Chapter Eight "Bridge Over Troubled Water": Popular Music in the 1970s

There are several dated biographies of Jackson Browne, all superseded by Dave Thompson's *Hearts of Darkness: James Taylor, Jackson Browne, Cat Stevens, and the Unlikely Rise of the Singer-Songwriter* (Milwaukee, WI: Backbeat Books, 2012). Popular music of the 1970s is well covered in a number of studies, including Ronald Brownstein's *Rock Me on the Water: 1974—The Year Los Angeles Transformed Movies, Music, Television, and Politics* (New York: HarperCollins, 2021); Andrew Grant Jackson's *1973: Rock at the Crossroads* (New York: Thomas Dunne Books, 2019); David Hepworth's *Never a Dull Moment: 1971—The Year that Rock Exploded* (New York: Henry Holt and Company, 2016); Alice Echols's definitive *Hot Stuff: Disco and the Remaking of American Culture* (New York: W. W. Norton, 2010); and in Bruce Schulman's *The Seventies: The Great Shift in American Culture, Society and Politics* (New York: The Free Press, 2001). Gillian Garr's *She's a Rebel: The History of Women and Rock & Roll* (Seattle, WA: Seal Press, 1992) offers good coverage of women rockers. Columnist Dave Barry has considerable fun with some truly awful music of the decade in *Dave Barry's Book of Bad Songs* (Kansas City, MI: Andrews McMeel Publishing, 1997). There are several good Patti Smith biographies: Dave Thompson's *Dancing Barefoot: The Patti Smith Story* (Chicago: Chicago Review Press, 2011); Eric Wendell's *Patti Smith: America's Punk Rock Rhapsodist* (Lanham, MD: Rowman & Littlefield, 2014); Nick Johnstone's short *Patti Smith: A Biography* (New York: Omnibus Press, 1997); *Patti Smith: An Unauthorized Biography* by Victor Bockris and Roberta Bayley (New York: Simon & Schuster, 1999); and *Patti Smith on Patti Smith: Interviews and Encounters* (Chicago: Chicago Review Press, 2020), edited by Aidan Levy. Mark

Paytress's *Break It Up: Patti Smith's Horses and the Remaking of Rock 'n' Roll* (Suffolk, UK: Portrait, 2006) focuses on the impact of that seminal album, as does Philip Shaw's *Horses* (New York: Bloomsbury Academic, 2008). Smith's own writings include *Just Kids* (New York: 2010), a 2010 National Book Award winner; *M Train* (New York: Alfred A. Knopf, 2015); *Year of the Monkey* (New York: Bloomsbury, 2019); and several volumes of poetry. Her *Collected Lyrics, 1970–2015* (New York: HarperCollins, 2015) reveals the breadth and depth of her captivating lyrics.

Chapter Nine "A Crisis of Confidence": National Politics and Foreign Policy

Shirley Chisholm's life and political career are addressed in her autobiographical *Unbought and Unbossed* (New York: Houghton Mifflin, 1970) while her historic campaign for the 1972 Democratic presidential nomination is the subject of *The Good Fight* (New York: HarperCollins, 1973). A more recent study is Barbara Winslow's *Shirley Chisholm: Catalyst for Change* (New York: Westview Press, 2014). The standard history of the 1972 election is Theodore H. White's *The Making of the President, 1972* (New York: Atheneum, 1973). Gerald Ford's political career is amply covered in *Ambition, Pragmatism, and Party: A Political Biography of Gerald R. Ford* by Scott Kaufman (Lawrence: University Press of Kansas, 2017). Studies that deal with his presidency are Douglas Brinkley's *Gerald R. Ford* (New York: Times Books, 2007) and Yanek Mieczkowski's *Gerald R. Ford and the Challenges of the 1970s* (Lexington: University Press of Kentucky, 2005)). A detailed account of the two assassination attempts on Ford can be found in Ronald L. Feinman, *Assassinations, Threats, and the American Presidency* (Lanham, MD: Rowman & Littlefield, 2015). The numerous works on the Carter presidency include Randall Balmer's *Redeemer: The Life of Jimmy Carter* (New York: Basic Books, 2014); J. Brooks Flippen's *Jimmy Carter, The Politics of Family, and the Rise of the Religious Right* (Athens: University of Georgia Press, 2011); Stuart Eizenstat's *President Carter: The White House Years* (New York: St. Martin's Press, 2018); Jason Friedman's *Jimmy Carter and the Restoration of Presidential Dignity* (New York: McFarland, 2020); and Kai Bird's *The Outlier: The Unfinished Presidency of Jimmy Carter* (New York: Crown, 2021). Foreign policy in the Nixon, Ford, and Carter years is examined in

Daniel J. Sargent's *A Superpower Transformed: The Remaking of American Foreign Relations in the 1970s* (New York: Oxford University Press, 2015). International affairs are addressed in Greg Grandin's *Kissinger's Shadow: The Long Reach of America's Most Controversial Statesman* (New York: Henry Holt and Company, 2015); Jussi Hanhimäki's *The Flawed Architect: Henry Kissinger and American Foreign Policy* (New York: Oxford University Press, 2004); and Justin Vaïsse's *Zbigniew Brzezinski: America's Grand Strategist* (Cambridge, MA: Harvard University Press, 2018). The failed effort to free American hostages in Tehran is examined in Justin Williamson's *Operation Eagle Claw 1980: The Disastrous Bid to end the Iran Hostage Crisis* (Oxford, UK: Osprey Publishing, 2020). The conservative wave that followed the 1980 general election is chronicled in Andrew E. Busch's *Reagan's Victory: The Presidential Election of 1980 and the Rise of the Right* (Lawrence: University Press of Kansas, 2005). Rick Perlstein's *The Invisible Bridge: The Fall of Nixon and the Rise of Reagan* (New York: Simon & Schuster, 2014) offers an encyclopedic examination of the events of the 1970s that led to rise of the New Right and the election of Reagan. Phyllis Schlafly's role in the New Right and the battle to defeat the Equal Rights Amendment (ERA) is examined in several studies, including Donald Critchlow's *Phyllis Schlafly and Grassroots Conservatism: A Woman's Crusade* (Princeton, NJ: Princeton University Press, 2005); Carol Felsenthal's *The Sweetheart of the Silent Majority: The Biography of Phyllis Schlafly* (New York: Doubleday, 1981); and Jane J. Mansbridge's *Why We Lost the ERA* (Chicago: University of Chicago Press, 1986). Schlafly was a prolific author, her bestselling book being *A Choice Not an Echo* (Washington, DC: Regnery, 1964, 2014).

INDEX

INDEX

ABOUT THE AUTHOR

Blaine T. Browne is a Texas native who has also lived in Colorado, Florida, and currently resides in Oklahoma City, Oklahoma. Having received a PhD in history from the University of Oklahoma, Browne taught history at Broward College, Fort Lauderdale for twenty-six years. Member and thrice president of the Florida Conference of Historians since 1994, Browne has co-authored and/or authored eight books, the most recent being *Mighty Endeavor: The American Nation and World War II* (Rowman & Littlefield, 2019). Since retiring in 2014, Browne has taught as an adjunct instructor at Oklahoma City University and as a lecturer at the University of Oklahoma.